THE COMPLETE METALSMITH

An Illustrated Handbook

———

Revised Edition

The smith also sitteth by the anvil,
And fighteth with the heat of the furnace,
And noise of the hammer and the anvil is ever in his ears,
And his eyes look still upon the pattern of the thing that he maketh.
He setteth his mind to finish his work,
And waiteth to polish it perfectly.

———————

Ecclesiasticus

The Complete Metalsmith

An Illustrated Handbook

Revised Edition

Tim McCreight

DAVIS PUBLICATIONS, INC.
Worcester, Massachusetts

ACKNOWLEDGMENTS
So many people contributed to this book that it is impossible to mention
them all. My students have helped in me in more ways than they can
imagine. Their keen eyes and sharp questions have honed the material
and its presentation. I will be always in their debt. Chuck Evans, Gary
Griffin and Bob Ebendorf reviewed the manuscript meticulously, con-
tributing greatly to the technical accuracy of the information. For help
on specific topics I'd like to thank Paula Dinneen, Will Earley, John
Cogswell, Bill Seeley, David LaPlantz, Heikki Seppa, Claire Sanford,
Adam Clark and Linda Threadgill. My colleagues at the Portland
School of Art have been generous not only in their moral support but in
the use of their printer and copier as well. Wyatt Wade of Davis Publications who supervised the project has been a constant source of support and sound judgement.

And for putting up with the late nights and lost weekends I especially
want to thank my family, Jay, Jobie and Jeff.

Printed in the United States of America
Library of Congress Catalog Number: 81-66573
ISBN: 0-87192-240-1

10 9 8

CONTENTS

INTRODUCTION

This book represents several years of intensive research and experimentation. Information from hundreds of sources has been collected, distilled and illustrated. It is intended to be both a text and a tool, a blend of instruction and reference. Like any tool, its value increases as you bring to it your own perceptions and skills. It is designed to make the information easily accessible, and built to stand up to years of bench-side use.

Like any craft, metalsmithing involves some chemicals and procedures that are potentially dangerous. Great care has been taken to omit hazards where possible and to give clear warnings wherever they apply. These will be only as effective as you make them. Before using this book, please take the time to read the health and safety suggestions on page 172. Because we can't be on hand to control the application of this information, the author and publisher cannot be held responsible for incorrect interpetations or use of this material.

THE COMPLETE METALSMITH takes a somewhat unusual approach to the material it presents. Unlike most books that progress from basic to advanced techniques, information has been arranged here according to the process involved. For example, you'll find all the information about holding things together, from simple tabs to sophisticated granulation is grouped in the chapter called *Joining*. In most cases each technique is confined to a single page. This makes it easy to get a quick overview of the nature of the process. The wire binding will allow the book to lay flat and take up only a little room on your bench top.

Dark rectangles along the edge of each page will guide you to the correct chapter. These may be augmented by adding your own index tabs at the beginning of each chapter or on frequently used pages. Buy plastic sleeves from an office supply store or cut the chapter heading tabs on the next page and glue one at the opening of each chapter.

Because the cost of chapter dividers is prohibitive, we've included this page of DO IT YOURSELF tabs. Pull out this page, then cut and paste as shown, covering up the chapter label on the first page of each chapter.

Materials	Surfaces	Shaping
Joining	Casting	Stones
Mechanisms	Tools	Reference

Chapter 1

Materials

Metallurgy

Metallurgy is the scientific understanding of metals. It includes classification systems, investigation into molecular and crystalline behavior and the effects and uses of metals.

Materials

Crystals

Face Centered Cubic
- Lead
- Copper
- Aluminum
- Gold
- Silver
- Nickel
- Iron (at high temps)

Body Centered Cubic
- Chromium
- Lithium
- Molybdenum
- Potassium
- Sodium
- Vanadium
- Iron (at room temps)

Hexagonal Close-Packed
- Beryllium
- Cadmium
- Cobalt
- Magnesium
- Titanium
- Zinc

Annealing

This is the process of reducing stress within metal by heating it to a prescribed temperature. Industrially this is done in a furnace where the temperatures can be monitored mechanically. In the studio it is more common to anneal with a torch. Temperatures are gauged by the color progression of the metal, with a dimly lit area being best suited for this purpose. Paste flux may be painted onto the metal to serve as a temperature indicator: it is clear at 1100° F (593° C). If quenching in pickle, beware of dangerous fumes and splashing acid. A safer method is to quench in water and then slide the work into the pickle.

Sterling **14K** **10K Gold**	Heat to a dull red; quench as soon as the redness disappears.
Red Golds **Copper** **Bronze**	Heat to a medium red; quench when the redness disappears.
Steel	Heat to a bright nonmagnetic red and cool as slowly as possible

Deformation

When a small stress (load) is applied to a sample, the metal will probably bend. If the metal returns to its original shape when the load is removed, the bend is called *elastic deformation*. If the load is increased in small amounts and retested at each increase, there will come a time when the sample no longer returns to its original shape.
This point is called the *elastic limit*, and the permanent change is called a *plastic deformation*. Properties that establish the elastic limit are the structure of the metal, its physical shape, purity and heat treatment.

Wonderfullest things are ever the unmentionable.
Herman Melville

Metallurgy

Though metals have been controlled for centuries, the science of metallurgy is as recent as 1864, when a microscope was first used to study the character of steel. X-rays and wave mechanics extended the understanding of metals with their introduction in 1925.

Recrystalization

When heated to its melting point a metal loses its crystaline organization and becomes fluid. When the heat source is removed and the metal cools, it re-establishes its crystal pattern, starting with the first areas to cool. Many clusters of crystals start to form simultaneously, all having the same order but not necessarily the same orientation.

Crystals move most easily within a semi-ordered structure. The crystals at a grain boundary are caught in a "log jam" with the result that the metal is tough and hard to work.

When worked, large crystals are broken into smaller ones, creating more grain boundaries. As a result the metal is work hardened. A similar condition is created when metal is rapidly cooled. Crystals do not have time to grow from a few clusters into an organized structure. Instead, the metal recrystalizes into many small unoriented grains.

In time, even at room temperature, crystals will realign themselves into an organized lattice. By heating the metal we accelerate the movement of atoms and the subsequent recrystalization. This process is called *annealing*.

In its annealed state, the crystal arrangement contains irregularities called vacancies. These facilitate crystal movement and so contribute to malleability. If nonferrous metals are held at annealing temperatures for long periods, the result is a more perfect arrangement and a less malleable material. This is called *heat hardening*.

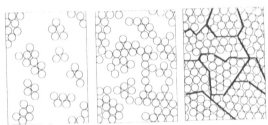

Vacancies & Dislocations

The amount of activity as a metal cools is quite astounding. At a slow rate of crystal growth, such as 1 mm per day, about 100 layers of atoms per second are being deposited. Crystalization normally occurs much faster than this, so it is not surprizing that few crystals are perfectly formed. Ironically, it is this imperfection that allows the metal to be worked. As various clusters of crystals organize themselves around differently oriented grains, they come to impinge on one another when they meet. The holes this creates are called *vacancies*. These accumulate to form a region in which the symmetry of the crystal lattice is disturbed, which is called a *dislocation*. As the diagrams indicate, it is this distortion that allows metal to be malleable. If the crystals were perfectly arranged they would have no place to move when stressed. Vacancies and dislocations distribute forces throughout metal and allow it to flex.

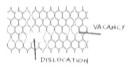

VACANCY

DISLOCATION

Gold

Gold was the first precious metal to be worked by man, being available as nuggets that required no smelting. Because of its rarity and luster and the ability to resist corrosion, it has been valued by many cultures.

DATA: **Au**
Melting Point:
 1063 °C
 1945 °F
Specific Gravity:
 Cast 19.2
 Worked 19.3
Atomic Wt: 197.2

- Gold was probably the second metal to be worked by early man, being discovered after copper. Quality gold work can be found from as early as 3000 B.C.
- If all the gold ever found (about 20,000 tons) were cast into a single ingot, it would make only a 20 yard cube.
- Gold has a face-centered cubic crystal.
- Pickles for gold would include Sparex #2 or a mixture of 1 part nitric acid (reagent grade) with 8 parts water.
- Gold dissolves in Aqua Regia and solutions of chlorine and potassium cyanide or sodium cyanide.

Gold-Filled

This term refers to a material on which a layer of gold has been bonded by fusing. The resulting ingot is rolled or drawn to make sheet and wire. A standard practice is to clad the base with 10% (weight) 12K gold. Since 12K is half pure it means the final result, if it were melted down and assayed, would equal 1/20 or 5% pure gold, marked as 1/20 G.F.

Voluntary Product Standard

This U.S. law has set legal tolerances since 1976. It allows variation of 3 parts per 1000 (.072K) on unsoldered goods and .007 (.168K) on soldered objects. This is called *plumb* (i.e. accurate) gold. Manufacturers were given until 1981 to dispose of their old merchandise made at lower standards.

Fineness of Gold

Since fine (pure) gold is too soft for most uses it is alloyed with other metals to achieve a desired hardness. During this process the color, hardness, malleability and melting point can also be altered. Silver and copper are the two most common additives but many other metals can be used.

The relative amount of gold in an alloy is called the *karat*. This word signifies proportion and should not be confused with *carat*, which is a unit of weight.

Decimal Equivalents of Karats					
1K	.0417	9K	.3750	17K	.7083
2K	.0833	**10K**	**.4167**	**18K**	**.7500**
3K	.1250	11K	.4583	19K	.7917
4K	.1667	12K	.5000	20K	.8333
5K	.2083	13K	.5417	21K	.8750
6K	.2500	**14K**	**.5833**	22K	.9167
7K	.2917	15K	.6250	23K	.9583
8K	.3333	16K	.6667	24K	1.000

One ounce of gold can be flattened to a sheet that will cover 100 square feet or drawn to a wire almost a mile long. Gold can be made into a foil that is less than 5 millionths of an inch thick, at which point it is virtually transparent.

Testing

To be scientifically accurate a sample must be assayed in a testing laboratory but these two tests have been used for many years and are often sufficiently accurate for the craftsperson.

Is It Gold?

With a small file, make a scratch in an inconspicuous spot. While wearing rubber gloves, use a wooden, glass or plastic stick to apply a drop of nitric acid to this spot. Observe the reaction. When done, rinse everything well in running water.

- No reaction _____ it's gold
- Bright green _____ it's base metal
- Green in scratch _____ gold layer over base metal.
- Milky in scratch _____ gold over silver

What Karat Is It?

Determining karat requires a testing kit:
- nitric acid
- aqua regia
- samples of known karat
- touchstone (slate or ceramic)

The object to be tested is rubbed on the stone (i.e. "touched") to leave a streak. A parallel line is made with one of the test needles. Both marks are flooded with acid and the reactions are observed. When the sample colors at the same rate as the test streak, a match has been made. Nitric acid is used for low karat golds; aqua regia is needed for higher karats.

Safety

Formulas

To lower karat

A. Amount to be lowered times its karat.
B. Same amount times the desired karat.
C. Difference between A and B.
D. Divide difference (C) by the quality being made.

To Raise Karat

A. Amount to be raised times its karat.
B. Same amount times the desired karat.
C. Subtract B from A.
D. Difference between pure (24) and desired karat.
E. Divide C by D.

Alloys

• A mixture of roughly equal parts of gold and silver is called *electrum*. This alloy shows maximum hardness at a 50/50 mix.
• The hardest alloy of gold, silver and copper is reached at 50/25/25. This is 12K yellow.
• Any increase of the copper content in a gold alloy will lower its melting point up to18% copper (melts: 880°C 1642°F). To continue lowering, add silver.
• Many kinds and colors of gold solder are commercially available, but in a pinch a gold of a lower karat may be used.

Fluxes

When pouring gold ingots use an even mixture of powdered charcoal and ammonium chloride (sal ammoniac) during melting. This will yield a bright tough ingot that will withstand rolling. **Dangerous fumes are produced.**

If iron or steel are present (for instance as a result of file wear) purify the scraps by melting with a flux of 1 part potassium nitrate (saltpetre) and 2 parts potassium carbonate. After cooling, remelt with the sal ammoniac flux and pour the metal into a warm (not hot) mold.

Platinum

Platinum is a dense white metal with a high resistance to corrosion. When encountered by the invading Spaniards in 1538 it was called *platina* because its appearance was similar to that of silver (*plata*).

METAL	SYMBOL	Relative Occurence	MELTING POINT		HARDNESS	SPECIFIC GRAVITY
Platinum	Pt	60%	3224° F	1773 °C	4 to 4.5	21.5
Palladium	Pd	30	2829	1555	4 to 4.5	12.0
Rhodium	Rh	4	3571	1966	5	12.4
Ruthenium	Ru	3	4530	2500	6.5	12.2
Iridium	Ir	2	4449	2355	6.5	22.4
Osmium	Os	1	5550	3066	7	22.5

Rhodium was separated from platinum in 1803 and takes its name from the Greek word *rodon* (rose) because of the colors of the metallic salts. Rhodium is often plated over sterling articles to provide a bright tarnish resistant outer layer. Its reflectivity index (85% of the visible spectrum) is slightly lower than sterling but this loss of shine is generally imperceptible. Worked rhodium has a Vickers hardness of 100 but electroplated rhodium has a Vickers of 775-820, showing that it is very hard and durable.

Platinum group metals can be cast but because of their high melting points a special investment must be used. When buying this, request a data sheet and follow mixing directions carefully. No flux is needed when melting.

Cleanliness is very important when heating metals of the platinum group. An oxidizing flame is recommended. Contamination by silver, aluminum, iron, lead, etc. will cause intercrystaline cracking at the grain boundaries. If contamination occurs there is no way to correct the problem metallurgically; the damaged area must be cut out and replaced with a patch.

Platinum group metals dissolve slowly in aqua regia.

• Because of their high melting points these metals require an oxygen torch for soldering and casting.
• Because of their toughness and great resistance to tarnish these metals are well suited to settings for precious stones.
• To test, heat a sample to bright red and air cool. Metals of the platinum group will remain bright and shiny. Because of this resistance, no flux is needed when soldering.
• More than half of all platinum metals mined are used by the jewelry industry.

Silver was known in the ancient world as *argentum*, and was held to be more precious than gold because it appeared less commonly in nature.

Pure silver, like pure gold, is too soft for most uses and is often alloyed. Though many metals may be used, copper is preferred since it greatly toughens the alloy without detracting from the bright shine characteristic of silver.

Sterling is the alloy most commonly used in jewelry making and silversmithing. It was adopted as a standard alloy in England in the 12th century when King Henry II imported refiners from an area of Germany known as the *Easterling*. The product they made was of a consistent quality and came into usage as currency by 1300 when it was known as Ea*sterling* silver.

Another common alloy contains slightly more copper, 10 to 20%, and is called *coin silver*. It melts at a temperature slightly lower than sterling and is more likely to tarnish. A 90% alloy was used in U.S. coins until 1966 but now no silver is used. This trend away from silver coins has been international.

An alloy popular in the Far East uses 90% silver and 10% zinc, producing a metal with a low melting point and a bright, tinny shine.

DATA: **Ag**
Melting point:
 960.5° C
 1761° F
Spec. gravity: 10.5
Atomic Wt: 107.88

STERLING:
Melting point:
 893° C
 1640° F
Spec. gravity: 10.41

Heat Hardening

In conventional work-hardening, metal is made rigid by upsetting the orderly arrangement of grains. A similar rigidness can be achieved by reducing the number of dislocations and vacancies; i.e. by creating extreme regularity. This is achieved by warming the metal sufficiently to begin recrystalization and holding at this temperature long enough to allow gradual ordered crystal growth.

> *For sterling*
> After all soldering is done, heat to 280° C (536° F) and hold for 2 1/2 hours. Quench in pickle and finish as usual.

Electrolytic Cleaning of Sterling

This procedure lends itself to the removal of tarnish from flatware or hollowware. In an aluminum pot (or a pot lined with aluminum foil) mix a dilute solution of equal parts of baking soda, salt and liquid soap. A quarter cup of each to a gallon of water would be a typical mixture. Set the sterling into the pot, bring the mix to a boil and allow to stand for a few minutes. Oxides are transferred to the aluminum. Rinse in water and wash before using.

Annealed fine silver has a hardness of Vickers 26 (tensile strength of 9 tons per square inch). Cold working increases the hardness to Vickers 95-100 (tensile strength of 20-22 tons per square inch).

Brittania silver: 958.3 parts per 1000 was the legal alloy in England from 1697 to 1719, contrived to discourage the melting of coins. It is still a legal alloy.

Silver resists aqua regia since hydrochloric acid forms a dense chloride film that resists corrosion.

Copper

Copper is relatively abundant, easily mined and extremely versatile in its many applications. It has a long history and has been used by many cultures for centuries.

DATA: **Cu**
Melting Point:
  1083 ° C
  1981° F
Spec. Gravity: 8.96
Atomic Wt: 63.54

Copper is available in more than 100 alloys. Comprehensive data is available from:
Copper Development
Association, Inc.
P.O. Box 1840
Greenwich, CT 06836
(203) 625-8210

Japanese Alloys
Shaku-do
  .5 to 4% gold,
  balance copper
  M.P. 1968-1980° F
    1070-1082° C
This is known for the deep purple color achieved through oxidation.

Shibu-ichi
  75% copper, 25% silver
  M.P. 1775° F
    968° C
This is a silvery pink alloy that darkens and reticulates easily.

Copper was probably the first metal to be put to use by our ancestors and remains important to us today. It conducts heat and electricity very well, can be formed and joined, and combines with many elements to form a broad range of alloys.

8000 BC copper discovered
6000 BC Egyptians used copper weapons
5000 BC beginning of Bronze Age
3800 BC evidence of controlled bronze alloying
2750 BC Egyptians made copper pipes

• Copper is sold in standard sheets 36" x 96" (3' x 8') and in coils 12 and 18 inches wide. When ordering specify Hard, Half-hard, or Annealed.
• When copper is hot-rolled it develops a slightly rough surface. For this reason most craftspeople prefer cold-rolled material. Copper alloy #110 is a common choice.
• When exposed to moist air, copper forms poisonous acetates, sulfates and chlorides known collectively as *verdigris*. The name comes from "vert-de-grice," Old French for "Green of Greece," a reference to metal sculptures of antiquity. Because of these compounds, workers should always wash their hands after handling copper for a long time. Copper cookware and serving pieces should either be plated with a non-corrosive metal such as tin or washed before each use.
• Most copper is electrolytically refined; i.e. electrically deposited on an anode. This product is pure but contains oxygen atoms scattered throughout the metal. When heated this forms CuO_2 which breaks down the bond between crystals and can weaken the metal as much as 60%. To alleviate this problem most copper is alloyed with a deoxidizer such as phosphorous.

If a man can keep alert and imaginative, an error is a possibility, a chance at something new; to him, wandering and wondering are a part of the same process. He is most mistaken, most in error, whenever he quits exploring.

William Least Heat Moon

Brass & Bronze

Brass is an alloy of copper and zinc, a combination that yields a yellow metal that is tougher than either of its components. Brass is widely used because of its malleability, machinability and its resistance to corrosion.

Archeologists theorize that the earliest brasses were the result of accidentally reducing a combination of zinc and copper ores. These earliest metals date back to the Neolithic Age and most references probably used the terms *brass* and *bronze* interchangably.

To distinguish brass from bronze:
Dissolve a small sample in 50/50 solution of nitric acid and water. Tin will be indicated by a white precipitate; metastannic acid.

DATA: **70/30 Brass**
Melting Point:
954° C
1750° F
Spec. Gravity: 8.5

Alpha brasses contain more than 62% copper and are known for their malleability and cold working properties. These are the brasses used for screws, pins and bolts. As the copper content goes up the malleability becomes even greater and the color becomes more rich. This trend peaks at about 90% copper, an alloy known as red brass. The addition of still more copper enriches the color of this alloy to a rich gold that is often used in fashion jewelry. *Pinchbeck, NuGold* and *Jewelers Bronze* are alloys in the 88/12 neighborhood.

Availability

Brass, like copper, is sold in 3 feet by 8 feet sheets. The most common system for measuring thickness among industrial suppliers is in thousandths of an inch. Brass can be purchased in hard, half-hard and dead soft tempers, but the hard is most typical. Brass and bronze are also commonly available as round and square rod, extruded molding, hexagonal bar and of course, round wires.

Bronze

Bronze is an alloy of copper and tin and was enormously important to the development of civilizations several thousand years ago. It gave its name to the third phase of man's material development (*the Bronze Age*) following the Paleolithic and Neolithic ages and was being made as early as 3000 BC. By medieval times specific proportions were alloyed for desired results.

Besides being tougher than its parent metal of copper, bronze is more easily melted and cast and is less susceptible to corrosion. By varying the proportion of copper and tin in the mix, several alloys of differing proper-

ties are possible. *Bell metal*, so named because of the tone rendered when struck, can have anywhere between 14 and 25% tin. *Statuary bronze* might have as little as 10% tin, and in applications such as bearings or weapons a small amount of zinc is added to increase strength. A small amount of phosphor improves the strength and quality of bronze as well. As little as 1% can significantly alter the resulting alloy. Manganese is also added to bronze to increase its strength and machinability, generally with zinc and sometimes without any tin at all.

Aluminum

Aluminum is the most abundant metallic element on the planet, making up 8% of the earth's crust. Because of its resistance to corrosion, its light weight and its low cost, aluminum is used in architecture, housewares and packaging.

DATA: **Al**
Melting point:
  660° C
  1220° F
Spec. Gravity: 2.7
Atomic Wt: 26.97

Pure aluminum	= 2S
Al + 1.25% Mn	= 3S
Al + 1.2% Mn and 1% Mg	= 4S
Al + 4% Cu, .5Mn, .5Mg	= 17S
Al + 4.5Cu., .5Mn, 1.5 Mg	= 24S

Properties

Because of its light weight, resistence to corrosion and ability to alloy well, aluminum is used structurally for buildings, aircraft, cars and for architectural trim such as siding. Aluminum is also popular for functional objects such as cookware, lawn furniture and outdoor fixtures.

Aluminum is the second most malleable and sixth most ductile metal. It is usually found in bauxite as an oxide called *alumina*: Al_2O_3.

Though the existence of aluminum was theorized in the 1700s it was not isolated until 1825. When the Washington Monument was completed in 1884, a 100 oz. pyramid of aluminum was made to crown it. At the time this was the largest mass of aluminum ever made. Before placement it was displayed in Tiffany's window in New York. Commercial production was devised in 1886 and many alloys have been developed since then.

Joining

Aluminum can be soldered and joined only with special solders, many of which are sold with their own flux. Welding can be done with 43S or #717 wire used with #33 flux. More detailed specifications are available from a supplier. Welding is made easier with a TIG (tungsten inert gas) welder, but can be achieved with gas/oxygen systems.

Alloys

As is the case with many metals, industry organizations have developed a universal system to identify components of an alloy. The first digit of a 4 digit number designates the principle ingredient, with the rest of the numbers specifying their proportions.

1xxx	pure or almost pure aluminum
2xxx	copper alloys
3xxx	manganese
4xxx	silicon
5xxx	magnesium
6xxx	magnesium & silicon
7xxx	zinc
8xxx	other elements

The 1000, 5000 and 6000 series are commonly preferred for anodizing, but many other alloys will work.

Anodizing

This is a process of electrically causing the formation of a resistant oxide film on the surface of aluminum. The film may be colored with dyes which can give finished aluminum products a wide range of color possibilities. See further information on pages 42 & 43.

Nickel

The word nickel means "deceiver" in German and was given to the ore (*niccolite*) because it was easily mistaken for copper ore. Nickel is a hard white metal used primarily as an alloying ingredient. It increases hardness and resistance to corrosion without impairing ductility.

Nickel alloys are familiar to most of us because of their use in coins. The alloy can be polished to a bright chrome-like shine, but will rapidly degrade to the matte silver color of an American nickel. The alloy is widely used as a base for plated flatware and is popular with beginning jewelers. Because it is tough and inexpensive, it is used in commercial findings such as pin stems, barrette backs and so on.

DATA: **Ni**

Melting Point: 1453° C
2651° F

Specific Gravity: 8.9

Atomic Wt: 58.71

Common Alloys

Nickel Silver (German Silver, White Brass)	Cu 60% Ni 20% Zn 20%	This metal is used in jewelry because of its low cost and generally favorable working properties. It can be forged, stamped, soldered, and polished. Though it can be cast, this is difficult because of its high melting point and tendency to oxidize.
Monel Metal	Ni 67% Cu 30% bal. Fe, Mn, C, Si, S	This tough, oxide-resistant metal has many uses in industry but is rarely used in the crafts. It melts around 1300° C, 2370° F.
Nichrome	Ni 80% Cr 20%	Because of its ability to reduce oxidation and its high melting point (1400° C, 2550° F), this wire is used as a heating element in electric kilns.
Nickel Alloy #752	Cu 65% Ni 18% Zn 17%	This alloy will "swell" when heated above 980° C, 1800° F. When its reticulated oxide skin is removed in a nitric acid pickle, the metal will be found to be dramatically perforated. It may be soldered and polished.

The important thing is not to stop questioning.
Albert Einstein

Iron & Steel

Iron ore usually contains sulphur, phosphorous, silicon and carbon. When all but 3 or 4% carbon has been smelted out, the resulting metal is poured into ingots and called *cast iron* or *pig iron*. Further refining is necessary to make a steel of good working qualities.

DATA: **Fe**
Melting Point:
    1539° C
    2802° F
Spec. Gravity: 7.87
Atomic Wt: 55.85

.15 to .3% carbon = mild (low-carbon) steel: cannot be hardened
.3 to .5% carbon = medium carbon steel: used for tools
.5 to 1.6% carbon = high carbon steel: specialty tools
2.5 +% carbon = malleable iron: for cast and machined parts

Code System

Set by the Society of Automotive Engineers (SAE) and the American Iron and Steel Industry (AISI).

- Letter indicates type of furnace used in smelting.
- Second two digits indicate major alloying material.
- Last two digits indicate the percent in this alloy.

B 1065

This is a plain carbon steel made in an acid Bessemer furnace that contains .65% carbon.

Steel Alloys

chromium for corrosion resistance; 10-20% used in stainless.
manganese increases hardenability and tensile strength.
molybdenum increases corrosion resistance and strength at high temperatures.
tungsten forms hard abrasion-resistant particles called tungsten carbide. Used for cutting edges, for instance on drill bits.

Hardening Steel (see also page 156)

Steel metallurgy is a complex field and deserves more space than can be given here. In a simplified way, however, this is how tool steels make their magic.

Annealed carbon steel contains **ferrite**, which is malleable, and hard particles of carbide called **cementite**. When heated to a glowing red the carbides dissolve into the iron; the result is called **austenite.** The temperature at which this occurs is called the *critical range*. If the steel is cooled quickly the result is a hard needle-like structure called **martensite**. This is what gives carbon steel its toughness. Unfortunately it also makes it brittle. By heating this to a prescribed temperature and cooling it at a certain rate, the stress may be relieved without removing all the hardness. The result contains hard cementite particles held in a tough matrix of martensite. This process is called tempering or drawing the temper, and usually takes place between 200-350° C (400-600° F).

It is important to distinguish between wear resistance and hardness. The former depends on the number and hardness of the particles; the latter on the strength of the matrix. In steel this property is mostly controlled by the alloy and not by heat treatment. Increased carbon (up to 1.6%) means more particles but less matrix, or increased wear resistance but decreased hardness.

Pearlite

Austenite

Martensite

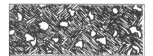
Tempered Martensite

White Metals

This general term refers to several soft, gray colored metals with low melting points and to the alloys having these metals as primary ingredients.

• These metals are also called easily fusible alloys, pot metal, and type metal, the latter name coming from the use of these alloys in making printers' type.

• Because of their low melting points, white metals can be melted with almost any torch. To help reduce oxidation, melting is best done in a small-necked crucible or ladle.

• During melting the metal may be protected from oxygen by a coating of olive oil, linseed oil or lard. These float on the surface of the melt. In pouring, the metal will slide out from underneath.

% Lead	% Tin	% Cadmium	% Bismuth	Specific Gravity	Melting Point °C	Melting Point °F
100				11.3	327	621
	100			7.3	233	450
		100		8.7	321	610
			100	9.8	271	520
27	13	10	50		60	140
34	33	33			94	171

CAUTION

The fumes produced by these metals are dangerous. Heat under a ventilating hood or arrange a fan over your shoulder to move fumes away from you. Lead can be absorbed through the skin. Wash well after handling any lead-bearing alloy. It is especially unwise to eat, drink or smoke in an area where white metal is being worked.

 Safety

Pewter & Britannia

Pewter, as used in antiquity and associated with colonial America, was an alloy of lead and tin. In the late 1700s a substitute alloy was developed in England and named Britannia Metal. Today the words pewter and Britannia are often used interchangeably and refer to this:

  91% tin
  7% antimony
  2% copper

It can be sawn, soldered, fused, formed and cast. Finishing can be done with fine steel wool and a mix of lampblack (soot) and kerosene blended to a paste.

Contamination

When heated above their melting point, white metals will burn pits into gold, platinum, silver, copper, brass, etc. Use separate files and soldering tools to keep these metals away from each other.

To remove white metal, file, scrape, sand or use either of these solutions:

  3 oz. glacial acetic acid
  1 oz. hydrogen peroxide
      or
  8 oz. fluroboric acid
  1.6 oz. 30% hydrogen peroxide
  22 oz. water

Allow work to soak for several hours.

13

Titanium Group

This term refers to a group of six tough gray metals that are lightweight, have a high melting point and are resistant to corrosion. They are of interest to jewelers principally because of the colors produced by their oxidation films.

Titanium and niobium cannot be soldered or annealed in the jeweler's studio, but both metals lend themselves to all other traditional processes. They can be drilled, filed, drawn, stamped, raised, etc. with conventional tools.

In addition to titanium and niobium, scientists would include in this group *tantalum, zirconium, tungsten* and *hafnium*. Only the first two are relevant to jewelers.

DATA: **Ti**
Melting point: 1675° C
3047° F
Spec. Gravity: 4.5
Atomic Wt: 47.9

Pure titanium is ductile and shows low thermal and electrical conductivity. It is twice as dense as aluminum and half as dense as iron. Its resistance to corrosion combined with light weight and toughness make it well suited to use in prosthetics. It has also found wide use as an alloying ingredient. It is added to steel to reduce grain size, to stainless to reduce carbon, to aluminum to refine grain development and to copper to harden it.

Titanium is the 9th most abundant element in the earth's crust and can be found in most rocks, clay and sand. It was first identified in 1791 but has been commercially viable only since 1947 when the development of the Kroll refining process was invented.

Titanium dioxide is a white powder used in paints and enamels.

DATA: **Nb**
Melting Point: 2468° C
4474° F
Spec Gravity: 8.57
Atomic Wt: 92.91

In its pure form niobium is soft and ductile and polishes to look like platinum. There is a good bit of niobium on the planet, being more plentiful than lead and less common than copper. Like tantalum, niobium is extremely ductile. In drawing wire, for instance, the cross section can be reduced by as much as 90% before annealing. This property can of course be a draw back for applications where strength is required.

When this metal was first discovered in 1801 it was called *columbium*, but it was rediscovered and renamed in 1844. After years of confusion the scientific community formally adopted the name niobium, but the older name is still sometimes encountered.

See pages 44 and 45 for information on anodizing reactive metals.

Plastic

The first plastics were made in the late 1800s and were based on wood fibers. Most of the ubiquitous plastics we see today are based on petroleum.

Thermosetting plastics are generally available as liquids that react with a catalyst or hardener to cross-link large molecules (polymers) with small ones (monomers) in a process called *polymerization*. After curing, the resultant material cannot be returned to its original state. Thermosetting plastics are usually epoxies or polyesters.

SAFETY
Thermosetting plastics produce fumes that can cause severe damage, even in small doses.

Serious ventilation facilities are a must.
Skin irritation is also likely to result from contact, so gloves should be worn. Specific health hazards are well documented in specialty texts. Anyone intending to work with these materials should do some serious reading before getting started.

Safety

Casting

Because they are liquid, thermosetting plastics are commonly used to fill a mold or encase an object. The sequence given here provides a general introduction to the process.

1. Careful measurement is important, so a sensitive scale is needed. Wax coated paper cups make handy containers for measuring, mixing, and as molds for small slabs. Pour out the desired amount of resin. Thinner may be added to facilitate the removal of bubbles. The mix may be set in a vacuum.

2. Weigh and gradually stir in additives. Add pigments to achieve the desired hue (usually a little goes a long way).

3. Weigh and add catalyst. Mix thoroughly (several minutes) but avoid whipping up bubbles. See chart below.

4. Pour the mixture into the mold. A release agent such as polyvinyl alcohol on the mold will make removal easier. The mold can be made of plastic, rubber, wax, plasticene, or sealed plaster.

5. Curing will usually take about 24 hours, less for castings under $\frac{1}{72}$" thick. Even when cured, the plastic will have a gummy layer on top. Test curing by poking through this with a pin. When the plastic is solid the gummy layer is scraped off and the material can be sawn, filed, sanded, and buffed.

Layering

Because of the slow rate of cure it is possible to build up layers of plastic with excellent bonding. In fact, layering is recommended for castings over 2" thick. Follow the instructions above through #4. At this point the resin/catalyst mix can be divided up and given various colors or properties. Each layer may be added as soon as the preceding one has begun to gel.

Embedding

Any water-free object can be embedded in plastic. The process is as above, with the object set into place midway into the pouring. As long as the first layer is gooey when the second is poured, there will be no division line.

Thicker castings require a smaller proportion of catalyst:

Casting Thickness	% Catalyst
1/4"	2
1/2"	1
3/4"	1/2
1"	1/4

Plastic

Thermosetting plastics are available as liquid resins and catalysts, which are mixed to induce a molecular bonding called *polymerization*. Thermoplastics have undergone similar processes during manufacture, but are sold in the solid state as rods, sheets and tubes.

Materials

SAFETY
The biggest problems here come from:
- Dust created by cutting and sanding.
- Toxic fumes released by the heat of machining.
- Toxic vapors given off by solvents and glues.
- When cutting thermoplastics on a power machine, ventilate and wear goggles and a respirator. These same precautions are needed when cementing, proportionate to the scale of the work being done.

Cutting
Thermoplastics can be cut, drilled and turned like wood. When possible, the paper coating should be left on for these operations. Sheets of 1/4" or thinner can be broken along a straight edge. Make a deep gouge using a scribe and straight edge and break over a table edge or dowel; use pliers for small pieces.

Joining
Thermoplastics can be held together with epoxy cement or cyanoacrylates (e.g. Super Glue) but a stronger and neater joint is made with a glue devised just for this purpose. It is a solvent that penetrates a seam by capillary action and chemically welds the joint. The area should be scraped and filed but not polished. Remove the protective paper and hold the pieces in place with masking tape. The solvent is applied with a brush or syringe and will dry quickly.

Finishing
Edges are smoothed with a file then scraped with a flat piece of steel (eg. the back of a hacksaw blade). Fine abrasive papers may be used. A muslin buff with white diamond or a plastic compound will remove scratches. Avoid building up heat.

Heat-Forming Acrylic
Thermoplastics may be formed at temperatures around 200°-350° F (100-180° C). Specific temperatures will depend on the material, the degree of deformation, and the thickness of the section. Forming may be done by hand, in forms pressed together, or with vacuum pressure.

The following sequence is given to provide a general introduction to the possibilities of this technique. Before trying this, read further and look for advice from someone familiar with plastics. A local supplier will have manufacturers' data sheets and can often help with specific projects.

l. After removing the protective paper, set the sheet or rod into a kitchen oven and heat to the point where the plastic will bend when pushed with a blunt tool (about 300° F).
2. Wearing clean cotton gloves, pull the plastic out and bend it or push it over a rigid form. Hold it in position until it cools - usually just a minute or two. If the plastic cools before forming is completed, return the piece to the oven and rewarm it.
3. A strip heater is used to achieve straight bends. These may be bought at a hobby shop or plastics supply company.

Chapter 2

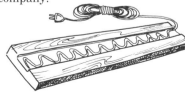

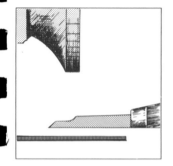

Surfaces

Hammer Marks

Hammers have always been central to metalsmithing. In fact the word smith is derived from the verb "to smite" which means to strike with a tool. While only a couple of hammers are needed to get started, most smiths collect specialized hammers as they develop their shop.

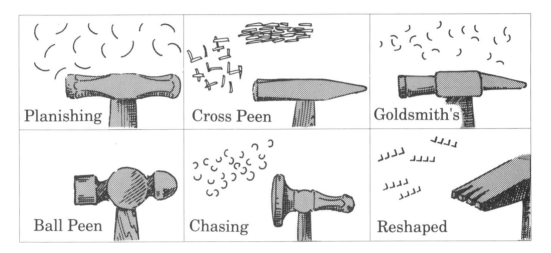

| Planishing | Cross Peen | Goldsmith's |
| Ball Peen | Chasing | Reshaped |

Improvised Hammer
To make a punch into a hammer, grip it in vise grips or a hand vise.

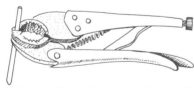

To mark both sides of a piece of metal, secure a punch or hammer in a vise and strike the metal between this and a hammer.

Fingerprint Protection
Hammer marks can be used stategically in places where handling will create unsightly fingerprints. Use a rough texture to hide tarnish on handles, flatware and the backs of pins and pendants.

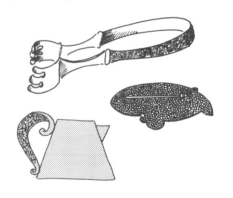

I have studied out a contrivance that I think may be of use to all brother smiths who think my way worth adopting.

C.H.W. writing in "The Blacksmith and Wheelwright" 1890

Stamping

Stamps are short steel rods used to impress a pattern or texture into metal. They can be commercially bought or made in the studio as a need arises.

Uses

1. As decoration. It is versatile, direct and permanent.
2. To provide recess for:
   solder inlay
   niello
   enamels
   amalgam
   resins
3. To give the illusion of depth.
4. To hallmark.

Tips

- Work on an anvil, preferably polished.
- Anneal the metal before starting.
- Use thick stock to absorb the blow.
- Hold the handle where it is comfortable. A lower grip increases power.
- You may also create a rich surface by hammering the metal onto a texture, such as rusted steel or concrete.

Tool Design

- Stamps should have a bevel to give the displaced metal somewhere to go.
- Punches with faces larger than 4 mm (3/16") tend to tilt and require a very heavy blow. They are not recommended for hand crafting.
- To make a clear, straight-walled imprint it is critical that the tool face be flat. Check with magnification.

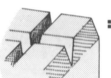

REMEMBER TO CONSIDER THIS THINNING.

Letters & Numbers

Commercially made letter and number stamps can be used for surface enrichment.

Found Tools

Carpenters' nail sets or Philips head screwdrivers with the point ground off make good punches. Leather working tools are not hard enough to stamp metal.

Hammers

Though any light hammer can be used, these two styles have evolved over the years for this technique. They are light enough to be used for hours, have a flat face and a comfortable grip. The handle is thin and springy so the hammer "spanks" the tool.

The Oriental style is simply a squat steel cylinder on a thin bamboo shaft. A chopstick works well.

Take what you can use and let the rest go by.

Ken Kesey

19

Surfaces

Chasing Tools

Chasing may be thought of as a refinement of stamping. In this technique, specially shaped punches are used to press a narrow line or large areas that become background.

Tips

- The tool is usually drawn toward the worker, held at such an angle that it propels itself along.

- The tool may be dipped in oil to lubricate its travel.

- Use a lightweight hammer and sit comfortably. The process should be delicate and controlled.

- For small radius curves, tilt the tool more or switch to a smaller tool. Since a sharper angle may cause the tool to slip, a different tool is the better solution.

- It is important that the workpiece be securely held.

- In some applications, a raised element is created by lowering the surrounding metal.

Definition & Uses

Chasing is an ancient and often misunderstood technique used to incise lines into metal. The result looks like engraving and the process resembles stamping, but chasing is a technique by itself. Unlike engraving, no metal is removed. Unlike stamping, the tool moves in a steady, unbroken motion. Chasing can be used to create linear patterns on flat or shaped sheet metal, and is used to sharpen details on castings.

Holding Devices

To keep clamps at a distance, use a strip of steel or a thin piece of wood. Protect against scratches with a rubber band.

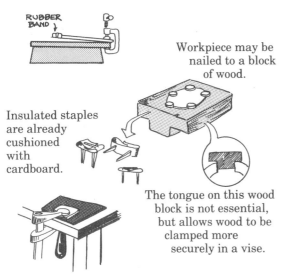

RUBBER BAND

Workpiece may be nailed to a block of wood.

Insulated staples are already cushioned with cardboard.

The tongue on this wood block is not essential, but allows wood to be clamped more securely in a vise.

When clamping directly onto the bench, use a wood, leather, or cardboard pad to prevent scratches.

Tools

The Western style chasing tool is held at an angle that allows the bottom edge of the tool to cut the line. The Oriental chasing tool features a symmetrical face and is held upright. The effect made by either tool should be identical, the choice being a matter of personal favorite.

In either case, a gradual taper on the shank makes it easier to guide the tool.

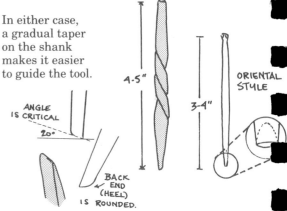

ANGLE IS CRITICAL

20°

BACK END (HEEL) IS ROUNDED.

4·5"

3-4"

ORIENTAL STYLE

For a note on hammers, see the preceding page.

Roll Printing

This technique uses the force of the rolling mill to press a pattern or image into a sheet of metal. It is quick and simple and opens many possibilities for invention.

Description

A sandwich made of sheet metal and a texturing material is passed through the rolling mill under great pressure. The metal is embossed, receiving the reverse image of the material.

Procedure

1. The workpiece is annealed and thoroughly dried.
2. When appropriate, the texture material is annealed.
3. Rollers are set by eye and sandwich is tried. Adjust rollers so the pressure is correct. The handle should be hard to move, but should not require two people.
4. Pass sandwich between rolls, trying to keep a continuous movement.

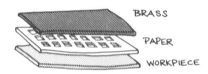

BRASS
PAPER
WORKPIECE

Variation

To create a raised pattern, prepare a sheet of metal by making indentations. This could be done by stamping, engraving, etching or roll printing. A hard metal such as brass is preferred. The print is then made on annealed metal as above.

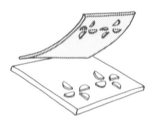

Suggested Materials

Burlap	Screen
Sandpaper	String
Lace	Binding Wire
Netting	Fabric

Paper Templates

Each variety of paper will leave a different surface when rolled. Experiment with card stock, drawing paper, tissue, etc. Cut and pierce the paper with a blade, lay it between annealed work metal and a stiff backing such as brass, and roll. Each paper template may be used only once, but where duplicates are desired, you can photocopy the images.

Engraving Process

Almost as important as the tool is the device used to hold the work-piece. It is this that controls the movement of the tool against the metal, which contributes to the gesture of the line that results.

Grip The graver is held between the fingertips and the length of the thumb. This will feel awkward at first but is worth getting used to. The handle should rest in the fleshy part of the palm. This is where the push comes from.

Posture Work should be at mid-chest height. When using a graver's ball, a table lower than a jeweler's bench will be needed. When using a shellac stick rested against the bench pin, sit sideways so the arm that holds the graver can be anchored.

Magnification Most engravers rely on a magnifying headset or loupe. If you can't see it, you can't cut it.

Cutting

Proper cutting involves a sliding rather than a scooping stroke. The graver is lightly pressed down into the metal at the beginning of the cut. The tool is then slid forward at a consistent depth. The scooping stroke can be

recognized by a telltale scar left behind the intended beginning of the line.

A line of varying widths is achieved not by changing the depth of the cut, but by rolling the graver on its side as it is pushed along. By rolling and returning to a vertical position, a graceful line can be cut.

In most cases the graver is held in one position as the work is brought into it. This is especially true of curved lines. Curves and circles are generally cut counter-clockwise.

Layout

Because engraving is a precise and demanding process it is usually unwise to plan on designing as you cut. Careful layout will allow you to concentrate on one task at a time. Drawing directly on the metal with a pen or pencil will create a wide line that can easily smudge. A better method is to coat the metal with a white paint (Chinese white, tempera, white shoe polish) and draw on this with a sharp pencil. The design is then lightly traced with a sharp scribe or sewing needle held in a pin vise. The white surface can be cut through or washed away. Though it takes a little longer, this kind of precision is needed for good engraving.

Wiggle Cut

A flat graver or liner is used to make this simple and versatile cut. The tool is held at a steep angle and "walked" forward, rocking from side to side. Any size graver may be used. The amount of swing in the wrist will alter the cut from being closed to open.

Engraving Tools

Engraved lines are made by slicing small bits of metal away with a sharp steel blade. These tools, called *gravers* or *burins,* are sharpened with great precision.

Gravers are made of high quality tool steel and are usually sold in the hardened, untempered state.

Square	▽	Lines, script, most cutting
Flat	▯	Carving, wiggle cuts
Knife	▽	Fine lines, shading
Round	▯	Wide lines, dots
Oval	◯	Carving, medium lines
Liner	▯	Textures, Florentine cuts

Handles

Graver handles are available in several styles; choice is a matter of personal preference. Since large bulbous handles can get in the way when making shallow cuts, those with a flat facet are generally preferred. Because gravers will get short with repeated sharpening, some engravers start with a short handle and later switch to a longer one to prolong use of the tool.

An EFB adjustable handle is often used with a square graver. The tool is held in place by a metal cone slid tightly along its shaft. A notched piece of brass provides for the changing length of the tool.

Most gravers are available with flat or bent shanks. The curved shape is usually preferred for working on a concave surface or on areas not easily accessible.

To determine the correct length of a graver, hold a pencil as shown. The end of the tool's handle will press into the heel of the hand where the flesh is thickest.

Holding Devices

It is impossible to engrave with control unless the metal is securely held. Here are several common solutions:

1. *The gravers' ball* A heavy steel sphere with vise jaws on top. It sits on a donut-shaped pad to provide for any angle and rotates on a bearing.

2. *A shellac stick*

This is a platform and handle that is held against the bench pin while cutting. The best style has a flared neck that facilitates angling the work. It can also be made from a piece of wood and dowel as shown. The platform is coated with a 3-5 mm layer of flake shellac, sealing wax, or a mixture of the two. To use, gently heat both shellac and object and press together.

3. *Vise stick* This is made when engraving several objects of the same shape. The outline of the piece is carved into the endgrain of the wood.

23

Graver Sharpening

All engraving requires a keen edge and repeated sharpening is needed to keep the cutting edge in shape. Although sharpening can be done by hand, an indexing device is recommended because it keeps each surface absolutely flat.

1. When purchased, most tools are too long and must be shortened. Determine the desired length as shown on the preceding page, taking into account the length of the handle. Tighten the graver in a vise at the right length and hit it with a sharp blow. For safety, catch the broken piece in a towel.

2. The tip will be sharpened many times. To speed this process the tip surface is reduced as shown. This is done on a grinding wheel (any size, flex shaft is OK). Quench often during grinding to keep the steel hard. If the graver gets blue you have undone the heat treatment. Refer to the page on hardening steel (page 156) to reharden and retemper.

3. The face angle for most gravers is 45° (less for soft metals and slightly more for hard materials). Use a protractor or similar aid to set this angle. The face is rubbed against a sharpening stone that has a coating of any kind of light oil. Set both stone and device on a smooth flat surface like a piece of glass or Plexiglas. The coarse stone is followed by a similar stroking on a fine stone. Continue this until all obvious scratches are gone.

4. Burs created by grinding are removed by jamming the tool a couple of times into a block of hardwood. The graver is then carefully polished by rubbing it along a piece of fine sandpaper held on a hard flat surface. The graver is usually removed from the device and held in the hand for this. A couple of slow, steady passes are usually sufficient. The graver is tested by setting the tip against the thumbnail. If properly sharpened it will "bite" rather than slip. When it passes this test the graver may be polished, which will cause it to cut a brilliant line. Rub rouge into a piece of crocus paper and stroke the face and belly of the tool lightly on this until it is mirror-like.

   To fasten the handle, grip the tool vertically in a vise and pound the handle onto the tang with a mallet. If the handle has a flat area it should lay along the underside (belly) of the tool.

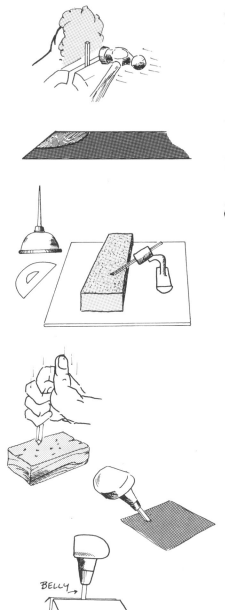

BELLY

Sharpening a Square Graver

The specific angles created in sharpening depend on the material being cut. The life expectancy of the edge will depend on the metal and the skill of the engraver.

1. If using an EFB handle prepare the back end by filing the edges like this. Heat the last half inch to bright red while holding the tool in pliers. Bend a slight curl and quench quickly. Be sure to bend up from the corner, not from a flat side.

NOT LIKE THIS

2. Prepare as in steps 1 and 2 on the preceding page.

REMOVE THIS PART

3. Grip the tool in the sharpener and set the bottom edge of the graver flat against the stone. Using a protractor, raise the tool to an angle of 8-12°. The tool is now rotated slightly by turning the barrel of the sharpener; note the amount of rotation by counting the markings on the sharpener.

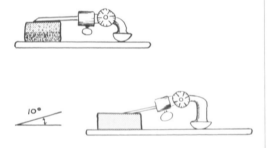

10°

4. Grind this surface (called the *belly*) first on a coarse stone and then on a fine one. Rotate the barrel back to its original position, then continue turning to the same number of notches used on the first side. Grind as before on the oilstone. The result, from below, should look like one of these:

Note that the angle can be modified to make a tool that will cut lines of various widths. The angles do not need to be identical, but their points must meet.

5. The barrel is then turned around so the face is downward. The angle is set at 45° and the face is ground on the coarse and fine stone.

45°

6. The tool is set into its handle and its three cutting planes are polished by rubbing on fine sandpaper held on glass. Test against a thumbnail. The tool should "bite" or stick to the nail without pressure. The face and belly may be polished on crocus paper as described on the preceding page.

DIP THE TOOL IN KEROSENE TO LUBRICATE.

Surfaces

25

Lamination Inlay

In this simple process sheets of metal are soldered together and then pressed until they are flush. This gives the appearance of an inlay. A rolling mill is helpful but not needed for lamination inlay.

1. One piece of metal must be thicker than the desired goal and the other must be very thin, around 26 gauge. The two pieces are cleaned and soldered together. The bond must be complete, extending all the way to the edges of the piece being soldered. Achieve this through careful preparation and heating, not by using surplus solder. Excess solder will make a yellowish ghost image around the inlay in the finished piece.

EXCESS SOLDER

2. After pickling and drying, the sheet is passed through the rolling mill or planished with a hammer until the two surfaces become flush. If rolling is to take place in both directions, anneal before changing the direction of the stretch. Lamination inlay cannot be used where specific shapes are required since distortion is inherent in the process.

3. Finish conventionally with files, paper, and buffing if desired. Subsequent soldering could spoil the effect. As a precaution use a lower melting solder and protect the inlay with yellow ocher.

A SINGLE BLANK CAN BE CUT TO MAKE A PAIR OF EARRINGS.

Variations

Complex patterns can be developed by borrowing a technique from glassblowers and sushi chefs. Make a *cane* by joining together several elements. In our case this means soldering together several wires of different color. This can be done in a planned or random way. Slice thin sections from this and solder these down to a base sheet. This is then rolled through the mill or planished until the surface becomes flush.

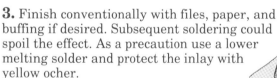

I am not a thing, a noun. I seem to be a verb, an evolutionary process, an integral function of the universe, and so are you.

Buckminster Fuller

Surfaces

Solder Inlay

In this simple and versatile technique, solder is allowed to flow into grooves made by hammering, engraving, roll printing, etching or similar means. Though many solders can be used, silver solder gives the cleanest and most durable results.

1. Prepare a recess by stamping, chasing, engraving, roll printing or etching. It should be about 1/2 mm (.020") deep.

2. Flux the piece well and flood the recess with solder. Wire solder works well but chips may be set in place if preferred.

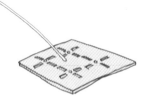

3. Some solder will spill outside the recess. This is unavoidable but should be kept to a minimum.

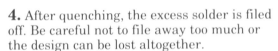

4. After quenching, the excess solder is filed off. Be careful not to file away too much or the design can be lost altogether.

5. To show up the pattern dip the piece into a liver of sulphur solution. This can be done throughout filing if necessary. The work is sanded, buffed and colored as usual. A high polish does not show the effect well and is not recommended.

Because the inlay material is solder and is flowed into place with heat, subsequent heatings must be thought out carefully. If the inlay is done before fabrication, IT (or at least Hard) solder should be used. If the inlay is going to be a final step, Easy or Easy-Flow is recommended.

Solder

Silver solder may be used on:
- steel
- nickel silver
- copper
- brass
- bronze
- 18K gold
- 14K colored gold
- 14K white gold

Gold solder may be used on:
- steel
- nickel silver
- copper
- brass
- bronze
- sterling: avoid colored & white solders

Soft solders like Sta-Brite and TIX work well for inlay but of course can't be heated above 600° F (300° C).

Puzzle Inlay

In this process pieces are cut out to fit together in the same way that the elements of a jigsaw interlock. While considerably more tedious than the lamination inlay, this method insures an undistorted image.

Method 1

- Saw out one unit, either the positive or the negative.

- After filing the shape to exactly what is wanted, trace around it on the other piece of metal using a sharp scribe. A sewing needle in a pin vise works well.

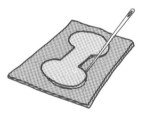

- Saw the second unit carefully and the two pieces should make a perfect fit. File or planish if necessary. Solder the pieces together.

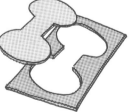

Method 2

- Clamp or glue pieces of metal together. Saw through both pieces simultaneously. Solder the pieces together.

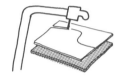

- When both convex and concave curves are involved, the kerf of the saw becomes a factor. This space will be filled by solder so must be kept small. Use a blade no larger than 4/0.

- Some cunning is needed when piercing to get started. Drill and saw to proposed line before gluing on the second sheet.

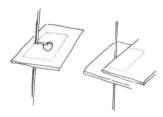

- Clamp or glue with epoxy or Super Glue. Generally, the inlay is completed before the object is fabricated but specific designs will require different sequences.

Surfaces

Niello

Niello (*ne-EL-o from the Latin **nigellum**, meaning blackish*) is a metallic alloy of sulfur with silver, copper and lead. It is first made as an ingot, then pulverized and fused into a recess.

1. The workpiece should be finished through a medium sandpaper stage. All soldering should be done, but stones should not be set. The niello will fill grooves as deep as one millimeter. These may be made by etching, stamping, chasing, roll printing, engraving, or by fabricating with overlay or channel work. After cleaning thoroughly, coat the metal with diluted (milky) paste flux or a thin solution of ammonium chloride and water.

2. Some people grind the niello ingot to a powder, which may be washed by swirling in a shallow dish under running water. The niello is carefully laid into place with tweezers, a brush or a small spatula-shaped tool. It is dried by setting it in a warm place or by gently playing a torch over it. When all moisture has been driven off, the piece is uniformly heated, either in a kiln or with a torch. The kiln should be set for 370°-540° C (700-1000° F). When using a torch, heat from below to avoid touching the niello with the flame. The niello will bead up and glow red-orange as it melts. If it does not flow, the niello may be spread into position with a steel or carbon rod. Be careful not to over-heat. Even with high-melting niello, the metal to which it is being fused should never go above a dull red. Most niello fuses around 380° C (700° F).

3. In an alternate method, niello is dripped onto a workpiece directly from the end of a rod-shaped ingot. Flux the piece and warm it in a soft flame until the flux is fully liquid. When the rod is touched to the metal it will melt and flow into recesses. The torch is lightly played over the surface, but should not be kept directly on the metal or the niello. Try to keep the fusing operation brief since prolonged heat can cause the niello to pit and attack silver and gold.

4. The work may then be finished by scraping, filing, burnishing and sanding. Machine buffing should be avoided because it will wear away the niello faster than the metal around it.

5. Working directly from the rod is recommended for repairs and filling small lines.

Note: Keep files, sandpaper and soldering blocks reserved for this work. Traces of niello will cause damage if accidentally heated to silver soldering temperatures. Because of the lead content, wash carefully after working with niello.

Making Niello

Though some recipes seem complicated, niello is really a simple mixture of three metals and all the sulfur they can hold. In general terms:

- sulfur causes blackness.
- copper deepens the blackness.
- silver raises the melting point.
- lead provides for fusion and ease in spreading.

1. Melt the metals in a borax-lined crucible and stir with a carbon rod.
2. Add sulfur and continue to stir. The resulting smoke is dramatic and acrid. **Provide very good ventilation.**
3. When no more sulfur can be absorbed, pour the mix into a warm ingot mold. A clean angle iron works well.
4. The ingot's surface should be smooth and shiny. If not, break the ingot into pieces, re-melt with additional sulfur and repour.

Recipes

Fike

6 g. silver	2 g. lead
2 g. copper	6 g. sulfur

Heinrich

1 oz. silver	3 oz. lead
2 oz. copper	6 oz. sulfur

Augsberg #1

1 oz. silver	2 oz. lead
1 oz. copper	8 oz. sulfur

Ruklin #1

1 oz. silver	4 oz. lead
2 oz. copper	5 oz. sulfur

Mokumé

In mokumé-gane, layers of contrasting metals create a multi-colored woodgrain effect. There are several possible methods for building up the billet of laminates and several others for making the pattern in the metal.

Diffusion is the best method of joining the layers of a stack. Such a block will be perfectly fused and may be treated like any other metal mass. This process is explained on page 77.

Soldering has a greater possibility of pitting, but is handy when a small piece of mokumé is needed and when very little forming is to be done.

1. Metal sheets are flattened, scrubbed with pumice, and degreased with an alcohol-type solvent.
Pieces about one inch square are a handy size.

2. Sheet solder is forged or milled as thin as possible and similarly cleaned. It is cut into sheets slightly smaller than the laminates.

3. Laminates are lightly fluxed on both sides and stacked up with a piece of solder between each one. This pile may have 4 to 8 laminate sheets, not counting the solder.

4. Heat the whole pile with a large bushy reducing flame. If your torch cannot be adjusted to a reducing flame, work on charcoal, perhaps with another charcoal block set behind. This will help absorb oxides.

5. Air cool. Do not quench, especially in pickle.

6. Forge or mill the sheet to about half its original thickness. Cut it in half, clean and flux the two surfaces. Using another piece of solder, join these two pieces. This will double the number of layers in the stack. Again, air cool.

7. Thin the sheet, cut, and repeat the last step. Do this until the desired number of layers is achieved. Generally 10-30 layers will yield pleasant results.

8. A disadvantage of this method is that subsequent soldering can endanger the bond between the layers. Use Hard solder for stacking and minimize soldering around the mokumé.

Bumping

The sheet of laminates is set on a medium soft surface like pitch or soft wood, and worked with small punches to create a bumpy sheet. The bumps may be random or arranged and may be made with a single or several tools.

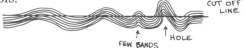

If a bump is made deeper than the thickness of the sheet, a hole will result in the next step when the tops of each bump are filed off. The metal is filed, sanded and polished using conventional techniques. The richness of the pattern will not show until the mokumé has been colored.

Carving

When the laminate stack is completed, the still thick billet is drilled, with care taken not to go all the way through. The pointed recess of the drill tip is converted to a round-bottomed hole with a spherical bur. An alternate method is to carve a recess with a round chisel. Further possibilities are opened by engraving or machining recesses. The carved ingot is forged or milled to cause the pattern to emerge. Repeated carving and forging steps are used to bring out the full pattern. Note that rolling will tend to emphasize a uniformity in the pattern while hammering will create a random effect.

Reticulation

Reticulation is a process by which metal is made to draw itself into ridges and valleys, creating a unique texture. Many alloys can be made to reticulate, but a formulation of 82% silver and 18% copper yields particularly dramatic results.

The buckling is the result of the different cooling rates of the two strata shown below. The copper oxide layer will remain solid while the interior of the sheet becomes molten. When heat is removed, the interior contracts, pulling the copper oxide skin into ridges. The effect may be achieved by careful heating of most nonferrous metals (heat scarring) but is much more dramatic when the metal is prepared as described here.

Process

1. Because the process is somewhat unpredictable, work on a piece of metal a little larger than your actual need. 16-20 gauge sheet will produce the best results. Heat the piece of sterling or 14K gold to 650° C (1200° F) and hold at this temperature for five minutes. This is most easily done in a kiln but can be done with a torch (keep the metal at a dull red). Do not use flux, since the purpose of this step is to create a layer of copper oxide. Air cool. The metal will be a uniform dark gray.

2. Pickle in hot fresh Sparex or a 10% sulfuric acid solution. This removes copper oxide from the surface leaving a silver-rich skin and "locking in" the copper oxide layer beneath.

3. After rinsing, heat as before to the same temperature, this time for at least 10 minutes. Oxygen cannot react much with the silver-rich skin so it penetrates and promotes growth of the copper oxide layer into the sheet (i.e. interior oxidation). Air cool. The sheet should be only slightly gray. Pickle as before.

silver skin
copper oxide
basic alloy

4. Reticulation is done with a torch. Since it is necessary to make the metal molten throughout its interior, it is wise to either preheat the soldering block and then allow the heat to rise up into the sheet, or to work on a wire mesh. The sheet is brought to red with a sharp hot flame. The torch is quickly passed over an area allowing it to cool intermittently. The cooling is what causes the metal to buckle. The skin may melt and crawl without damaging the results, but this should be minimized since this flowing softens the sharpness of the ridges and diminishes the effect. Allow the piece to lose redness before quenching.

5. Reticulated metal may be soldered, colored, and finished like its original stock. It is brittle, and extensive forming is not recommended. The copper oxide layer seems to be porous and "soaks up" solder when joining an exposed edge. To make a neat and strong joint, burnish the edges before soldering.

Because copper plays an important role in reticulation, higher copper content generally enhances the results. 14K yellow or rose gold will work better than 14K green or white, or any color of 18K. An alloy of 820 parts silver, balance copper, produces especially dramatic results. It may be made by adding 10% (by weight) copper to sterling or can be purchased from Hauser & Miller, Inc. or Hoover & Strong, Inc. (see page 189).

Granulation

This ancient process uses a delicate solderless bonding to attach small pieces such as granules to a surface. It was highly developed in ancient times, particularly by the Greeks and Etruscans.

 Granulation is an ancient decorative process in which a metal object is ornamented by the application of many tiny beads (granules). The techniques involved will work for other shapes of applied ornament and rely on a diffusion process related to eutectic bonding. The term granulation is often expanded to include all these aspects of the procedure. The stunning quality of proper granulation is achieved by having granules adhered to the surface by an almost imperceptible bond at the tangent point. Because this fine precision is impossible with conventional soldering, a diffusion reaction is created. A detailed description of this is given on page 77. In brief, by one of several methods a small amount of metal (usually copper) is introduced to the contact area. When appropriate heat is reached, the metals form an alloy of a lower melting point than the metals being joined. This alloy flows, creating a strong bond.

Process

When working on fine silver or high karat gold it is necessary to supply the metal that will make the bonding alloy.

1. The metal and granules are coated with a mixture of flux (containing a metallic salt) and a glue that contains carbon. At high temperatures the metal becomes an oxide (such as CuO_2). The carbon from the glue then unites with the oxygen and passes off as carbon dioxide gas. This leaves a small amount of metal to alloy at the joint.

Fluxes used include Prip's, antimony trioxide, copper chloride, verdigris or a copper nitrate made by dissolving copper into ammonia (allow scraps of copper to sit in a closed jar of ammonia until the solution turns blue; about 24 hours). Any organic glue can be used: gum tragacanth, mucilage, hide glue, etc. Thin these with water to a pale soupy consistency.

2. Copper can be supplied by plating the granules before applying them. Set granules in a steel container such as a jar lid and pour in old (copper-saturated) pickle. The plating should be thin (rosy colored) because too much copper will cause a flooding of the bonding alloy. When using coated granules, any flux may be used and the glue may be omitted.

When granulating on sterling, the copper content of the alloy itself provides the metal needed to create a low melting solution at the point of contact. Use any flux and a trace amount of glue. A disadvantage is the proximity of the fusion point (1500° F, 815° C) and the melting point of sterling (1640° F, 960° C).

Two Ways to Make Granules

• Line a coffee can with about 3/4" of powdered charcoal, made by filing briquets. Sprinkle tiny chips of metal on top of this layer, keeping the number small enough that the chips won't touch each other. Build up alternate layers of charcoal and metal. Set the can into a kiln until it glows red hot and hold it at this heat for about 15 minutes. To test for granule formation, remove a spoonful of the mixture and rinse away the charcoal. If the shot is not completely spherical, continue heating. When ready, air cool the can and rinse in water. The charcoal will float off, leaving the granules on the bottom of the can.

• Cut metal into chips and sprinkle onto a clean flat charcoal block. Hold the block in a gloved hand about 12" above a dish of water. Use a torch to melt the metal, holding the block at an angle that allows each granule to roll off as it is drawn into a sphere.

Firing

Granules are set onto clean metal with tweezers or a brush. A scribed line can be used to help locate the tiny beads. Avoid a single line of granules if possible because it is weak. Dip granules in the flux/glue mix before applying, but avoid excess liquid by soaking it up with a tissue. Allow the work to dry thoroughly (half hour) before applying the torch. With a broad flame, bring the whole piece to bright red. When joints "flash" which looks like solder flow, remove heat. Pickle and finish, avoiding rough handling. Scratch brushing is recommended.

Surfaces

Amalgamation

This ancient technique uses mercury to create a paste that carries fine gold to the surface of an object. It involves high health risk and is not to be taken lightly. If you try it, work outside with the wind at your back. Wear rubber gloves and wash thoroughly when done.

1. In a mortar and pestle, knead equal weights of mercury and filings of fine gold.

2. If you want an inlay effect, prepare the work piece with recesses made by chasing, engraving, or etching. These do not need to be very deep, say 1/4 to 1/2 mm. Amalgam can also be used as an all-over surface wash.

3. The surface of the thoroughly cleaned piece is primed by rubbing it with a paste made of mercury and chalk dust.

4. For inlay, the gold amalgam is pressed like putty into the grooves and recesses of the piece. A slight excess is mounded above each filled area.

5. Leave the piece exposed to air, preferably outdoors, for at least two days. Occasionally press the amalgam further into the recesses with a smooth wooden stick. **The mercury is being driven off in the form of a poisonous gas.**

6. Place work in a warm area, such as near a radiator or a sunny window sill to drive off further fumes. Again, ventilation is very important. Leave for several hours or longer.

7. Set the work piece on a soldering block and heat to a dull red. Fumes are still being driven off. If possible set a fan beside you to blow the gases away. This assumes there is no one sitting across from you.

8. After air cooling, burnish the amalgam into the recess, scrape off excess and reburnish.

A DAPPING BLOCK CAN BE USED FOR THIS

Safety

Coloring

It is difficult to overstate the importance of color to the effect of a finished piece. Thoughtful care at this stage is needed to bring a piece to its fullest potential.

Surfaces

Preparation

The metal to be colored must be clean. Try to avoid greasy materials like steel wool and buffing compounds when possible. Alternate finishing materials would include pumice, sandpaper, Scotchbrite and a scratchbrush. When grease is present, clean the work in an ultrasonic machine or scrub it in a strong solution of ammonia, soap and water. When metal is thoroughly clean, water will "sheet" or cover the whole surface rather than bead up. When the work passes this test, dry it with a soft cloth or drop it in a box of sawdust. From here on, handle the work only by the edges. Just before coloring, clean the metal by wiping with an alcohol-type solvent.

Simple Copper Plating

Brass, gold and platinum are notoriously hard to darken. One solution is to plate the work with a thin layer of copper, which can be readily colored. Because it is thin this layer will not withstand wear, but if the area to be darkened is recessed this method offers a useful solution.

Saturated pickle (blue-green in color) is actually a copper plating solution in that it is an acid charged with free copper ions. These have a tendency (especially when electricity is introduced) to attach to a metal object. An easy way to create a slight electrical charge is to put into the same acid solution a ferrous and a non-ferrous metal. The electrolytic reaction is increased with heat.

- If used pickle is not available, set copper scraps in pickle overnight or until it shows color.
- Wrap the object lightly with iron or steel wire. Binding wire works well.
- Set the object into warm pickle. Note that everything in the pickle at this time will be plated. After removing the steel, the pickle can be used as normal. It has not been damaged.
- Rinse and color the object and buff the copper from raised areas if desired.

Preservation

It is the nature of most metals to react with their environment. This produces (among other things) their colors. In choosing a particular patina we are singling out one point on a continuum and trying to preserve it. To do this, the metal must be either returned to its original finish periodically or sealed off from the environment. A hard film (lacquer) will resist marring but can eventually be chipped away. A soft film (wax) is more vulnerable to wear but will smear across the protected surface, keeping the film more or less intact. In articles to be worn, wax can rub off on clothing.

Lacquer

Use only top quality lacquer. Apply a thin coat, taking care to avoid bubbles and trapped dust. A couple of thin coats are preferred to a single thick one. Porous materials (ivory, wood, clay, etc.) are likely to contain oils that can never be completely cleaned away. Because this can cause lacquer to bead or discolor, a test sample is a good idea. For small areas, clear nail polish is a good lacquer. It might need to be thinned to spread well. Lacquer thinner can be bought at a paint supply store.

Wax

Beeswax or paraffin are commonly used to protect metal objects. Popular commercial preparations are *Museum Wax* or *Renaissance Wax*. One method of application is to warm the object and rub the wax over it. Another method is to reduce the wax to a paste by melting it and pouring it into turpentine. Use about 1/3 as much turpentine as wax. This is then rubbed onto the piece. Paste wax (like *Butcher's, Trewax* or *Johnson's Wax*) can also be used, but avoid polishes that contain other additives such as silicone.

Patina Recipes

Liver of Sulfur (Potassium Sulfide)

This sulfur smelling yellow liquid is one of the most commonly used chemicals to darken metal. It will quickly produce black on sterling and copper, but it's capable of much more. By moving slowly through the development of the sulfide layer, a range of colors present themselves. They are not permanent enough for an exposed surface such as a ring shank, but they are satisfactory for pins, earrings and pendants.

Liver of sulfur quickly looses its strength when exposed to air or light. For this reason it is commonly sold in large chunks and kept either in a can or a brown glass jar. Break off just what you need and carefully seal up the rest.

Dissolve a small amount of liver of sulfur in warm water. A pea-sized piece to a cup of water is usual. If the solution is too strong the resulting sulfide layer is brittle and will be easily chipped off. The solution may be warmed, but should never boil. The solution may be brushed on or the work may be immersed. I recommend the dip-rinse method to slowly create a wide range of colors.

Work at the sink, warming the piece under a running stream of hot water. I dip the piece briefly into the liver of sulfur solution then quickly rinse it off. This dip-rinse cycle will allow you to see the full spectrum of colors, which, on sterling, runs from gold to brown to vermillion to blue to gray. A small amount of ammonia added to the solution will enhance the blues and a little baking soda will deepen the browns.

On copper, use a weaker solution and brass brush between each dip to create a purplish gray. It's especially important that you remove all fingerprints before darkening copper. Liver of sulfur will have almost no effect on brass or nickel silver.

Copper

Along with its malleability and low cost, one of the features that makes copper so popular is its ability to turn many beautiful colors. Chemicals in the air and earth will achieve these given time, but most metalsmiths prefer to control the process themselves. Be warned that the metal will take an active role in the process, often behaving in ways that defy explanation. Those who undertake patinas in the spirit of adventure are more likely to enjoy the process than those who want to dictate every nuance of the color.

This very brief description will deal in generalities, but in fact the surface (smooth or textured), the state (annealed or work-hardened) and the environment will all affect the outcomes of the recipes given here. There is no substitute for experimentation, and no shortcut to a unique patina.

Green

1 Tbsp ammonium chloride
   (sal ammoniac)
1 Tbsp salt
1 oz. ammonia
1 qt. water

Mix the chemicals in a plastic carton or bowl that will never again be used for food. Warm water will hasten the dissolving process. Unless your tap water is pure and neutral, use bottled water.

The copper surface must be chemically clean and dry. Use Scotchbrite, pumice or a commercial scouring powder. Avoid steel wool because of its oil content. Spritz the metal with a pump spray until it is uniformly wet. Allow it to dry naturally, for instance in a sunny spot or near a radiator. Do not try to speed up the drying with a torch, because this creates a patina that is too flaky to adhere well. When dry, respray and again allow to dry. Repeat the process at least four times.

This recipe is also recommended for a smothered patina. Mix the liquid with sawdust (or leaves, grass, kitty litter, etc) until damp, place in a plastic bag with the workpiece and seal.

Patina Recipes (on copper)

These recipes continue the list started on the preceding page, and refer to patinas on copper. In many cases they will give similar hues on brass.

Surfaces

Blue

water
salt
ammonia

After the piece has been thoroughly cleaned, wet the surface with clean water. Sprinkle on a layer of table salt and trap the piece in a sealed environment with an open dish of ammonia. A plastic bucket or trash bag are typical enclosures. An alternate patina uses the same process but replaces the water coating with vinegar.

Brown

1 Tbsp ferric nitrate
1 qt water

Mix the solution in a spray jar and spritz lightly onto a clean surface. Allow the surface to dry before applying another coat. Several coats are needed.

Peanut Oil
available from grocery or health food stores.

After cleaning and drying the metal, apply a drop or two of the oil to the palm of your hand and spread it across your palms. Rub this gently over the piece, developing an extremely thin film of oil on the piece. Warm the piece with a soft bushy flame, just until the oil starts to smoke.

Red

5 gm 'rokusho' *
5 gm copper sulfate
1 liter water

* homemade rokusho
3 parts copper acetate
1 part sodium hydroxide
1 part calcium carbonate

Immerse the cleaned workpiece in a boiling solution for at least an hour. When the desired color is achieved, remove and rinse in cold water.

Rokusho is a traditional Japanese patina preparation which is difficult to obtain in the West. To make your own, thoroughly mix the ingredients listed and allow the solution to settle for a week. Gently pour off the liquid on the top and substitute for rokusho.

Taken from <u>The Colouring, Bronzing and Patination of Metals</u>, by Hughes and Rowe. Used with permission.

Grey

Gold oxidizer
Available through most jewelry supply companies.

On gold, steel is required to create the reaction. Use a nail or piece of wire (paper clip) to color specific areas. For broader applications, grip a bit of steel wool in tweezers and use this as a dauber. To color small pieces or chains, dissolve steel wool in solution and immerse.

Patina Recipes

As the old saying goes, there are three ways to learn about patinas. Experiment, experiment, experiment.

Surfaces

Bronze
• Gray to dull black

Birchwood Casey Gun Blue
Available at most sporting goods stores, or from
 Birchwood Casey Co.
 Eden Prairie, MN 55344

Use the solution full strength by brushing onto or immersing work. On brass or bronze, apply the solution with steel wool.

Aluminum
• Gray to dull black

Birchwood Casey
Alumina Black
(address above)

Use full strength from the bottle by wiping, spraying or immersing. The transparent oxide must be removed from the aluminum, preferably by a mechanical abrasive like bead blasting. When sufficiently dark, rinse the work in water and seal the color with a wax or lacquer. The solution contains phosphoric acid, so goggles and rubber gloves should be worn.

Pewter
• Gray to dull black

Dilute nitric acid.

Mix a very weak solution, using the precaution of gloves, goggles and a rubber apron. The solution may be wiped on or the piece may be immersed. The color change will be immediate.

Steel
• Gray to blue black

Birchwood Casey Gun Blue
Available at most sporting goods stores, or from
 Birchwood Casey Co.
 Eden Prairie, MN 55344

Use the solution full strength by brushing onto or immersing work. On brass or bronze, apply the solution with steel wool.

• Red-orange

Salt water.

Mix a strong solution and spray onto clean metal. Allow the oxide to form naturally. Several coats will be needed. It's important that the metal be free of oil and dirt.

37

Etching

In this process chemical rather than mechanical force is used as metals are given controlled exposure to acids for specific durations to create the desired effects. Protective clothing and ventilation are required.

A design may be cut into metal with acid by covering part of the metal with an acid-proof material (resist) while leaving areas exposed to the corrosion (bite) of the acid. The following tips apply to all etching:

- Work only in a ventilated area. Acid fumes can do you no good.
- Wear rubber gloves, apron, goggles and a respirator.
- Keep baking soda handy to neutralize acid mishaps. Always add the acid to water. Acid is the denser fluid of the two and will fall to the bottom of the dish and begin the mixing. When water is added to acid it will float on top making a limited interface between the two liquids. The rapid build-up of heat might cause the acid to splatter.
- Because they are slow to mix, make acid solutions (called *mordants*) at least an hour before using them.
- Store acids in narrow-necked glass or plastic jars with glass or plastic lids. Store in a cool dark place; never up high. Label the vessels clearly, including the strength and date of the solution.
- Don't pour acid down the drain or toilet. Neutralize with baking soda and pour into the ground. Large quantities should be disposed of through a waste removal company.
- Generally, the slower the bite, the more even it will be.
- To check the depth of the bite, remove the piece, rinse it in water and set the point of a needle into the etch, feeling the height of the wall. To allow for polishing, etch a little deeper than desired.

Acids

Chemically pure (C.P.)	100%
Reagent	approx. 70%
Commercial	approx. 50%

Most acids are available in these three grades. The first is very expensive and not necessary. Most people use reagent grade and most formulas, including those on the next page, are written for this. If you have a more dilute acid, modify the formulas accordingly.

By its nature, acid is a temperamental commodity. In some cases it gets stronger as it absorbs other chemicals, so "old" acid is better than a fresh mix. Increased temperature will accelerate the action of acid but once it gets going it produces its own heat and so will continue a strong bite. The only rule is that there are no rules and each time you etch you must pay attention to what is happening.

Process

Many variations are possible, but typically a design is either painted on or selectively scratched away after the whole piece has been painted and dried.

To achieve different heights, etch a while, pull the piece out, rinse it, and stop out the areas that have sufficient depth. Allow the fresh resist to dry and resubmerge. The opposite approach can yield the same effect. Scratch out only that part of the design you want deepest and begin etching. After a while pull the piece out, rinse, and scratch away more of the design. The first design will continue etching deeper along with the newly cut design. This may be done repeatedly to achieve several distinct layers.

38

Mordants

Mordants are the chemicals, generally acids, that are used to deliberately corrode metal. Protective clothing and ventilation are required.

Unless specified these are fluid measures. The figure in parenthesis is %. For brevity the word "acid" has been omitted.

Gold	1 part nitric (25), 3 parts hydrochloric (75)	*This is Aqua Regia.*
Silver, Sterling	1 part nitric (25), 3 parts water (75)	
Copper, Brass, Nickel	1 part nitric (50), 1 part water (50)	
Aluminum	1.5 oz ammonia (2), 5 gm copper sulfate (2) 14 oz. sodium hydroxide (6), 2 gal. water (90)	
Lead, Tin, etc.	1 part nitric (20), 4 parts water (80)	
Iron, Steel	2 parts hydrochloric (67), 1 part water (33)	

Safety

Supplies

None of these resists will bond well to unclean metal. Since a slightly roughened surface is also helpful, clean by scrubbing with pumice. Rinse, pat dry and avoid touching the surface.

Resists	Solvents
asphaltum	turpentine
oil base paint (spray paint)	turpentine
shellac (color with dye)	alcohol
lacquer (e.g. nail polish)	lacquer thinner
press type, grease pencil	turpentine

During etching, gases are released in the form of bubbles. If these remain on the metal they will prevent the acid from reaching it, causing an uneven bite.
To remove bubbles, brush the work lightly with a feather or a mop made from string.

To safely lower work into the acid bath, use a loop of string. Tweezers may also be used but they often scratch the resist.

A very clean etch can be achieved on copper and brass with a *ferric chloride* solution. This is a salt rather than an acid and behaves a little differently. Work must be level and should be suspended just below the surface of the fluid. Electrical tape or contact paper can be used to protect the back. In addition to the resists listed above, permanent felt tip pen can be used with this mordant. The etch will take 1 to 4 hours. Rinsing in water will not stop the corrosive action.
Scrub with ammonia.

Available in gallons from Mouser Electronics, 2401 Highway 287, Mansfield, TX 76063, (817) 483-4422.

Photoetching

In this process, photographic techniques are used to lay down the resist on the metal sheet. Acids are then used as described previously to cut the design into the metal.

In simple terms, a piece of metal is coated with a light-sensitive material so it will react in the same way as photographic paper. It is then exposed to light passing through a piece of film. A chemical developer is used to remove those areas exposed to light. When the resist has dried, the metal is etched. This process is fundamental to the micro-electronics industry and is growing and improving at an amazing pace. Metalsmiths pursuing this technique are encouraged to consult technical magazines, industry, and technical colleges for more information.

The image must be a high-contrast negative; that is, one without gray areas. This can be made with Kodalith film or by drawing on acetate with black ink. Some copying machines will print an image on acetate, allowing the use of drawings or printed images from books. The film image must be the actual size you want on the metal.

Process

1. Cut the metal slightly oversize, drill a hole in one corner and hook a 6" piece of wire by which to handle and hang the metal.
2. Check metal for flatness and clean it thoroughly with pumice until water runs off in sheets. Do not shortcut on cleanliness. Dry with a lint-free cloth.
3. Under a safe light, coat the metal with resist by dipping. **Fumes from the resist are dangerous.** Wear a proper respirator. Remember to put the resist away before turning on room lights because exposure will ruin it.
4. Hang the metal to dry in a light-tight box, preferably covered with a tightly woven dark fabric. Warm air will speed up drying. This can be supplied with a hair dryer. Since this will kick up dust, be sure the box is clean. Do not heat above 100° C (200° F). Drying will take about 45 minutes with heat, 2-3 hours without.
5. Still using safe-light conditions, contact print the negative onto the metal. The exposure time will depend on the brand of resist, freshness of light bulbs and distance from the light source to the metal. It will probably be between 5 and 20 minutes. A standard step test with 2 minute intervals is recommended.
6. Develop in normal light for 1-2 minutes by setting the metal in a tray of developer made for the resist being used. Agitate slightly to provide a fresh wash of chemicals to all areas. Though hard to see, the image should be visible as a pattern of coated and bare metal. Rinse in cool water.
7. Dry in heated box for 30 minutes or in warm area for about 2 hours.
8. Coat the back and edges with a conventional resist such as asphaltum or lacquer.
9. Etch as described on the preceding two pages with the mordants listed. A detail-preserving slow etch is recommended. After etching remove the resist with acetone or lacquer thinner.

Chemicals

You'll need photoresist, thinner, emulsion and developer. Enough chemicals for several dozen plates will probably cost around $80.

Freundorfer, Inc.
1551 Commerce Dr.
Elgin, IL 60123
(708) 931-7300

Materials

1. A darkroom or light-proofed closet or bathroom
2. A respirator.
3. A drying box
4. A light box.

Surfaces

Low-Tech Photoetching

While not as precise or predictable as the technique described on the preceding page, this very simple method makes photoetching as accessible as a photocopier.

In this process the toner used in copiers and laser printers is transferred to a metal plate where it becomes the resist for traditional etching. Copies are made from a high contrast black and white image onto acetate film. The toner is then transferred with a household iron.

1. The metal must be very clean. A mild abrasive such as Scotch-Brite is recommended because it removes surface oils while also creating a little "tooth." Follow this with a wipe of solvent (nail polish remover, acetone, paint thinner, etc.) Use ventilation and keep away from flames for this step. When the metal is clean, handle it only by the edges.

2. Photocopy the image onto either side of a plastic film. For most copiers you'll need to be sure the acetate is a standard size. Small pieces can sometimes be taped onto a standard sheet of paper to help them feed through. If there is any sign of dirt or oil on the film, gently clean it with solvent.

3. Lay the film, toner side down, onto the clean metal and make a tape hinge along one edge. Set a piece of paper or light fabric on top of it and press with a hot iron (265-295° F, 130-150° C). This is a typical "cotton-linen" setting. Use a firm pressure and allow the heat to soak through the plastic. Insufficient heat will result in an incomplete transfer, but too much will cause the lines of the image to "bleed" outward. I suggest doing a practice piece to develop a feel for the process. If some sections of the image did not transfer, you can often touch up specific places by lightly rubbing them with the edge or the tip of the iron. This calls for a gentle touch.

4. An alternate method is to set the metal on a hotplate or an inverted iron. Allow the heat to flow upward until it softens the toner image, then burnish through the plastic. A jeweler's burnisher, a brayer or a small graphics roller can be used. When the metal has cooled, peel away the film to reveal the transferred image. Do this slowly so you can make repairs if necessary. If you are not going to etch immediately, leave the film in place to protect the resist. Etch as usual, then remove the transfer with paint thinner or a similar solvent.

1.

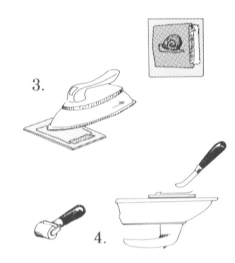

3.

4.

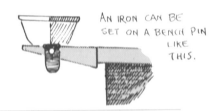

AN IRON CAN BE SET ON A BENCH PIN LIKE THIS.

While most acetate sheets seem to work, a plastic film called TEC 200 was developed specifically for this purpose. It is available from Meadowlake Corporation, Box 497, Northport, NY 11768.

Anodizing Aluminum

Aluminum can absorb a dye if its surface layer is electrically treated to create a porous corrosive film. This process is called anodizing.

SAFETY

Anodizing involves the use of acids and electric current. Considerably more expertise than what is presented here is needed to safely work with either of these. Always turn off the electric apparatus before handling, ventilate the area and wear protective clothing, goggles and gloves before handling acid or caustic solutions. Always.

Equipment & Supplies

As with any process, there is almost no limit to the maximum cost. Those interested in experimenting with anodizing on a small scale are generally more interested in the minimum investment required. You will need a rectifier or battery charger, a number of stout plastic vessels, a stainless steel pot, several immersible thermometers, an acid-proof apron, gloves and goggles and several chemicals. A small experimenting setup can be assembled for $100-150.

In its relatively brief history (the process was patented in 1924), anodizing has matured to a complex and exact science. Those interested in pursuing this topic are advised to read further, both in texts and in industrial literature. The intention on this page is to provide a synopsis of the process and a review for those already familiar with it.

While the oxide layer is significantly tougher than untreated aluminum, that is not to say it can withstand the rigors of metalworking. The layer is brittle and thin, and will crack when worked. For this reason all cutting, filing, bending,

forming and finishing should be accomplished before the anodizing process begins. Cold connections are well-suited to this technique, and with care, clean joins may be made by careful gas and TIG welding.

To the casual observer, the process of anodizing aluminum seems a lot like coloring Easter eggs. In both cases you dip, rinse, and dip again. The diagram below shows a synopsis of the anodizing process. The time notations refer to minutes in the bath. In all cases these are merely suggestions for typical applications. Experimentation is needed.

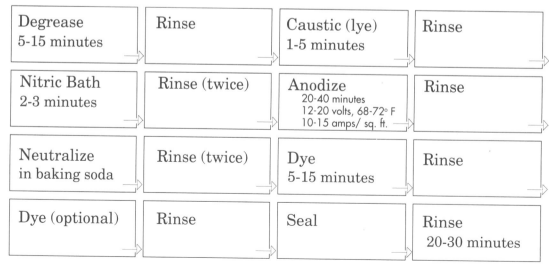

Degrease 5-15 minutes	Rinse	Caustic (lye) 1-5 minutes	Rinse
Nitric Bath 2-3 minutes	Rinse (twice)	Anodize 20-40 minutes 12-20 volts, 68-72° F 10-15 amps/ sq. ft.	Rinse
Neutralize in baking soda	Rinse (twice)	Dye 5-15 minutes	Rinse
Dye (optional)	Rinse	Seal	Rinse 20-30 minutes

Safety

The whole process should take no more than two hours, and of course you are not constantly working during that time.

Anodizing Aluminum

Simple anodizing is like dipping Easter eggs, but with the introduction of pens, resists and overdying techniques a huge range of subtle effects become possible.

Though we refer to the whole process as anodizing, this term correctly refers to one specific step. In a solution of 15-18% sulfuric acid (the *electrolyte*) the aluminum is attached to the positive (+) pole of an electric current, called the *anode*. The negative pole is connected to a sheet of lead, aluminum or stainless steel, called the *cathode*. Lead is the most commonly used cathode. When current is passed through the electrolyte, oxygen is compelled to combine on the metal's surface, creating clear tough porous aluminum oxide.

Structure

When aluminum combines with oxygen, the compound aluminum oxide (Al_2O_3) is formed as a thin transparent coating. When this process is accelerated by electricity and performed in an acid bath, the result is a much thicker layer that looks like this. It is these pores or 'tubes' that allow the clear coating to accept dyes. As a final step, the oxide layer is sealed, either with hot water or a nickle salt.

Dyes

Because the anodized surface is porous, it will absorb many kinds of colors, including most dyes, inks and stains. To insure color fastness, richness and control, dyes made specifically for coloring aluminum are recommended. These are generally sold as powders to be mixed with water as needed. Follow the manufacturer's instructions, paying special attention to the need for chemically pure water. The dyes may be mixed to achieve a new color (e.g. red and blue may be combined to achieve purple). A more popular approach is to achieve mixes by overdyeing the original hues. In this way the original colors may be mixed and kept pure, leaving the fullest palette available. Of course where production runs of a specific color are required, mixing the desired hue is a more reliable solution.

Familiar jewelers pickle (Sparex) can be used to bleach out unwanted colors. Reserve a container of pickle for this purpose, kept at room temperature. Other acid solutions can also be used, but involve more dangerous chemicals.

Racking

One of the keys to successful anodizing is the unobstructed flow of electricity. This requires clean solid contact between the power source and the work piece. Use titanium or a piece of aluminum of a similar alloy to that being anodized. Here are a few examples of racking systems.

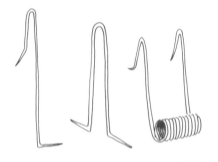

For more detailed information I recommend *Artists Anodizing Aluminum* by David LaPlantz. Available from Press de LaPlantz, 899 Bayside Cutoff, Bayside, CA 95524, (707) 822-6009.

Surfaces

Reactive Metals

Titanium, niobium and the four other reactive metals have the unique property of developing surface films of precise and controllable thickness when charged with small voltages of electricity. The colors created by these oxide films are predictable and permanent.

Electrical Hazard!
This technique uses electric current and is potentially dangerous. Do not proceed until you have understood and accommodated all the safety requirements. For additional information about reactive metals, see page 14.

Safety

Titanium, niobium, tantalum, zirconium, tungsten and hafnium are called the *reactive metals*. They exhibit a wide and varying range of properties that make them of interest to metallurgists and engineers. Because of their workability and other factors, titanium and niobium are the metals of interest to jewelers and the ones that will be addressed here.

These metals develop oxide films of consistent, specific and uniform thickness. Once formed this film is inert and tends to remain unchanged.

The oxide film is incredibly thin, something on the order of one millionth of a centimeter or less. You'll never see it, but you will see the results of this layer as it bends light that passes through it and is reflected back. The result is a predictable palette of colors that include vibrant blues, hot vermillions and frigid greens.

Control is achieved by using electricity to form the oxide film. A controlled electric current running through a liquid bath will form oxygen at the positive (+) pole. This pole is called the anode, and the process is called *anodizing*. Increased voltage creates a thicker oxide film and a resulting change in color. The technique is simple to understand, but to exploit the process fully requires more information than is available here. The following is provided as an outline and stimulus to further reading.

Equipment

Miscellaneous supplies can be picked up in a department store for about $10 and include a plastic container with a tight fitting lid, rubber gloves, a sponge, several alligator clips, electrical tape and assorted paintbrushes with metal ferrules. Nylon bristles are preferred over natural hair.

The heart of the equipment is a transformer and current rectifier with a current limiter. This apparatus converts alternating current from a wall plug into direct current and harnesses it for control over both the amperage (volume) and voltage (force of the supply). The device is similar to that used for electroplating and for aluminum anodizing, but the needs are sufficiently different that neither of these setups is quite right for coloring reactive metals. Informed and industrious people can put together the equipment from components available through an electronics supply store. Plans are available from Reactive Metals Studio (see Suppliers, page 188), which also sells ready-to-use equipment and supplies for the jewelry studio.

Sequence

At any given voltage the film will grow to a specific thickness and stop, having reached a thickness where current will no longer pass. An area of oxide created with any specified voltage will not pass current of a lower voltage. Multiple anodizing, then, proceeds in decreasing voltages.

Reactive metals are tough but will yield to most conventional jewelry procedures. They can be sawn, filed and ground with the same tools used for silver or gold. In industrial settings, titanium filings and dust can ignite, but conventional metalsmithing equipment should create no danger. Because heat is not readily transmitted, lubricants are recommended to preserve bits when drilling. When sanding, lubricate with dilute soapy water, using a waterproof abrasive paper. Reactive metals cannot be soldered and must be joined with cold connections such as rivets, screws, tabs, bezels or adhesives.

Bath Method

1. Prepare the metal by sanding, sandblasting, chasing or any other surface technique associated with jewelry. Polished surfaces offer the brightest colors, but if viewed obliquely they will appear dull and dark. For this reason scratch finishes are the most common. Degrease and handle only by the edges.

2. Set up equipment as shown, being certain that the power is OFF. The electrolyte is made by dissolving a tablespoon of TSP (trisodium phosphate) or Sparex into a quart of water. It is kept cool and used at room temperature. With a tight lid to prevent evaporation, the solution will last indefinitely. Do not allow clips or leads to touch the electrolyte (bath). Double check that the anode and cathode do not touch. Wear rubber gloves.

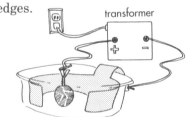

3. Turn on the power supply and increase the voltage until the desired color is achieved. To check midway, turn off the power and lift the workpiece out of the bath. Bubbles forming on the surface will slightly distort the color while anodizing.

4. Turn off the power.

5. The metal may be rinsed and lightly dried to reveal the final color. It can be reimmersed for further coloring, remembering that changes will occur only at higher voltages. You can never go back if you pass the color you want.

Applicator Method (Anodic Painting)

1. Prepare the metal as before, by sanding, sandblasting or polishing. Degrease and handle only by the edges.

2. Connect the anode (+) to the workpiece and secure it to the table. Double-sided tape is handy.

3. Prepare an applicator so it can carry an electric current. Brushes will work. It is critical that the metal cathode be insulated. Cover it with electrical tape or the rubber coating sold in hardware stores to cover tool handles.

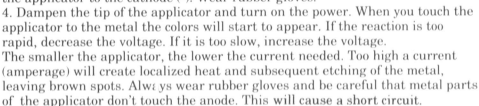

3. Be sure the machine is OFF and connect the lead from the applicator to the cathode (-). Wear rubber gloves.

4. Dampen the tip of the applicator and turn on the power. When you touch the applicator to the metal the colors will start to appear. If the reaction is too rapid, decrease the voltage. If it is too slow, increase the voltage. The smaller the applicator, the lower the current needed. Too high a current (amperage) will create localized heat and subsequent etching of the metal, leaving brown spots. Always wear rubber gloves and be careful that metal parts of the applicator don't touch the anode. This will cause a short circuit.

The liquid electrolyte is the carrier of the electric current. By keeping an area dry you can prevent oxides from forming. Typical masking materials include electrical tape, high quality masking tape or frisket, dilute asphatum and fingernail polish. When using tape it is important to burnish down the edges to prohibit traces of liquid from seeping underneath. This will be enough to create a fuzzy edge.

This material is drawn from *Studio Preparation and Coloring of Titanium*, by William Seeley, used with permission (and thanks).

Polishing

Hours of careful fabrication can be nullified by sloppy or unconsidered polishing. Experience is the best teacher, but a solid understanding of the procedures and their effects is a vital foundation.

• A polished appearance is the result of a perfectly flat surface. Under magnification, the cross section of scratches looks like this. Light is reflected around the scratches like sound being echoed in a mountain valley. A flat surface gives no "echoes" so all the light is bounced back, resulting in a highly reflective surface.

• Good finishing begins when you first handle the metal. Avoid making unnecessary scratches by storing the stock carefully. Don't scribe a line until you are sure of your plans.
• Generally a file is used to smooth edges or define shapes. The next step is usually abra-sive papers. Silicon carbide (wet/dry paper) is a popular choice. This can be bought at a hardware store or jewelry supply company. Other choices would include emery, garnet and crocus (rouge) papers. Whatever your preference, the paper should be wrapped around a board or dowel to increase your leverage. The cutting power of the paper depends on the force behind it.
• Polishing sticks can be made by gluing leather or felt onto wood and then saturating it with a polishing compound. Another effective method of hand polishing is the use of strings or thongs, called *thrumming*.

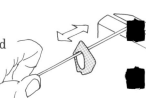

Grits

100's	very coarse
200's	coarse
300's	medium
400's	fine
500's	very fine

Advance from coarse to fine papers, taking care not to skip or abbreviate any step. As you switch grits, change the direction of your stroke. This will make it easier to tell when the marks of the previous abrasive have been worked out. To achieve a mirror finish you'll probably progress to a 600 paper. Keep in mind that there is no universal "right" finish. You can stop at any point that complements the piece.

Rules for the Buffing Machine

• Pay attention! If your mind wanders, turn off the machine and take a break.
• Use a pinch or breakaway grip. Don't entwine your fingers into the work.
• Wear goggles. Keep long hair and loose clothing tied back.
• Work only on the lower quarter of the wheel.

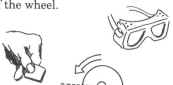

WORK ZONE

Compounds

A typical finishing sequence moves from files to papers to the use of tough powders called oxides. These may be natural sands or man-made particles. They are usually bought already mixed with a vehicle or bonding agent, typically grease or tallow. A wide range of compounds are available. Consult a supply company catalogue for a detailed list. Try a couple and choose those that meet your needs. Here are some popular choices:

BOBBING	a gray material that contains pumice powder. It is especially good for fast cutting.
TRIPOLI	a brown colored sandstone material that removes scratches well.
WHITE DIAMOND	contains no diamonds, but is a very fast cutting all purpose choice. It cuts as fast as tripoli but leaves a brighter finish.
LEA	another fast cutter, and especially good for steel, as when polishing hammers and stakes.
ZAM	a man-made compound that will give a bright final finish to most metals and many gem materials.

Chapter 3

Shaping

Layout

This simple step is critical for precise work and predictable results. Careful thought and geometric accuracy from the beginning of a piece will make subsequent steps easier.

• Avoid making scratches that will need to be removed later.

• Before any surface is applied, the metal must be degreased. Clean with a solvent such as alcohol or a waterless hand cleaner (available in paint stores). Or you can rub the metal with pumice powder, fine sandpaper or Scotchbrite. To allow drawn lines to show up better, rub these abrasives in a circular motion.

• To show up a pencil mark, paint the metal with white tempera, white shoe polish or a proprietary layout fluid such as DyeKem.

• Drawings may be made on label paper (one brand is called *Crack-n-Peel*), available from office supply stores or commercial printers. A second choice is white contact paper, sold to line shelves.

• After piercing, any of the above may be removed with solvents or by burning. **Ventilation is suggested.**

• Photocopies can sometimes speed up layout. Copy a pale graph paper onto label stock, for instance, or duplicate production templates.

• Sometimes several pieces should be laid out at the same time, but in other cases the dimensions of one piece are affected by some other one. In those cases it might be best to cut out (or bend, etc.) the first piece before laying out the second. Consider these factors and develop a plan of events before you get started.

STORE SHEET METAL BETWEEN LAYERS OF PAPER.

LAYOUT DYE — NURSE SHOE POLISH — TEMPERA WHITE

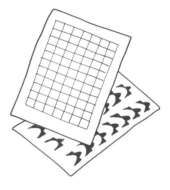

When making a circular bend (a ring, for instance) add two thicknesses of the metal being used to compensate for the compression of the metal as it bends. When laying out a right angle bend, remember that the thickness of the sheet will create a difference between the inside and outside measures of a corner. This can be critical when laying out a small box, for instance as a stone setting.

INSIDE DIMENSION IS SMALLER THAN OUTSIDE DIMENSION.

See page 181 for some guidelines and formulas for layout geometry.

It's better to make one thing right than a million things wrong.
William Shepard

48

Piercing

Though it is a deceptively simple technique, piercing is not only an extremely versatile process, but a preliminary step in many other procedures. When done correctly, sawing is a relaxed and rhythmic experience.

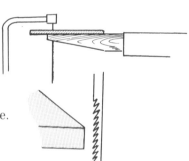

• The piece being sawn should be horizontal and securely held. A wooden bench pin is the typical arrangement.
• The blade must be tightly strung in the sawframe. See below.
• The teeth of the blade must point toward the handle. To determine the direction, look closely or stroke the blade against fabric. The blade will snag in only one direction.
• The blade should always travel at a right angle to the workpiece.
• The hand holding the sawframe should be relaxed. Do not clench or jerk the frame.
• The correct size blade has three teeth on the metal at a time.

Blade Insertion

Method 1 Clamp one end of the blade in place and tighten the screw (A) finger-tight. Adjust the length of the frame so the tip of the blade just overlaps the other gripping plate, then tighten (B) the frame screw well. Lean the frame against the bench, blade uppermost, and press hard enough to "spring" the frame. Slide the loose end of the blade into place and tighten the last screw (C). The frame springs back, putting tension on the blade.

Method 2 After loosening the screw on the back of the sawframe, set the blade into position, being sure the teeth are pointed outward and toward the handle. Tighten the gripping plates at each end of the blade. Use both hands to slide the frame open as shown, laying a thumb into position to hold the back of the frame once it is fully extended. While holding it, tighten the screw on the back of the frame (B).

Lubrication
This is not necessary but it sometimes speeds sawing, especially on "gummy" metals such as sterling or copper. Beeswax or a proprietary wax ('*Bur Life*') can be warmed and fused onto the base of the bench pin like this.

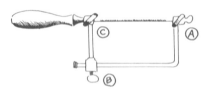

Alternately, Oil of Wintergreen is applied by touching the blade to a wick every couple of minutes.

Piercing
This is the term given to sawing when working within a piece. Begin by drilling a hole in each compartment to be sawn. Only a tiny hole will be needed. With the blade secured into the frame at one end, thread the other end through the hole and connect to the frame as usual.

After completing the cut, it is often helpful to refine the shape by 'filing' with the blade, rubbing it along the sawn edge. To remove, loosen either end of the blade and withdraw it.

49

Drawing Wire

This simple tool will allow a craftsman to create the thickness and cross section of a wire as it is needed. It is an example of a tool whose shape and function has not changed since its invention 500 years ago.

Process

1. The plate is held in a vise so it is well supported.

2. A gradual taper is filed on the tip of the wire to be drawn. A notch filed in the bench pin makes this easier.

3. The tip of the wire is fed through the unnumbered side of the plate into the first hole it fits snugly. Heavy-duty gripping pliers called *draw tongs* are used to pull the wire through the plate in a slow smooth motion.

4. The wire is pulled through successive holes until it feels tough and springy. It is annealed, dried, and drawing can continue. Often the point will need to be refiled as drawing progresses.

5. In most cases the numbers on a drawplate have no correspondence to wire size.

Annealing Wire

Coil wire closely to avoid melting it. If it is wrapped with non-ferrous wire, the coil can be quenched in pickle immediately after annealing.

Lubrication

A piece of rag or sponge is clamped onto the plate after having been moistened with a light oil like wintergreen or olive oil. The wire may also be rubbed with wax but this can clog small holes.

If a vise is not available, hold the draw-plate on a board with a hole in it, braced across a door jamb. Native American silversmiths used to anchor their plates against pegs in the ground.

To draw half-round wire in a round drawplate, slightly flatten two strips of wire and solder them together for about an inch at one end. Taper this and draw as usual, annealing as necessary. In the same way, rectangular wire can be made in a square drawplate.

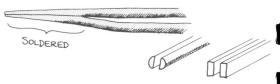

SOLDERED

Rolling Wire

The slotted rolling mill is a great convenience when reducing the size of heavy gauge wire or rods. As shown here, it can be used for some decorative techniques as well.

Process

• Unlike rolling sheet, the gap between the rollers is adjusted only slightly, because the progression of sizes is more or less built into the decreasing size of the grooves.

• Feed the tip of a wire into an opening that is larger than the wire itself. For very large stock it might be necessary to open the rollers or prepare the wire by forging the tip.

• Roll the wire through, making an effort to pull it straight out of the mill. A small amount of tension on the wire will help to keep it from curling.

• Rotate the wire 90° and run it through the mill again.

• Move to the next groove and repeat the two rollings

Rolling a Taper

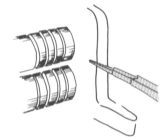

Follow the directions above, but roll only part way along the wire. Reverse the direction at the top of the intended taper to remove the wire. Rotate it 90° and roll to the same spot. Either move to the next groove or tighten the rollers (sometimes both) and roll again, this time stopping a short distance before the last "step". Reverse, remove, rotate and repeat. Continue until the taper is roughly formed, then smooth out the gradations with a planishing hammer. If the taper is to be made round, anneal it; then planish while rotating the wire in your hand.

Decorative Uses

The wire mill can be used to create some interesting patterns of parallel lines and ridges on sheet metal. Keeping in mind that only annealed silver, gold, copper or brass should go through the machine, experimentation is your best guide here.

Try rolling a sheet through then rotating it and rolling again.

Planishing can be used effectively after patterning to create a subtle transition.

I don't want to achieve immortality through my work, I want to achieve it through not dying.

Tubemaking

There are many cases where a jeweler will need a tube of a specific size and wall thickness. Tubes are easy to make and handy for stone settings, bails, findings and hinges.

With scissors, cut a strip of metal having parallel sides; dividers are handy for marking this. Cut a point on the strip. Lay the annealed strip in a V-block, across the open jaws of a vise or on a lead block.

Set a rod along the center line and strike it with a mallet. With pliers or a mallet, continue bending this trough into a tube near the point.

Once this is curled enough to fit in the drawplate the rest of the strip will curl evenly.

Try to pull the tube straight out; i.e. perpendicular to the drawplate. Continue pulling until the edges just meet.

If the seam looks rough, pause before closing to even the edges with a needle file. Do not overlap the seam. If the tube ripples, anneal it before proceeding.

In most cases it's a good idea to solder the seams. Use a bushy flame and draw the solder into the seam.

Calculations

•For a given *outside diameter:*
O.D. + thickness* x 3.14 (π)

•For a given *inside diameter:*
I.D. - thickness* x 3.14 (π)

*Thickness of the sheet being used.

Tubemaking works best with metal 24 gauge or thinner. To make thick-walled tubing, follow the directions above, making a tube of a much larger diameter than what is needed. Solder the seam. After pickling and drying, the tube may be drawn, making it smaller in diameter, longer and thicker walled.

To achieve a desired inside diameter, set a steel or brass wire of this diameter into the tube midway in the process. Oil the wire lightly and be sure it is longer than the tube. To remove it, put the wire through the plate from the front and pull it out with tongs.

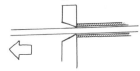

Shaping

Bending

As simple as it is, bending is a venerable aspect of the jeweler's art. Thoughtful use of fingers and pliers can create a huge vocabulary of forms.

- Use your fingers as much as possible. Wood or rawhide tools are used next, and steel tools (hammers, pliers, etc.) only when absolutely needed.
- Whenever possible, anneal the metal. This step takes less time than removing the marks that might be the result of working on hard material.
- To achieve a sharp bend, score the metal at least 3/4 of the way through. After bending, the crease should be reinforced with solder.

Shaping

Scoring

Scoring is the process of removing metal along the line of a proposed fold. On thin sheet, it may be achieved with a sharp scribe. On metal over 24 gauge, scoring is done with a graver, a file, or an old file tang converted like this. It is pulled to scrape a groove.

Shallow Forming

Shallow forming (also called "Bossing") is a method of giving a minor curvature or doming to sheet metal. It usually makes a piece look thicker and because curved surfaces show more reflections than flat sheets, the result is often more dynamic. Bossed areas are also more rigid.

1. Saw out the shape.
2. If the piece is to be stamped, chased, textured or to have married metals these are done next.
3. After annealing the metal is set on a medium soft surface and worked with a mallet, hammer, or punch.
4. If the edges do not blend into the piece, they may be formed over a dapping punch or hammer held in a vice.

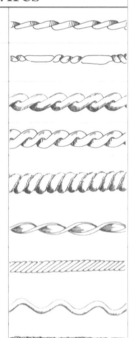

Twisted Wires

A square wire twisted	
Square wire, twisted left & right	
Round wire, doubled & twisted	
As above, flattened	
Round wire twisted on itself, then wrapped with a smaller twist.	
Rectangular wire, twisted	
3-7 strands twisted together	
Wires twisted together, one then removed	
Square wire and twist wound on a thick wire	

Working Surfaces

pitch   lead (scrub hands and metal after using)

micro-crystaline wax

leather

soft wood (pine or plywood)

53

Forging

The shaping of a rod through the controlled use of a hammer is an ancient and basic technique of metalsmithing. Beginners are often surprised to discover how plastic metal can be.

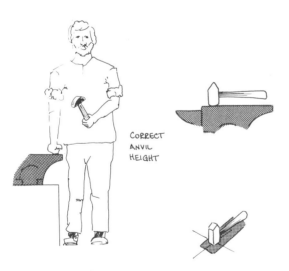

Forging may be defined as the controlled shaping of metal by the force of a hammer. This technique lends itself to graceful transitions from plane to plane and appealing contrasts of thick and thin sections. It is equally appropriate for large and small work. Gold, sterling and copper forge very well. Low-zinc brasses can also be forged but will require frequent annealing. It is a sign of good forging to require very little filing. Force and control must work together.

Directional Control

Control in forging comes from the cross peen of the hammer. Its wedge shape can push the metal in only two directions. This "push" can be directed along the axis to increase length or outward from the axis to increase breadth.

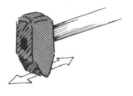

Tips

- Sit or stand close to the work in a posture you can comfortably maintain.

- Work on a smooth, hard, stable surface.

- Keep fingers and thumb wrapped around the hammer handle, not pointing along it.

- Anneal as needed; don't press your luck.

- Keep the hammer face polished.

- Don't hold the work piece where you intend to hit it.

- The hammer must make solid contact with anvil.

CORRECT ANVIL HEIGHT

Certain tools of the manual crafts scarcely changed in form for ten or more centuries, because they were perfectly suited to the requirements of these crafts.

Maurice Daumas,
A History of Technology & Invention

Shaping

Forging

Control and force must play equal roles in proper forging. Careful attention to the height of the anvil and the shape of the hammer face will help in both areas.

Forging A Taper

Work on square stock striking all sides equally.
Planish out bumps by rotating.

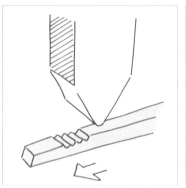

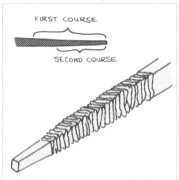

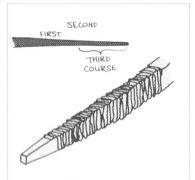

The Rhombus

This refers to a cross section shape that is easy to make but hard to correct. Either file off the shaded areas or forge into round rod and from there return to square section.

An alternate forging method uses the curve of an anvil horn or a stake to force the metal to flow outward from the point of contact.

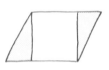

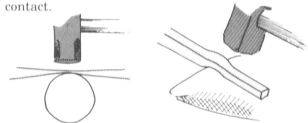

Hammers

Haste in every business brings failures.   Herodotus, 450 B.C.

Repoussé

This ancient process gives form to a sheet of metal by pressing it out from the back and in from the front. In addition to a range of punches, repoussé depends on the plasticity of a supporting material that holds the work metal.

Repoussé is one of the oldest metalsmithing techniques in the world. Virtually every ancient culture has left examples. It is a versatile process appropriate to any scale and all malleable metals, from aluminum to steel. Many approaches are used, so the outline below must be taken only as an introduction and point of departure. The word comes from the French verb meaning "to push back." Simply stated, repoussé is the process of creating volumetric forms by pushing metal. The pushing is usually done on both the front and the back.

Process

1. Draw the design on annealed metal.

2. Warm the pitch with a gentle torch flame and set the metal right side up onto a smooth area. Pitch may be pulled onto metal with a popsicle stick to achieve a better grip.

3. Go over the design lightly with a tracer punch.

4. Lift the metal out of pitch by prying, rapping the pot, or warming it and lifting with tweezers. Remove excess pitch by burning or (better) by dissolving it in baby oil or turpentine. If burned, do not allow ignited pitch to drip back into the bowl. It is brittle and must be discarded. **Ventilation is needed when burning pitch.**

5. Turn the metal over and set it back into the pitch. Boss up forms with whatever round-tipped tools will fit. When the metal feels stiff and the corners are curling out of the pitch, remove the work, clean off pitch and anneal.

6. Dry the metal and return it to the pitch for further work on either the front or back as needed.

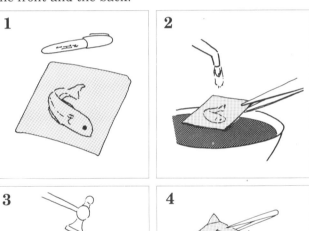

1

2

3

4

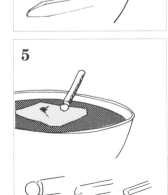

5

6

Repoussé

One of the special characteristics of repoussé is the ability to watch the form evolve, and to continually refine the forms and ideas as the work progresses.

Although tools can be bought, many people prefer to make their own. Only a few are needed to begin but a collection of 40 or 50 is typical. These tools, especially the modeling punches, do not have to be hardened and tempered but most people prefer to do this. Tool steel may be bought or salvaged from broken tools. See Toolmaking on page 156.

Tracers, for making lines

Modeling & planishing

Curved punches

Matting tools

To make a matting tool, file a line around a tool steel rod, harden it, then snap it off. A fine grain pattern will result. Textures may be added as the metal is being formed by using sharp-edged punches. For a smooth surface use mirror-finished planishing tools.

The material used to support the metal is very important. The most commonly preferred support is pitch.

Too hard
  metal is thinned.

Too soft
  no control.

Good pitch
  hard enough to
  hold its shape,
  but soft enough
  to yield.

Pitch may be bought from many tool supply companies (see Appendix) or:

Northwest Pitchworks
5705 26th Ave., N.E.
Seattle, Washington 98105
(206) 525-4136

Holding Devices

Pitch pot-allows rotation and can be tilted to any angle.

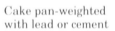

Cake pan-weighted with lead or cement

Wooden tray (note the lip for clamping)

Cast iron skillet

Shaping

57

Stretching & Sinking

Flat sheets of metal are given their simplest volumetric form by pressing them into a hollow in the process called sinking. Stretching creates volume by thinning the center of a form.

Stretching is a technique that causes sheet metal to dome by forging it against a solid flat surface such as an anvil. As tension is created between expanded (stretched) and unhammered areas, the metal is pulled to a domical shape. The advantages of stretching are the thick edge that results, its rapid progress, and the fact that the overall size does not change. This might be important when fitting, as in the case of a lid. A disadvantage is that, since all the hammering is done from the inside, depth is limited by access of a hammer.

Sinking is a versatile technique used to create domical forms in sheet metal by pounding the metal into a hemispherical die. Sinking is used by itself and often as a first step in raising.

1. Cut a disk using the formula **diameter + $\frac{1}{2}$ height** to calculate the diameter of the starting blank. 20 to 16 gauge stock is usually used. 	**2.** You may want to draw pencil guidelines using a compass on the inside of the form. After a little practice these become less necessary. 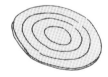
3. With the edge of the disk held across the center of a carved depression, the metal is sunk with a ball-faced hammer or mallet. Work progresses from the circumference inward toward the center. 	**4.** When the desired depth has been reached (and this could take several annealings and courses from edge to center) the form is made less lumpy in a step called *bouging* over a mushroom stake. 

Sinking Blocks

These are usually made of wood, preferably using the end grain. Carve depressions with gouges or turn them on a lathe. The die shapes are general forming aids and do not exactly fit the final shape.

Crimping

Crimping is a specialized technique that uses gentle radial folds in sheet metal to begin the process of raising. While many smiths use crimping regularly, others prefer to move from sinking to raising.

Process

• The disk is marked into segments and held across a notched stake so the line is over the center of the notch.

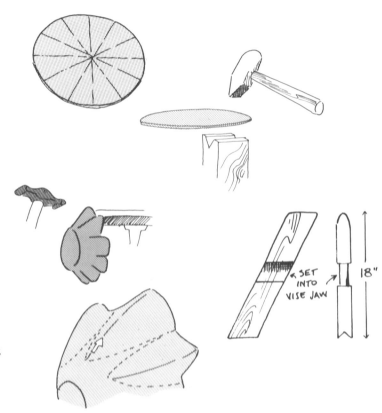

• A cross peen mallet or hammer is used to make a fluted bowl shape.

• These flutes are then smoothed out over a T-stake in a usual raising operation.

• Always raise from the point of the crimp out to the edge.

Hammers versus Mallets

A familiar axiom in regard to crimping and raising is *Wood-On-Steel* or *Steel-On-Wood*, but rarely *Steel-on-Steel*. Until a craftsperson has a finely trained sensitivity, a wooden (or plastic, fiber or horn) mallet should be used with a steel stake. If a steel hammer is preferred, work over a form made of wood.

To travel hopefully is better than to arrive.
Sir James Jeans

Shaping

Raising

This ancient and basically unchanged technique is a foundation stone of metalsmithing in all cultures and all times. It requires only a hammer and a solid form against which the metal is bent. Oh, and a little practice.

There is only one right way to raise: the way that works. Methods will differ depending on the size and shape of the piece, the metal and thickness being raised, the tools available, and the preferences of the smith. The illustrations below show in general terms the steps in raising a vessel. This information, along with the adjacent pages, will get you started. Only by actually doing the work will these tips synthesize into a method.

Shaping

1. Make an actual size drawing and a template from it. The diameter of the starting disk is the sum of the widest and tallest measures (AB + CD) or, for a dome, twice the length of line AB.

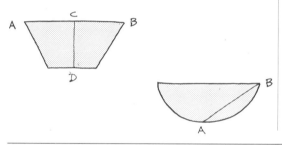

2. The center is punched and a circle drawn and cut. File and burnish the edge, and anneal the disk. The flat sheet is bent upwards by stretching, sinking, or crimping. After annealing, any of these methods may be repeated to quickly bring the sides up. Most people have a favorite method and stick with it, but they may be used in combination. If the vessel is to have a flat bottom, this area is left untouched.

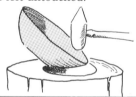

3. When the metal is too thick to crimp or its curve restricts access for a hammer, the vessel is worked from the outside over a stake, made of wood, plastic or steel. A cross peen hammer or mallet is used. Starting at the baseline, with the sheet held at about a 30° angle, the hammer is brought down so the handle is parallel to the floor. As work proceeds, the disk is rotated and the hammer falls in even blows. After going around the form once, the disk is slid back (off the stake) about a half inch and raising continues. The effect is to make a bulge and then work it to the edge, as you would in smoothing out a carpet.

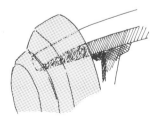

4. The progress from the base line to top edge is called a *course* and consists of concentric circles about a half inch apart. These may be drawn in pencil with a compass after each annealing to serve as guidelines. Keep in mind that the edge has to move a lot more (i.e. cover a greater distance) than the metal near the base line. That makes it easy to create a bugle horn shape. To prevent it, strike more gently near the base and take special care near the top edge. If the bowl flares out too much, raise a course or two starting at mid-height.

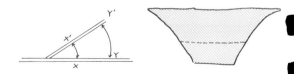

Early attempts at raising might make it seem like an ineffective process, but with practice the technique can create volumes in a surprisingly short time.

5. As raising continues, the top edge will thicken. This may be exaggerated by tapping the edge with a cross peen at the end of each course. Support the work on a sandbag or in the hand while doing this.

6. In an open vessel, planishing is done after the form is complete. On a necked-in shape, the lower section must be planished midway in the process while the stakes still fit inside.

7. Curved forms are usually raised as a series of flat sections like this. These are then given roundness with blocking hammers on a wooden block, steel stake or sand bag.

8. The straightness of the form is checked with a surface gauge or by drawing pencil lines as shown. The top is cut as needed and filed smooth.

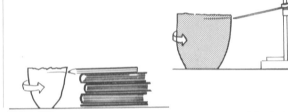

Planishing

This word comes from the Latin *planus* which means to flatten or level. It refers to the smoothing, toughening and polishing of metal by hammering. The effect of planishing can be only as good as the surfaces being used. Hammer faces and stakes or anvil must be mirror-finished. Overlap blows and don't hurry.

Hammers

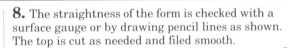

Any smooth-faced hammer may be used for planishing but it's a good idea to have the one made for this purpose. It will have the two faces shown. To get maximum contact but avoid leaving marks, use the flat face on curved surfaces and the domed face on flat or nearly flat surfaces. A heavy hammer (12-16 oz.) is best for quick work and flattening wire but a lightweight hammer (3-6 oz.) is recommended for final finishing.

Some Common Situations

A hammer held in a vise can be handy

Cow's tongue stake

A dapping punch held in a vise

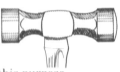

When planishing a tall form it is a good idea to alternate rotation directions after each annealing. This will help prevent the form from twisting.

Shaping

Anticlastic Raising

In this variation of traditional raising, an upward curve in one axis is countered by an opposite curve on the right angled axis. The result is a structurally rigid form with a vast vocabulary of possibilities.

Synclastic
In this family of forms, the two major axes both curve in the same direction. A bowl is an example.

Anticlastic
In this family, the curves of the two major axes travel in opposite directions. An example is the surface of a saddle.

Tools

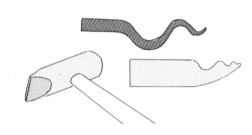

Process

This example uses a strip, but the process is the same for a square, circle or irregular shape.

1. Cut a pattern and smooth the edges. This process allows the use of thin gauge metal. 24 gauge is a good place to start for jewelry scale objects.

2. By hand, bend the strip along its long axis. As you work, hold these ends together so this curve is preserved.

3. Lay the strip into a curve in a stake so its outer edge touches a slope. Strike a series of overlapping blows to make a trough along the edge of the sheet.

4. Turn the strip around and repeat the same process on the opposite edge. In each case, move along the entire length of the strip.

5. Still holding the ends of the sheet close together, direct another line of blows just inside the first. Again, turn the piece around and repeat this on the other side. The blows should fall at a right angle to the stake. If they are slanted the piece will become skewed. Anneal.

6. Continue in this way to develop the form. The shape can be manipulated by hand as the forming progresses.

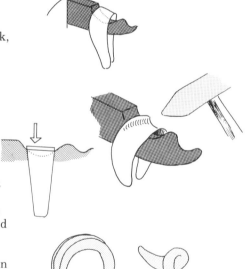

For extensive coverage of this topic I recommend:

Form Emphasis for Metalsmiths, by Heikki Seppa. Kent State University Press Kent, Ohio 44242 (800) 666-2211

Shaping

Seaming

It is sometimes more efficient to fabricate a shape that approaches the desired end result and apply forming techniques from there. The solder seams in such pieces will receive a lot of stress so some special provisions should be made.

Preparing the Joint

To provide more surface area for the solder, the edges are filed to a bevel equal to about 5 thicknesses of the metal. The two ends of the strip are filed in opposite directions to make a smooth joint.

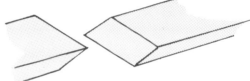

Because of the bevel it's likely that the two edges will slide over and past each other. To prevent this, tabs are cut and bent as shown. The edges are then brought together and the form is tied with binding wire. The tabs are malleted down as the cylinder is held on a stake. Flux is applied both inside and outside along the seam. Solder is usually set inside.

Examples

Interlocking Finger Joint

1. Planish the two edges to be joined so they thin out evenly over about a 1/2" area.

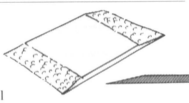

2. Mark a line 1/4" in from each edge and lay out the same number of tabs on each edge. Generally, the tabs are of equal size, but all that matters is that the two sides be identical.

3. Saw these lines on both sides, stopping at the 1/4" mark. On thin stock (20 ga.) a single cut is sufficient but for heavier sheet, cut a skinny V.

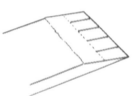

4. On one edge, bend the even-numbered tabs up slightly. On the other edge bend the odd-numbered tabs down. Paint the whole area with flux, slide the edges together, and tie with binding wire.

5. Set over a stake and mallet the tabs down. A burnisher might be needed to press the end of each tab down.

6. Soldering is usually done from outside the form. Wire solder lends itself to this job. Raising and planishing are as usual.

63

Die Forming

Dies are rigid and reusable forms that give shape to a work piece. They can be made in a range of materials and can have a lifespan from only a few to thousands of pieces.

Description & Uses

There are several families of dies, so the topic can quickly get confusing. Simply put, dies can be categorized by the amount of detail they impart and their strength. This latter is important not only because it determines the lifespan of the die, but because it controls the difficulty in making the die in the first place. It is easier to cut a die of wood than one of steel, but of course the steel tool will last longer.

Die forming has many applications but is especially good for:
- matching halves like spouts and fabricated containers.
- matching parts as with a box and lid.
- certain production methods.

Conforming Dies

Dies in this category consist of two corresponding parts. For instance a ridge on one matches a groove on the other. Conforming dies are generally held in a superstructure of some sort to guarantee that the parts line up when they are brought together. This die controls every aspect of the form and ensures exactly duplicated units time after time.

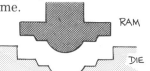

Nonconforming Dies

(also called Silhouette Dies)
A rigid material is pierced with an outline (silhouette) of a desired shape. The work metal is then held against the die and pushed into the open area. The process is extremely versatile because the contour and depth of the image can be changed each time the die is used.

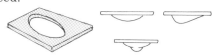

Sequence

This shows the usual progression of tooling, moving from outside edges inward. If a punch is used, it is held at a slight angle so that the hammer blows push it along.

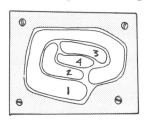

The Flange

The flange left around a die-formed shape keeps the form intact through moderate surface decorating. If much deformation is planned, fill the piece with pitch by pouring from a pan, or melting lumps right in the formed area. Keep the flange intact for later refitting into the die.

A unique feature of die forming is the flange or skirt that surrounds the form. Before cutting it off consider its use.

Die Forming

Dies can be cunningly complex or surprisingly obvious. The silhouette die is simply an outline shape cut from a tough material such as Masonite, plywood or steel.

Process

1. Make a die block by gluing together pieces of plywood and tempered Masonite as shown. Use a white glue and clamp or weight.

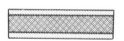

2. Mark the design on Masonite and cut out the die hole. Use a coping saw. If a band saw is used, the sawn opening should be glued closed. Insert a strip of wood (like a tongue depressor) and clamp. Take care in sawing that the sides of the hole are **vertical**. The opening in the top must be the same size as the opening in the bottom.

3. Plan the location of hold down screws and drill holes. These should be about 5mm (1/4") from the die hole.

4. To cut the right size piece of metal, make a rubbing of the die. Use this to cut metal and drill holes for screws. The holes should be oversized.

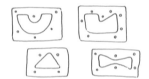

5. Fasten the metal onto the die with 3/4" sheet metal screws. To "find" the outline of the form, tap the metal lightly with a mallet or hammer handle. While working, the die may sit on a bench, sandbag or vise. To anneal the workpiece, remove the screws and take the metal off the die.

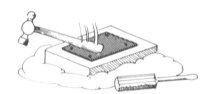

This is a reversible die. This means it can be used to make two pieces that fit together. To make the other piece, turn the die over and start with #3.

When a specific contour is needed, like the angle shown here, it may be built into the die by filing the Masonite to the correct shape. Note that this is not a reversible die; two dies must be made for matching halves.

A Masonite-faced die may be used several times before the edge starts to break down. Its durability depends on the kind of metal being worked and its thickness. For a more lasting die, cut a piece of thin steel sheet with the same hole as the rest of the die and fasten it onto the Masonite with countersunk flathead screws.

Steel Dies

Because steel is so much stronger than wood, a thinner die will provide equal support. Steel dies are less cumbersome and more durable than wooden dies. Because the die material is thinner, it is easier to guarantee that the wall of the die hole is vertical.

Process

1. Draw the design on 1/4" steel sheet with a permanent marker. Sheet steel is probably locally available. Look in the Yellow Pages under *sheet metal* or *steel*. Many suppliers will give cheaper prices on scrap pieces. Any kind of steel, including stainless, will do. When drilling a hole for piercing, cool the bit with a generous bath of oil. Pierce with a jewelers' saw using a large blade (eg. #5). After sawing, smooth off the edges with a file and sandpaper.

2. Plan the location of screw holes and centerpunch for each, about 1/4" from the die hole. Again, use oil when drilling. Be sure to use the correct size bit for the tap to be used next.

3. Cut threads with a tap using oil to lubricate. A tap and handle can be bought at a hardware store for a couple of dollars. Cut slowly with the tap, advancing a quarter turn, then reversing to clear the threads.

Any size tap may be used, but you must be sure that the bit, tap, and screws all coordinate in both diameter and number of threads per inch. Short screws will make the screwing and unscrewing go faster.

4. Make a pencil rubbing of the die to determine the sheet of metal needed and the location of the holes for the hold down screws. These holes should be about 1/4" in from the edge and a little larger than the screw shanks.

5. With the annealed metal screwed onto the die, the forming proceeds as shown previously.

6. To anneal, unscrew the workpiece to remove it. After each annealing, forming begins from the outside edge.

A CLAY WALL MAKES A RESERVOIR FOR OIL.

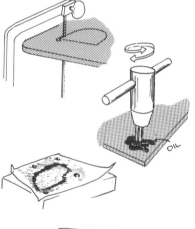

OIL

Supports

A steel die must rest on something to keep it up off the table while forming.

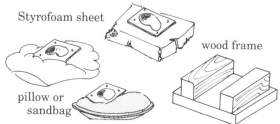

Styrofoam sheet

wood frame

pillow or sandbag

When the die hole is less than 4 square inches, steel thinner than 1/8" may be used. Though this may still be threaded (#3 above) an alternate method is to use sheet metal (also called self-tapping) screws. Drill a hole only as large as the shank of the screw and force it in. It can be unscrewed without damage and will work from both sides.

Shaping

Press Dies

A press die consists of a matched pair of complementary shapes made of any hard material. When a softer substance is set into position, the parts of the die are pressed together, causing a deformation of the softer material.

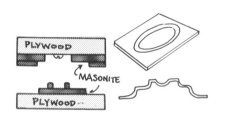

1. Plan the design and draw a cross section of the piece. From this, plan and draw the die.

2. Cut pieces from wood, Masonite, brass and/or steel. As you measure, allow clearance. As shown, more clearance gives a softer form. The thickness of the metal being used will also affect the sharpness of these contours.

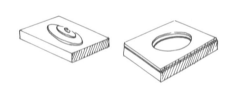

CLEARANCE

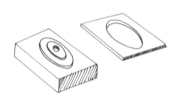

3. Die pieces may be made of hardwood, screws, or metal pieces that have been silver soldered onto a brass backing plate.

4. Complete the die assembly by gluing, soldering and/or screwing.

5. Use a standard hardware store hinge to hold the two die sections in alignment. Use chalk dust, paint or clay to transfer locations from one side to the other.

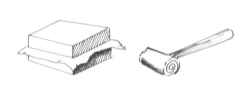

6. Check results on a thin metal such as heavy duty aluminum foil.

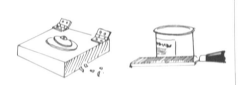

7. File, carve or build up with epoxy or auto body filler if needed.

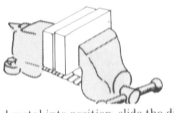

8. Put annealed metal into position, slide the die into a large vise, and squeeze.

Electroforming

Conventional plating deposits a thin film of metal onto the surface of an otherwise finished piece of work. Electroforming uses this technology to build up a substantial layer of metal, often on a matrix of a non-metal such as wood, plastic or paper.

As anyone blessed with bronze babyshoes knows, it is possible to electroform over non-metallic objects. The only requirement is a coating of a conductive paint. This can be painted onto a matix of wood, plastic, paper, stone or about anything else. In some cases (like the babyshoes) the object will remain encased in its metal shell. In others the original form is burned away once the metal is sufficiently strong to stand without it.

Equipment

An extremely simple experiment can be conducted with two lantern batteries. The process will work, but this setup lacks power and control. A boost in power is possible with a battery charger or a 6V car battery. In order to have control, either of these will need to be fitted with an ammeter and a rheostat. By the time you've invested in these, you probably would have been better off buying a rectifier, which combines all these parts into a single system. The initial cost is justified by the greater control and the more efficient and cheaper use.

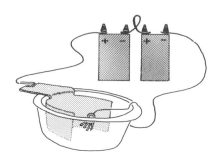

Process

1. Create the model, using any combination of materials and techniques. Be certain that the final assembly is completely free of oils by washing in an alcohol solvent. Everything to be coated must be conductive, either as clean metal or by coating it with a conductive paint, which is available at electronics stores. Porous materials (paper, leaves, etc) should be sealed with several coats of varnish before this step. All metal parts to be left unplated should be covered with stop out varnish. Delicate objects such as shells, organic gems and so on should be stopped out to protect them from the relatively harsh electrolyte solution.
2. Prepare enough electrolyte to completely submerge the object. Using protective clothing and ventilation, mix one pound of copper sulfate with 100cc of sulfuric acid and a half gallon of distilled water. Stir gently until the copper sulfate dissolves. This solution is used at room temperature.
3. Clean a piece of copper roughly equal in surface area to the piece being electroformed and connect it to the positive (+) pole. This is the anode. This can be a single piece bent around the object or several pieces hanging from bus bars that are connected by a wire. The objective is to provide sufficient and evenly spaced supply of copper to the solution. Allow at least a half inch between this copper and the object. They should never touch!
4. Suspend the workpiece from a stout copper or silver wire that is connected to the cathode (the negative (-) pole. When you are certain that the elements are not touching each other, turn on the rectifier.
5. The thickness, texture and speed of the plating reaction is dependent upon many factors including heat and strength of the solution, voltage and amperage and the size and shape of the anode. Experimentation will be required to teach you to control your setup.
6. When the object is sufficiently rigid, turn off the power and remove the work. Cut away support wires and, if appropriate, remove the matrix material. Wax can be removed with boiling water. Neutralize the work by soaking it in a baking soda solution, then finish as usual. Electroformed objects can be soldered and colored as usual, but they are too brittle to withstand much forming.

Shaping

Joining

Soldering

Reliable soldering can only be learned from experience at the bench, but it helps to have an understanding of the physics as well.

When a metal is heated to temperatures approaching its melting point, the crystals of which it is made move apart opening up microscopic spaces. The idea behind hard soldering is to introduce an alloy that is fluid just at the point of maximum expansion. This alloy, called *solder*, flows into the spaces of the expanded metal.

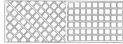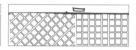

This should not be confused with soft soldering, which uses an alloy of tin, lead and similar metals. Soft solder flows at temperatures about a third of those needed to cause the crystal spaces to open. The holding power of soft solder comes from its ability to fuse onto clean metal. Since the grip is only surface-to-surface, soft solder cannot be filed flush without weakening the joint. This is not true of gold or silver solder.

Silver Solder

It is the amount of zinc in silver solder that controls its melting point. When making solder, care must be taken to avoid overheating, because the zinc will go off in a vapor, changing the proportion. This vaporization is also a factor when soldering. Each time solder becomes fluid its melting point is raised. Overheating a previously soldered joint will burn out the zinc and can leave a pitted seam.

Name	Ag	Cu	Zn	Cd	Melt. Point °C	°F
"IT"	80	16	4		809	1490
Hard	76	21	3		773	1425
Medium	70	20	10		747	1390
Easy	60	25	15		711	1325
"Easy Flo"	50	15	15	20	681	1270

Gold Solder

Gold may be joined with silver solder but to achieve a color match a gold-based alloy is usually used. Gold solders are available in many colors and melting points. When buying solder, specify the metal you are joining. *14 karat yellow solder* refers, not to the quality of the alloy, but means it is used on 14K gold. In fact, solder will be a karat or two lower than the metal it will join. Any gold of a lower karat can be used as a solder. 10K will be a solder for 14K; 14K will solder 18K, etc.

Spelter is another name for zinc. Today the word is used to describe brass when it is used as a solder for steel in a process called *brazing*. Fluxes for brazing include cream of tartar, table salt, and the paste fluxes used in silver soldering. The chart on page 182 shows the melting points of common brasses. These can be used in the same way as the different grades of solder.

Joining

Soldering Process

Almost all work in jewelry and metalsmithing shares a dependence on soldering. Knowledgeable and confident soldering is a prerequisite to skilled work in these fields.

Rules

GOOD FIT — Neater and stronger joints will result from care on this point. Hold work up to the light to check for gaps.

WORK CLEAN — Joint and solder must be free of dirt: no grease, finger oils, tape, pickle, buffing compound, pencil marks, etc.

FLUX — Flux is needed to absorb oxygen. See page 73 for more information.

EVEN HEAT — All pieces being soldered must reach soldering temperature simultaneously. Take into account heat sinks such as binding wire, steel mesh and tweezers.

SOLDER FLOW — Because solder flows toward heat it is often possible to position the torch in such a way that the solder is drawn through a seam. Avoid directing the flame at the joint; let the heat travel through the piece.

RIGHT SIZE — Use just enough solder to fill the seam; don't settle for whatever piece of solder is handy. It takes a lot less time to cut a new piece of solder than to remove excess later.

STEAM VENTS — When soldering an enclosed area, provide an escape for steam and gases trapped inside. These will expand rapidly and unless vented can cause the piece to explode.

Troubleshooting

Incomplete or unsoldered joint.	Not enough heat, metal was dirty, no flux, prolonged heating.
Solder balls up.	Heat may be flowing away from the joint. Metal or solder may be dirty. Avoid playing flame directly on solder.
Solder jumps to one side of joint.	One side is hotter than the other. Reflux and try again.

Lead/tin alloys such as soft solder will create pits in gold, silver, copper or brass when heated above 260° C (500° F). Where scraping or filing won't work to remove white metals that have accidentally adhered to a workpiece, soft solder can be chemically removed.

> Mix *3 oz. glacial acetic acid* with
> *1 oz. hydrogen peroxide*.
> Heat but do not boil.

Brush onto the affected area and allow several days to work. Tin will be left as a white powder that can be brushed off.

Lighting

Metal temperatures are judged by color changes which can be seen best in a dimly lit area. Whatever your lighting, keep it consistent.

Torches & Blocks

The history of civilizations can be traced through the ability of each to control fire. The range of possible heat sources available to today's jeweler would make him the envy of his predecessors through the ages.

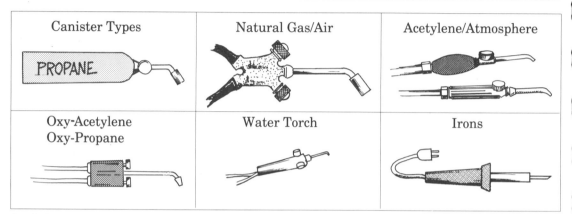

Canister Types	Natural Gas/Air	Acetylene/Atmosphere
Oxy-Acetylene Oxy-Propane	Water Torch	Irons

Soldering Blocks

Charcoal This creates a reducing atmosphere and is soft enough to imbed work. It's expensive and a little messy. It will remain glowing for a long time, which can be a fire hazard. Quench in water after each use. The life of the block can be extended by wrapping a sheet of thin copper or brass around it. Tie this in place with binding wire.

Fire Brick These are soft, inexpensive and safe. They crumble, especially when a lot of flux is used. Available through ceramic suppliers.

Coiled Asbestos This is flat and relatively soft. Particles are great respiratory danger. This is best avoided.

Ceramic & Synthetics Generally good but are heat sinks and give off disagreeable fumes when first heated. When new, set into a kiln and bring up to soldering temperatures. Allow the block to "cook" for a few minutes and cool slowly.

Wire Nest & Pumice The old standby. Very good for annealing or in cases where a flat surface is not needed. A cake pan makes a convenient dish.

Maintainance

Like any other tool in the shop, soldering surfaces have to be kept up to provide consistent service. The greatest problem is the build up of flux glass, especially when paste flux is used. To avoid this, apply flux as the work is held in the fingers rather than when it is on the soldering block. Several materials, especially charcoal, should be quenched in water at the end of the work day to prevent their burning up.

With use, most surfaces will become irregular. A piece of coarse abasive paper can be used to periodically dress a soldering block, or two blocks can be rubbed against each other.
Work over a waste basket.
WEAR A RESPIRATOR.

Joining

Flux

Flux comes from the Latin word for *flow*, and refers to the chemicals that facilitate the flow of solder by preventing the formation of oxides.

Generally fluxes work by forming a coating that protects metal from oxidation. Most fluxes use water to make a liquid that can be sprayed or painted onto the workpiece. When the water is evaporated, the resulting skin is often a clear glassy coating. Flux acts as an "oxygen magnet" by providing a compound that is more attractive to oxygen than the metal being soldered. As oxygen and other elements combine with this coating, the protective power diminishes, a change often seen as a blue or green tint in the flux.

Borax
sodium borate
$Na_2B4O_7 \cdot 10H_2O$

A mineral, usually ground to a powder and mixed with water to form a paste. It is probably the most commonly used flux worldwide, though it's less commonin the US. It can be purchased in solid form as a cone that is ground into a dish and mixed at the bench as needed. Borax melts at 75° C (167° F).

Handy Flux
(paste flux)

A white borax-based compound available from jewelers' and welders' supply companies. This provides substantial oxide protection and leaves a tough glassy skin. This flux becomes clear and fluid at 600° C (1100° F) which makes it a reliable temperature indicator.

Battern's
(Allcra, Hillco, etc)

A flouride-based flux with a watery consistency that is often yellow or green. It is called *self pickling* because it doesn't leave a resilient flux glass like those above. This does not have the oxygen absorbing power of the borax-based fluxes, and is not recommended for "dirty" metals such as copper, brass and nickel silver.

Boric Acid & Alcohol

Make this yourself by adding boric acid to denatured alcohol until it stops dissolving and makes a thin paste. This will need to be shaken or stirred periodically. In use, work is dipped into the solution, set on the soldering block and ignited. The alcohol burns off, leaving a white film of borax. Many jewelers paint a little handy flux on the joint in conjunction with this.

Prips Flux

Griffith Distrib.
Box 662
Louisville,
CO 80027

This flux is a popular firescale protection. The piece is dipped and warmed until dry. Several applications are recommended. The resulting glassy skin is waterproof, so it can be sustained throughout several solderings if you quench only in water .

Borax	75 ml (2 oz. troy or 2 fl. oz.)
TSP *	75 ml (2 oz. troy or 2 fl.oz.)
Boric Acid	90 ml (3 oz. troy or 3 fl. oz.)

Boil in 2 quarts of water until dissolved.
* Tri-Sodium Phosphate, available in paint and hardware stores.

Cupronil
4S Labs,Box 11819,
Phoenix, AZ 85061

This is a commercial flux similar to Prips but especially good at preserving a finish through a heating operation. This makes it handy for repair work.

Hydrogen peroxide

Mix 2 parts hydrogen peroxide (3% solution) with the same amount of Sparex and 1 part water. Pickle first in plain Sparex then soak in this for 5-10 minutes to remove the pink skin often remaining on pickled brass. Exposure to sunlight will weaken the solution.

Joining

73

Soldering Methods

With experience each metalsmith develops a personal approach to soldering. Here is a summary of the most commonly used methods.

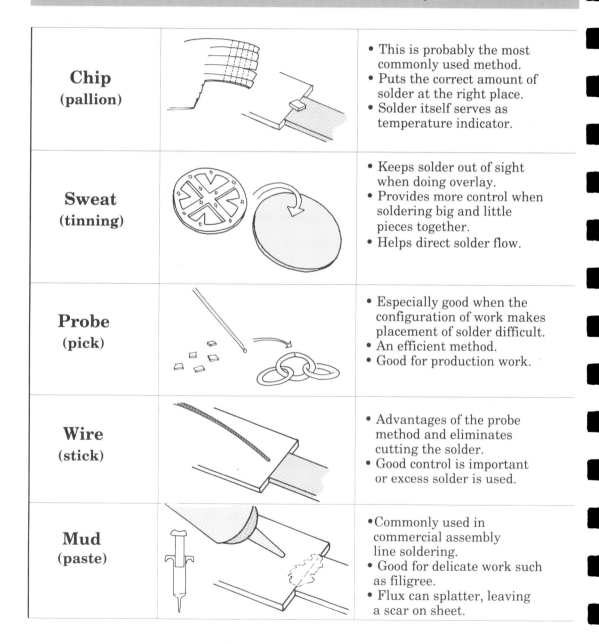

Chip (pallion)		• This is probably the most commonly used method. • Puts the correct amount of solder at the right place. • Solder itself serves as temperature indicator.
Sweat (tinning)		• Keeps solder out of sight when doing overlay. • Provides more control when soldering big and little pieces together. • Helps direct solder flow.
Probe (pick)		• Especially good when the configuration of work makes placement of solder difficult. • An efficient method. • Good for production work.
Wire (stick)		• Advantages of the probe method and eliminates cutting the solder. • Good control is important or excess solder is used.
Mud (paste)		• Commonly used in commercial assembly line soldering. • Good for delicate work such as filigree. • Flux can splatter, leaving a scar on sheet.

Find what you are and you may show us what the world is.
Robert Hughes

Joining

This is a strong chemical bath used to dissolve surface oxidation and flux residue from a metal's surface. Pickles work at room temperature but the reaction is hastened with heat.

SAFETY WARNING When mixing, always add acid to water. Protect yourself from splashes by wearing safety goggles, an apron and rubber gloves. Always wash hands after working with pickles or other acids. Keep baking soda close at hand to neutralize spills.

Pickle Plating

As pickle is used to clean sterling or karat gold it absorbs copper ions, creating what's called a *super saturated solution*. This is in essence a

copper plating solution, loaded with excess copper it is eager to transfer to a metal object. The plating reaction can occur at room temperature in an inert bath, but both heat and electrical

charge will increase the plating response. The introduction of steel into an acid creates an electrical charge. Copper, brass or wooden tongs are used with pickle because they will not create a charge.

Note that if a steel item is used in the pickle it will activate the bath on anything in it at the time, usually causing a thin coating of copper to be deposited on everything in the bath. The thickness of this coating is dependent on the strength of the solution. Heavily used, bluish pickle will create the thickest coat. Freshly mixed pickle has no copper and therefore no plating reaction will occur. When the steel is removed, the pickle is "de-activated" and will no longer cause the plating reaction.

Pickle Solutions

- Ferrous Metals **Sparex #1**
- All Non-Ferrous Metals
    Sparex #2
    (Sodium Bisulphate)
- Sterling - 1 part Sulfuric
    10 parts Water
- Gold -   1 part Nitric
    20 parts Water

Heating

Sparex works best at about 80° C (180° F) It should never be heated to a boil, because dangerous fumes will then be generated. A convenient tool is a crock pot that has had its seams sealed with tub caulk.

Substitutes

In a pinch, a swimming pool additive called *Ph Plus* or a comparable product can be used as a pickle. It has the same active ingredient as Sparex.

Flame Types

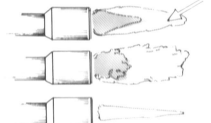

Neutral Sharp point, gentle hiss, medium blue color. All gas is being ignited. Hottest point is at the arrow.

Reducing Bushy, pulsing flame, deep blue color. This fuel-rich flame absorbs oxides and is best for soldering.

Oxidizing Thin cone, angry hiss, pale lavender. This fuel-starved flame has no advantages when soldering.

Joining

Firescale

The Jeweler's Bane, firescale is an insidious deposit of cupric oxide that grows within the structure of some copper alloys such as sterling and low karat gold.

Also called
Fire Coat
Fire Mark
Fire Stain
#*!!*!

- ○ CuO
- ● CuO$_2$
- ○ Silver

What Happens
When copper-bearing alloys are heated in the presence of oxygen, oxides are quickly formed. Cuprous oxide (CuO) is a black surface layer that can usually be dissolved in pickle. Cupric oxide (CuO$_2$) is a purplish compound that forms simultaneously within the metal. This is firescale.

Prevention
Strictly speaking, the only way to eliminate firescale is to heat the metal in an oxygen-free environment. This is the solution used in industry, but it is rarely appropriate for the craftsperson. By following these suggestions, however, it is possible to minimize the growth of firescale.

- Use a "hit and run" soldering technique.
- Avoid prolonged heating.
- Use a big enough flame to get the job done efficiently. A small flame can cause, not prevent, firescale.
- Use enough flux. Flux absorbs oxygen and prevents it from combining with copper. Just like a sponge, there is a limit to its absorbing capacity. Flux will become saturated, so be sure you have enough.
- Do not overheat metal when soldering. There is no advantage to keeping the work hot after solder has flowed. In dim light, silver and gold alloys should never need to go above a medium red when soldering.

Bright Dipping
If firescale has formed, it can often be removed by dipping the work in a strong nitric acid solution. After all soldering and rough finishing are done, but before stones are set, attach the piece to wire and dunk it for only a few seconds into a 50/50 solution of nitric acid and water at room temperature. Firescale will turn dark gray. Rinse and scratchbrush. Repeat until the scale is gone, neutralize the piece in baking soda and water, and polish. Wear rubber gloves, protective clothing and a respirator.

Plating
A commercially popular solution is to electroplate over scale. This is especially good for work that is subject to little wear, which would rub off the plating. A process called *depletion gilding* can be used to simulate this action without special equipment. After all soldering and finishing is complete, create a skin of pure metal by heating the work to the point where a gray oxide forms, and immersing it in clean pickle. Repeat the procedure 3-5 times, rinsing in water and lightly scratchbrushing each time. Remember to protect yourself against splashing pickle.

Fusing

It is possible to connect pieces of metal by heating them to their melting point and allowing the puddled surfaces to commingle. This technique has limited control but can create rich textures and unusual effects.

Fusion

Similar materials, when fluid, tend to mix readily. When you pour water into milk, the two mix. A similar mixing occurs when two pieces of metal are heated above their melting point. Molecules from the two pieces intermingle. When the material solidifies (cools) the interface between the two units has disappeared. Another name for this, usually referring to ferrous metal, is welding.

The disadvantage of fusion for metals that are good heat conductors is a lack of control over melting. This usually makes fusion inappropriate for precise work. An important exception is platinum, for which fusing is a common fabrication technique.

Where control is not essential, fusing can be used to generate interesting forms and textures. Pieces of metal are coated with flux and heated to their melting point, with care taken to heat all units simultaneously. With sufficient time and heat, the mass would draw up into a lump, but if the torch is lightly played over the surface it can guide the mirror-like flashes of fusion. Precious metals will respond better to this than copper, brass or nickle silver.

Diffusion

Somewhat related to fusion, this term refers to the nature of electrons in metals to be constantly "wandering" (technically, *delocalized*). If two pieces of metal were clamped together and left at room temperature, this electron exchange would eventually bond the two pieces together. The movement of electrons and consequently the rate of diffusion, is accelerated by heat. For careful discussion of this topic I recommend *Metalsmith Papers* (see page 187). A simplified description of the diffusion process used to form a billet of laminates for mokume-gane follows.

Diffusion is best between similar metals. Alloys of gold, silver, and copper are commonly used. Pumiced sheets of equal size and similar thickness are piled up and bonded tightly between sheets of steel. No flux is used. As the stack heats, it will expand more than the steel, having the effect of 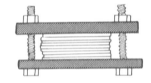 squeezing the laminates together. This tightness prohibits oxygen from entering and allows diffusion (electron migration) between the sheets.

The unit is heated in a kiln or forge until it glows red and shows a liquid-like film ("sweating"). The pile is pulled out, tapped lightly, and quickly removed from its steel enclosure. If it is still red the billet may be forged to insure that all areas are in contact and diffused. If properly done, diffusion results in a bond that is as strong as the parent metals. Subsequent forming and soldering won't disturb it.

Eutectic Bonding

The term **eutectic** defines the specific proportion of metals in an alloy that has the lowest melting point. This alloy will also be characterized by changing directly from a liquid to a solid without passing through a slushy state. Technically, this is a meeting of the *solidus* and *liquidus* temperatures. See the phase diagram on page 182 for further information. If two pieces of metal were coated with their eutectic alloy, they would easily join as soon as heated to the eutectic temperature. This is the principle used in bonding granulation, discussed on page 32.

Investment Soldering

This technique uses a plaster-like material to hold small pieces into position for soldering. It takes a little longer to set up, but in some cases it is the only way to achieve a desired precision.

1. Prepare the pieces to be soldered in the usual manner. That is, they should be well finished, edges should be refined and the surfaces being joined must make a good fit.

2. Hold the pieces into position by pressing them partially into clay. An alternate method uses an adhesive such as Super Glue to temporarily locate the pieces. Use it sparingly. It will burn away during soldering and creates unwanted fumes.

3. Mix a small amount of investment to a thin paste. Conventional investment is okay and in fact even plaster of Paris will do in a pinch, but the best material is called *soldering investment*. It has the advantage of curing quickly and remaining tough at high temperatures (unlike plaster). This can be mixed in a paper cup or in the palm of the hand.

4. Gently trowel the mixture over the workpiece, taking great care that it doesn't penetrate the seams to be soldered. Use a brush, stick or finger, depending on the scale of the work.

5. Set the resulting lump aside in a warm place to dry. This can take from 5 minutes to an hour depending on the wetness of the mix, the thickness of the application, and the choice of material. Abbreviating the drying step can cause the investment to shatter when soldering begins, which means you have to start all over. So show a little patience.

6. Apply a thick flux (one that won't remoisten the investment) to each of the seams being joined. Soldering proceeds in the conventional way, remembering that the investment will act as a heat sink.

7. When all soldering is complete and verified, quench the work in water. This will break off a lot of the investment, but some scrubbing with a toothbrush or a bath in an ultrasonic will be needed. Note that there is a similar product that does not harden and can be reused. In that case do not quench, but follow the manufacturer's directions.

Art exists not in objects but in a way of seeing.

Robert Irwin

Joining

Rivets

This is one member of a large family called *Cold Connections*. Rivets are pieces of rod that are slid through a snug hole and upset or bulged over on each end to lock pieces together.

Making a Standard Rivet

1. Drill matching holes in the pieces to be joined. If many rivets are being made, set two before drilling remaining holes. This will prevent the pieces from sliding or rotating.
2. The rivet is made of annealed wire that makes a snug fit in the holes. After being cut and filed flat, this should extend a half a diameter on each side.
3. Holding the assembly slightly above a steel surface, tap the wire with a small cross peen in two directions making a **+**.
4. As a head develops and the rivet is held in place, use the flat face of a hammer to shape and smooth the rivet.

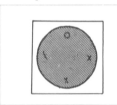 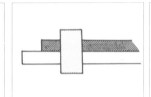  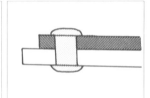

Preparing a Rivet   (Forming one head before inserting.)

1. Drill holes and select a tight-fitting wire.
2. Hold wire in vise or in pliers supported against the bench. Form a rivet head on one end of the wire, as in #3 above.
3. Slide the wire into the workpiece, tap lightly to seat it, cut off excess wire and form second head to lock the rivet in place.

When connecting soft materials such as wood, leather, etc. use a washer to keep the rivet head from pulling through. This can be of almost any shape and offers a good chance for design enhancement.

If the wire on hand is a little too large to fit a rivet hole, sand or file a gradual taper. This is faster than drawing the wire down.

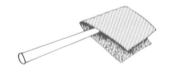

When forming a rivet head in a tight spot, a flat punch held in a vise is a useful anvil.

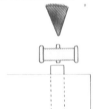

To Allow Movement

When a riveted piece is supposed to swing side-to-side, add a thin piece of cardboard to the assembly and rivet as usual. Remove the cardboard by burning it or soaking in water to provide clearance.

Shaping

Rivet heads can be shaped and burnished by a beading tool set into a drill press. Tools may be made for any size head that is needed. Lubricate the action with a light oil or wax.

Special Rivets

Rivets can be simple or complex, delicate or bulky, dominant or invisible. By understanding all these possibilities, a jeweler enlarges the range of solutions to any particular joining problem.

Nailhead Rivets

This popular variation on the rivet is useful when a larger head is needed, either for the look of it or because the material being held requires a wider grip. It is also handy when one end of the rivet is difficult to reach, for instance inside a cup, or when the material is fragile enough to warrant minimum hammering.

1. Draw a bead on a wire that fits tightly into the rivet hole. Use a hot, sharp-pointed flame. Gold and silver will form balls more easily than copper or brass.

2. Slide the wire into a tight hole on numbered side of drawplate as it is laid across vise jaws or anvil hole. Strike with a planishing hammer.

3. The resulting nailhead may be shaped with punches or a nail set while still in the drawplate, or removed and filed to a desired shape.

4. Slide the wire through the holes, tap lightly to seat, and form a standard rivet head on the other end.

Nailhead rivets are recommended for 16-24 gauge wire. Smaller wire doesn't leave enough head to show. Heavier wire does not easily form a bead.

Traditional Rosette

These decorative nailheads are made with four angled blows of a ball peen hammer.

Flush Rivets

These rivets are made as described on the previous page (standard rivets) except that the hole is prepared by beveling so that the swell of the rivet is below the surface.
If the rivet is made of the same metal as the piece it is holding, the rivet will blend in completely. This is called a ***disappearing*** or ***invisible*** rivet.

Any of these tools may be used.

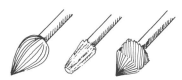

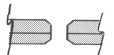

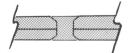

Either or both ends of a rivet may be made flush.

After forming the rivet head with a small cross peen, file, sand, and finish as usual.

Other Cold Connections

These special kinds of rivets are rather unusual but can provide intriguing design possibilities when considered from the earliest stages of a piece.

Uses

These "gentle" rivets are recommended when the hammering needed to form a standard rivet head might cause damage. This would include enamels, shells, delicate mechanisms, and stones.

Plastic rivets also add color to a piece, especially where light can be seen through the rivet. Tube rivets can be used to perforate a piece.

Tube Rivets

1. As with other rivets, the first step is to drill a hole through all the pieces being joined. This must make a tight fit with the chosen tube.
2. The tube seam should be soldered and the tube annealed.
3. The tube is slid into position and sawn to leave an amount equal to about half the diameter sticking out on each side.

4. A scribe is set into the tube and swung around to flare out the mouth. This is repeated on the tube's other end.

5. To further curl over the ends of the rivet, set it on a round punch or hammer face and tap or burnish like this.

Projecting Rivets

Blanks for these rivets are made by filing, casting or fabricating a rod of stepped diameters.

Cutlers' Rivets

These rivets are borrowed from the knife-maker's tradition and are especially handy when you want a large rivet head. Fabricate the units with a solid rod on one side and a tightly fitting tube on the other. File a blunt point on the solid piece, and assemble the rivet by squeezing or tapping the rivet halves together.

Plastic Rivets

Plastic rivets may be made from rod or sheet, in either opaque or transparent material. Since each kind of plastic has its own melting properties it's a good idea to do some test pieces. Plastic may be bought from distributors who often have scrap pieces available and can be scavenged from housewares and toys.

1. As before, start with a hole (or slot) that pierces all the pieces to be joined. Plastic may be easily filed or sanded to fit.
2. Slide plastic into place and saw it to the correct length. This can be from 1/2 to 1 diameter or thickness of the rivet.
3. Heat a steel tool in a torch or alcohol flame and press it firmly onto the plastic while supporting the rivet on the other end. The tool should not be too hot to hold in the hand. Avoid heating the plastic to the point of bubbling.
4. Invert the piece and repeat the steps above to form the other rivet head. Plastic may be finished with files, sandpaper and rouge.

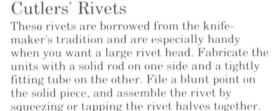

81

Adhesives

Adhesives used as a substitute for a properly made mechanical connection are generally considered a sign of poor craftsmanship. There are situations, however, when adhesives are a legitimate and important technique of heatless connecting.

To pursue this topic I recommend a trip to the library, where you will find technical information and an annual directory of suppliers called *The Adhesives Red Book*.

1. All Purpose

These include household glues such as *Elmer's, SOBO, Duco Cement*, mucilage, etc. Their primary advantages are their low cost, easy use, and broad application. On porous materials like wood, these glues penetrate and harden to form a strong mechanical bond. Most can be thinned with water and are waterproof when dry.

2. Epoxies

This is a category of thermosetting plastic known for its strength. It is available from most hardware stores in brands that offer different rates of cure (i.e. setting time), color, and specialized application. All epoxies consist of two parts (resin and hardener) that must be mixed to start the hardening reaction. Incomplete mixing will greatly decrease bond strength. Use a mixing tool that provides a good grip (not a broken match)

and stir/fold the two parts for at least a full minute. The hardening reaction is usually hastened by heat, up to about 40° C (100° F). Specific guidelines will be on the package. Hardened epoxy can be dissolved in a commercial solvent such as *Attack*. Most epoxies will start to break down at about 200° C (400° F).

3. Cyanoacrylate

This recently developed family of adhesives is sold as *Super Glue, Krazy Glue* and other brand names. It is anaerobic, meaning that it hardens when air is excluded. For this reason it will not fill a gap or bond porous materials. On tight-fitting nonporous surfaces, it is quick and strong. Its drawbacks are its high cost and the inability to reposition pieces during gluing.

Rules

Many adhesives are delicate compounds that require certain temperatures or environments to properly harden. Read label directions and follow them meticulously for maximum holding power.

Surfaces to be joined must be absolutely clean. Since metal is nonporous only a thin surface film of glue will be doing the holding. On this scale, even a trace amount of oil or debris will affect bond strength. Though clamping is not always necessary, it is a good way to assure proper fittings and will keep pieces from being bumped apart.

Cleaning

Proper cleaning before gluing will usually follow a sequence like this:

1. Abrade surface
2. Pickle (if metal)
3. Rinse in water
4. Wipe with a solvent.
5. Warm slightly to drive off solvent.

Casting

Charcoal Casting

In this ancient technique, molten metal is poured or pressed into a mold carved from charcoal. What the process lacks in precision it makes up for in ease and simplicity.

Open Molds
The mold deteriorates with each use but can provide 3 or 4 castings.

1. Carve a recess in a flat block of charcoal to the thickness and shape of the desired piece. If the surface of the block is irregular, prepare it by sanding it flat.

2. Melt the metal directly in the mold cavity. Flux is not usually needed because of the purifying atmosphere created by the charcoal.

3. As soon as the metal is molten, bring a second charcoal block down on the first with even pressure. Avoid slamming and splashing the metal. Work while standing to avoid a lapful of hot metal.

Closed Molds

1. Carve a depression in a flat charcoal block or blocks. If both sides are carved, the alignment will be approximate. Careful measurement will help.

2. Carve a sprue funnel.

3. Tie the blocks together with binding wire.

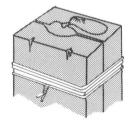

4. Pour molten metal from a pouring crucible, or carve a melting reservoir in the top of one of the charcoal blocks and connect it to the sprue with a channel. When the metal is molten, grip the whole assembly in tongs and tip to pour.

Alternate Molds
Other materials can be used for either of the methods shown here. Native American Indians in the Southwest use a rock called Tuff or Tufa (compacted volcanic ash) to make casting molds.

 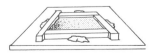

Plaster or investment can be formed into blocks by pouring into boxes or wooden frames laid out on a sheet of glass or plastic. When thoroughly dry these can be carved and used as above.

Water Casting
Metals may be poured into water to create unusual shapes and to reduce large pieces to smaller, easier melting pieces. Use a deep enough bucket to allow the pieces to cool before hitting the bottom.

Cuttlefish Casting

The skeleton of a squidlike saltwater fish can be used to create simple one-use molds for casting. The growth lines of the fish, which resemble the grain pattern of wood, create a fascinating texture.

The use of a cuttlefish skeleton as a mold is an ancient device. This technique provides rich texture and immediate results at a low cost and with very little equipment.
A disadvantage of the process is that it is limited in size and thickness. Most cuttlefish are about 3" wide and 7" long.

1. Use two bones or cut one in half. Remove the pointy end.
2. Rub the pieces together (soft side to soft side) in a circular motion to make flat surfaces.
3. Carve an indentation for the desired form. Remember that the depth of cut equals the thickness of final piece. Position the cavity about 3/4" from the big end.
4. Carve a sprue funnel in both sides.
5. If the grain pattern is to be emphasized, the mold is eroded with a soft brush.
6. Scratch vents upward to allow the escape of gases from inside the mold.
7. Tie the mold halves together with binding wire or masking tape. Set the mold into sand.
8. Melt metal in a pouring ladle and fill the mold with a smooth even pour.

A flat back can be made of firebrick or charcoal.

Three Part Molds

1. Cut off three bone pieces.

2. Rub B and C together until flush. Bind with tape.

3. Rub A along the top edge of BC until flush.

4. Open BC, set pins and model into position.

5. Press B & C together; bind with tape.

6. Press A down on the part of the model that extends out of mold. Mark location with tape or ink lines.

7. Open, remove the model, carve a sprue and pouring funnel (gate).

8. Put the mold back together, tie, and cast.

Sand Casting

In this ancient technique, moist sand is tightly pressed around a model which is then removed, leaving a mold cavity to be filled with molten metal. Sand casting has been used by many cultures for centuries and is still an important technique today.

Preparing Sand

Almost any sand can be used, but beach sand is not recommended. Fine pumice, sold as a finishing medium works pretty well and has the advantage of being presifted. Casting sand is commercially available or may be easily prepared. The finer the sand, the better the detail on the resulting casting.
- Get a bucket of sand from the hardware store or highway department.
- Sift it through a sieve several times to remove debris.
- Sift through screen or cheesecloth to remove large particles.
- Mix with water or oil by massaging. Baby oil or used motor oil are common binders. Avoid making the sand too wet. If you goof, spread sand on a board and dry in the sun. It is right when it holds together after being squeezed into a ball.

Casting a Flat-Backed Object

1. Set the *drag* (frame piece without pins) onto a flat surface such as glass. Fill with dampened sand, packing it down firmly with a block of wood. Strike off (make flat) as shown.

2. Flip the drag over and set the other frame piece (called the *cope*) into place on it. Dust the packed sand with pounce* and lay the model into position.

3. Sprinkle sand over the model and pack it layer by layer until the cope is full. Strike off as before.

4. Carefully lift the cope and remove the model with tweezers. Remove sand with a brush to create a sprue.

5. Set the cope and drag back together, covering each with a piece of wood, glass, or plastic. Tie with wire, tape, or use a clamp as shown. Don't tighten the clamp too hard.

6. Pour molten metal into the mold using a pouring crucible.

*Pounce

This is a powder used to keep mold sections from sticking together. Talc, cornstarch, chalk dust or graphite can be used. It is often kept in a bag of loosely woven material like gauze or muslin for dusting onto a mold.

Casting

Sand Casting

Sand for casting can be bought commercially or can be dug and refined by straining it through a sieve. The fineness of the grains will determine the amount of detail on the final casting.

Casting a Heavy Ingot

1. Put moistened sand in a pan that is 2" deeper than the ingot you intend to make.
2. Fill pan half full, packing firm, not hard.
3. Prepare a model of wood (dowel), plastic, or metal by coating with pounce.
4. Slide the model into the sand, leaving about an inch of sand below the model.
5. Add sand to cover model, packing hard. Create a funnel.
6. Carefully slide the model out, and pour molten metal into the mold.

A Homemade Flask

A casting flask is a one-time investment, because they last almost indefinitely with normal use. They do not need to be closely fitted to the size of the workpiece, but they cannot be too small and are a nuisance if they are too large. A typical jewelry caster might want 2 or 3 of various sizes.

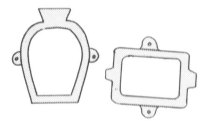

To make a flask, weld a 1" angle iron like this. The walls of the flask are angled to secure the sand when it is packed in. The lugs can be made from a section of pipe, a stack of washers, or an oversized nut. Note that the pin will slide (not screw) into position. The pin is a bolt that is screwed and welded into one side and ground down to slide onto the other lug. Remember to grind away a small area for the gate, where the metal is poured in.

A Two Part Model

The preceding page shows the technique for a flat or almost flat object. A fully dimensional form will require the making of a 2 part model, which is usually of a well-dried soft wood such as poplar.

The model is designed to come apart at the parting line. Every surface will slope inward from this line, as shown. The model may be made and then sliced in two, or built from two pieces of wood. If it is to be turned, glue two pieces with a sheet of newspaper between them, and make sure this seam is in the center of the turning. When the form is complete, strike it with a chisel and it will fall open.

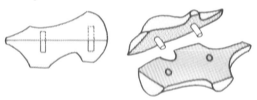

Drill a couple of holes in one unit and line up registration pins in the other side. A short piece of 1/4" dowel will do for these. As a final step the wood is sealed with shellac or varnish.

87

Lost Wax Process

Most jewelry casting today uses a variation on the lost wax method developed in ancient Egypt. This page provides a summary of the process, which is explained in more detail throughout this chapter.

When the metalsmiths of ancient cultures first developed this technique they made models of beeswax and coated them with layers of clay. The outer layers were reinforced with straw or linen and the dried assembly was set into an oven to harden. Simultaneously the wax was burned away, leaving a cavity into which molten metal was poured. The clay shell was broken away to retrieve the finished casting. Because the mold was destroyed in the process, the technique is called a ***waste mold casting***.

Safety

1. A ***model*** is made of wax or another completely combustible material.

2. The model is mounted on a wax rod called a ***sprue.***

3. The sprue is mounted onto a base and fitted with a watertight section of pipe called a ***flask***.

4. A plaster-like material called ***investment*** is mixed to a creamy consistency. Steps are taken to insure that this mix is free of air bubbles.

5. The smooth investment is gently poured over the prepared model as it stands in the center of the flask.

6. The investment is dried and then heated (***burned out***) in a kiln. This cures the mold and removes all traces of the model.

7. While the mold is still warm from the burnout, molten metal is poured or forced into the mold, where it assumes the shape of the original model.

8. After brief cooling the mold is quenched in water. This breaks the mold and releases the casting.

Casting

Modeling Wax

Modeling wax can be shaped in the fingers or with simple tools at room temperature. It is generally an additive process, building up layers and elements as needed to create a form.

Tips on Working

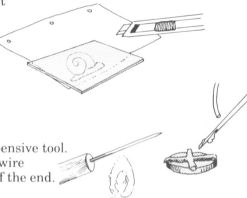

- Keep wax sheets between pieces of paper to prevent them from sticking together. Store in a cool place.
- Before working on sheet wax, soften it by dipping into warm water or breathing on it.
- Sheet wax can be cut with a razor blade knife. Because wax is transparent, a design drawn on paper can be traced.
- Soft wax can be folded, twisted, stamped, pinched, pierced, built up or pressed to receive a texture.
- All kinds of wax can be used together.
- A biology, or clay needle, makes a handy and inexpensive tool.
- To add wax to an area, heat a needle, touch a wax wire to this and allow the wax to slide down and drop off the end.
- When heating a needle, hold it as shown, with the flame hitting it at mid-length. This will preserve the tip and keep the needle warm for a longer time.

Casting

To Make a Lamp

Use a glass jar with a metal cap. A piece of rope or shoelace can be used for a wick. To make the hole for the wick, pound a nail through from the inside. This makes a sharp bur that will grip the wick.

ALCOHOL

Fuel

- Commercial lamp fuel
- Methyl Alcohol-also called wood alcohol, methanol and carbinol
- Alcohol-based solvent

*Never use gasoline.
Never expose any fuel
container to open flame.*

Safety

Establishing a Ring Size

Wrap tape around a dowel until the correct size form is made. To allow the wax pattern to slip off easier, lubricate the tape with Vaseline or oil. The mandrel may be held in a vise if needed.

Wax Extrusion

Wire of unique cross section can be made by extruding soft wax through dies you make yourself. Buy 3 sizes of telescoping brass tubing at a hobby shop. Cap the smallest to be the ram. The die is soldered onto a 3" piece of the largest tube and held in place while extruding. You might want to make several of these, in different shapes. Wear gloves.

Carving Wax

Carving waxes are sold by most jewelry supply companies and by some hobby shops. Although other waxes can be used, they do not carve as well as waxes blended for this purpose.

Carving tools can be purchased or made from discarded dental tools, steel wire (eg. paper clip, coat hanger) or old silverware. Handles can be a dowel or a pin vise.

Coarse files (soft metal files) and utility knives are used.

A spiral blade fitted in a standard sawframe is used to cut off sections of wax.

A nonclog wax bur is made for a flexible shaft. Very handy.

Use a coarse paper towel or fabric for removing scratches.

Scraps

Melted wax poured on water causes interesting effects. Variations include pouring wax onto ice, steel, wood, concrete, etc.

Leftover bits of wax may be remelted and formed into a usable block as long as they are not contaminated with debris. Line a cardboard box with aluminum foil and heap the scraps into it. Warm the box slowly in a kiln just until the wax starts to melt. Hold at this temperature until the whole mass is fluid. Tap lightly to ease out any air bubbles and allow the box to cool slowly.

Welding

Blocks of wax can be welded to create forms in preparation for carving. Be certain that both surfaces are glossy and press them together. If done right there will be no seam.

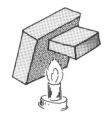

Stippling

Uneven carved surfaces may be made more uniform by repeated working with a scribe, needle tool or beading punch.

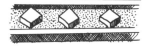

Because the starting point for wax carving is usually a large block, a common error is to make models too large. Final weight may be calculated as shown on page 93. To reduce, carve out the inside with a chisel or a flexible shaft bur.

If at first you don't succeed, try, try, again. Then quit. There's no use being a damn fool about it.

W.C. Fields

Casting

90

Other Models

Wax is the most common material used for casting models but plastics, wood and organic substances can also be used. In some cases special ventilation during burnout will be required.

Organic Materials

Many organic objects, such as leaves, twigs, flower petals and insects will burn out completely when encased in an investment mold. This means they can be cast directly, often with very clear detail. Burnout usually takes longer for organic materials than for wax, and higher temperatures may also be needed. Experimentation is required.

• Porous materials such as paper, cardboard, popcorn should be sealed by spraying, painting or dripping with lacquer, wax, or thinned white glue.

• Thin and delicate models also require some treatment. Flower petals or insect wings can be sprayed with several coats of hair spray, fixative or paint. Often a model may be reinforced by adding wax wires on the back.

Clay Relief

Attractive wax models rich in texture can be made by pouring or brushing molten wax over clay. The result will be a reverse image of the shape and markings of the clay.

• Injecting wax or a mix of hard and soft wax will give best results.
• Use earthen clay, not plasticene (kids' modeling clay) which will melt under hot wax.

• Always use a double boiler arrangement to melt wax. Wax has a low flash point and can ignite violently on an open burner. **Never leave wax unattended on stove!**

Plastics

• Most plastics will burnout completely, so found objects like these can be cast in accurate detail. Plastics may be modified by heating or used in combination with wax.
• Pieces may be glued together with white glue or sticky wax.

• Styrofoam can be used to make models, too. Pieces are held directly in the flame to shape, or may be carved with a heated needle.

 CAUTION
The fumes of burning plastic are toxic and must be ventilated.

91

Sprues

Sprues hold a model in its correct position while making the mold, they also provide a passageway for the escape of melting wax, and allow entry for molten metal.

Proper placement and attaching of sprues is one of the most important factors in achieving a successful casting. Unfortunately it is also one of the most difficult to describe, because each situation has unique requirements. As best as possible, satisfy each of these rules.

	Wrong	Right
1. Arrange sprues to supply sufficient metal to each section of the model.		
2. Plan sprues to avoid flow-backs and sharp curves.		
3. Attach sprues where they will cause the least damage to the model's surface texture and where they can be easily removed.		
4. Avoid spruing work dead level. Sprues should not enter at a right angle.		
5. Sprue to the thickest section of the model. The sprue itself should be the thickest mass of the whole assembly.		

Porosity

As metal cools it contracts, so additional metal is needed to fill a space that was previously filled by molten metal. If no extra material is supplied at the instant of contraction, the metal will crystalize with voids (pits) as it tries to fill the cavity. To control this the sprue and button should be the last area to cool (contract). If pits occur here no damage is done. To achieve this, the thinnest section of the model is set furthest from the sprue base. The thickest is attached to the sprue, and the sprue is thicker than any part of the model.

Vents (Also called **gates**)
In small models, fumes in the cavity escape into the investment as metal enters. For large models it is wise to provide a vent for gases. In large industrial castings sometimes many vents are used.

Avoid constricted, pinched-neck sprues. These will spray the metal, causing it to chill (harden) prematurely.

The man who makes no mistakes does not usually make anything.
W.C. Magee

Casting

Preparations

The moldmaking process is not daunting, but can seem complex to a beginner. Careful preparation can ease the panic of this important step.

Determining How Much Metal to Use

• Guess, pray, ask a wiser person.

• Attach the sprued model to a wire and push it into a container of water. Note the raised level. Remove the model and add metal to bring the water back up to the marked level. A graduated cylinder is handy but not necessary. To this amount add $\frac{1}{3}$ more for the button.

• Multiply the weight of the model by the specific gravity of the metal being used. Add about 20% more to allow for the button.

Example	Wax with sprues	x	specific gravity	=	total needed
	6 grains	times	10.4 (for sterling)	=	62.4 grains, or 1 oz/6 dwt.

Specific Gravities

Aluminum	2.7
Brass (70-30)	8.5
Nu-Gold (88/12)	8.7
18K Yellow Gold	15.5
14K Yellow Gold	13.4
10K Yellow Gold	11.6
Iron	7.9
Lead	11.4
Nickel Silver	8.8
Platinum	21.4
Fine Silver	10.6
Sterling	10.4

To Help Investment Better Coat a Wax Model

1. Coat the model with a commercial debubblizer by brush or by dipping.
2. Paint with alcohol. A lamp wick may be used as shown.

3. To make a wetting solution:

> 50% hydrogen peroxide
> 50% liquid soap

Timing

Investments have 9-10 minutes of working time. If your pace is too slow, the investment will harden before it can coat the model. If you work too quickly and the investment is poured into the flask too soon, water in the mix is free to come out of solution and will travel along the model. This will result in water trails (raised streaks) on the finished casting. To avoid these problems, time yourself as you invest and adjust your pace accordingly.

Plastics

The specific gravities of common plastics range from 1.2 to 1.7. To calculate the metal needed for a plastic model add 10% to the specific gravities listed, then multiply as before.

93

Investing

Investment is a plaster-based material that has been made heat resistant with the addition of silica. Though the process takes only about 10 minutes, carelessness here can ruin hours of modelmaking.

 SAFETY NOTE
Investment is extremely dangerous to inhale because of the silica it contains. Always wear a certified respirator when mixing investment.

Vacuum Method

1. Mix the investment thoroughly with your hand or a spatula. Investment should look like sour cream.
2. Set the bowl on a vacuum table, wet the rim of bell jar and set it over the investment.
3. Turn on the motor and direct vacuum to the table. Press down on the bell jar to guarantee that suction is achieved.
4. Leave vacuum at maximum (25-28) for about one minute. Investment will swell and bubble. When it "spits" and the jar condenses, turn off vacuum.
5. Pour creamy investment into flask by allowing it to run down the side. Set the flask back onto the vacuum table and repeat. If the investment is starting to thicken (looks like pudding) omit the second vacuum operation.
6. Remember that the investment will swell in the flask. Allow for this by not filling flask to the top or by using a collar of rubber, plastic, paper or masking tape.

Hard Core Method

1. Mix investment and vibrate the bowl to remove bubbles.
2. Paint investment onto the model with a fine brush. Spread the mixture so as to avoid bubbles, especially in crevices.
3. Sprinkle investment powder onto the coated model to absorb moisture and begin setting of this shell or core.
4. Set a flask over the model, secure base, and pour in the investment. Keep weight off model by pouring it down the side of the flask. Be sure to hold onto the base while pouring.

Alternate Flasks
Use a can with both ends cut out. The can may be bent as long as it will fit the casting machine. Note that steam or vacuum methods can tolerate odd shaped flasks. Do not use a thin beverage can.

94

Burnout

This is the important step in which the model material, usually wax, is removed from the mold. Noxious fumes can be released, so ventilation is recommended.

The purpose of burnout is to
- cure or harden the mold
- eliminate wax or other model material
- heat the mold for compatibility with the molten casting metal.

VENTILATE!
Wax fumes are not good for your body. Plastics are worse. Keep kiln in a large room, near a window, and in a cross draft. An exhaust fan is needed.

Safety

Burnout is usually done in a small electric kiln, though gas kilns may also be used. Burnout is best done within 48 hours of investing. If casting must wait, remoisten the flask by soaking it in water for a few seconds before burnout. Recent developments in investment technology have created a product that will tolerate faster temperature changes than what was available 10 years ago. The progression and pace of burnout will vary depending on the size and number of flasks in the kiln, the temperature of the kiln, and the preferences of the caster. As a rule of thumb, allow two and a half hours for a typical jewelry-scale burnout.

Flasks are placed in the kiln with sprue holes facing down. Prop up in any of these ways to allow the wax to drip out.

LUMP OF INVESTMENT   PUMICE

Hot flasks are handled with tongs sold for this purpose or with household jar lifters sold for canning and handling baby bottles.

Because aluminum melts at temperatures used for burn-out (660° C/1220° F) it can be used as an indicator in the kiln. Set a small piece near but not touching the flask. When it curls, the flask is probably ready.

Casting

Temperatures (approximate)

°F	°C	
300	150	Wax melts and drips out.
450	235	Wax ignites.
600	325	Woody materials ignite.
1000	550	Plastics vaporize.
1250	650	Wax residues vaporize.
1350	740	Gypsum binder in investment breaks down, releasing sulfur that will cause oxidation. Do not go to this temperature!

Fume Reduction

The amount of fumes can be reduced by catching the wax at around 150° C (300° F), before it ignites. This is done in a stainless steel tray sold by suppliers or in a similar affair which you can make from a cookie sheet. Wax caught in this way usually contains too many impurities and has been too changed by melting to be used again.

To know that you do not know is the best. To pretend to know when you do not know is a disease.

Lao Tzu 500 BC

Steam Casting

This ingenious process uses the heat of the molten metal to create steam pressure which forces metal into a mold cavity. It requires very simple equipment and can yield consistently fine results.

Steam Handle

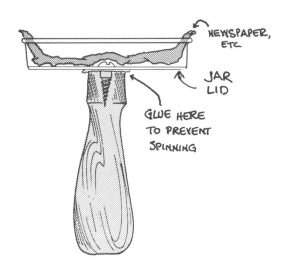

NEWSPAPER, ETC

JAR LID

GLUE HERE TO PREVENT SPINNING

Sprue Size

Because this technique calls for the metal to be melted in the mouth of the flask, the sprues must be a small enough size to prevent the metal from dripping into the mold cavity prematurely. If the model is large or thick and therefore requires a lot of metal, compensate by using more sprues.
Sprue with 16 gauge or smaller wax sheet or wire.

The carving of the model, location of sprues and mixing of investment are the same for steam casting as for more conventional techniques.

1. If the sprue base did not form a large enough reservoir for melting, a funnel shape is carved in the top of the invested flask.

2. After standard burnout, metal is melted in the mouth of the flask. Flux as usual.

3. When metal is molten, the torch is withdrawn as the steam handle is simultaneously clapped firmly onto the flask. Hold it in this position until the metal solidifies.

Sling Casting

This casting technique uses very simple equipment and the power of centrifugal force to push molten metal into a mold. It involves just enough risk to keep the process exciting.

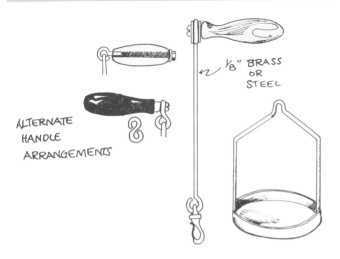

ALTERNATE HANDLE ARRANGEMENTS

⅛" BRASS OR STEEL

In this straightforward technique, molten metal is forced into the mold cavity with centrifugal force generated by hand. The prepared flask is set into the casting device described here and swung in a large arc. Though perfectly safe, this is not a technique recommended for low ceilinged studios or for the timid. As described on the preceding page, sling casting uses the mouth of the flask itself as the melting crucible.

Process

1. Make a sling in any of the ways shown. For small flasks, the pan can be a jar lid. For a larger sling, fabricate a ring and base from copper, brass, or steel sheet.

2. Prepare the model with 16 gauge sprues.

3. After burnout, set the flask into the basket of the sling and set this on a fireproof surface.

4. Melt metal to be cast in the funnel at the top of flask. Flux as usual.

5. When the metal is molten, pull the torch away and swing the flask in large even arcs. A steady motion is more important than a fast or mighty swing.

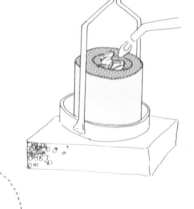

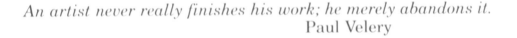

An artist never really finishes his work; he merely abandons it.
Paul Velery

Centrifugal & Vacuum

These two methods are the most commonly used means of filling a mold in today's jewelry industry. The first requires a spring-loaded arm that uses centrifugal force to throw molten metal into the mold and the second uses vacuum methods to achieve the same results.

Process

1. Before burnout, balance the machine by setting the cool flask into it and adjusting the weights until the arm is level.

2. Wind the machine 3 times and secure it into position. This is probably achieved by sliding a steel pin against the arm, but there are several styles of machine so yours could be different.

3. Set the hot flask into the machine with tongs and load your metal into the crucible. Heat the metal, adding flux a couple of times. Direct the torch flame on the mouth of the crucible as well.

4. When the metal is molten, plant your feet squarely and get a good grip on the arm of the casting machine. Release the pin so it is only you holding the arm. Release the arm as you simultaneously lift the torch.

Melting

Care in melting the metal is important in every kind of casting.

- use a flame that is hot enough to be efficient, but not so hot it will burn the metal.
- Use a fuel-rich, reducing flame. This is a bushy or feathery flame. It should not make a hissing sound.
- When the metal is red and again when it is molten, sprinkle on borax, boric acid, powdered charcoal or a commercial flux.

Vacuum

A strong vacuum pump (one that can produce a vacuum equal to 25-29 inches of mercury) is needed for investing and vacuum assist casting. After burnout, the hot flask is set into place on a silicone rubber pad. Turn on the vacuum pump to check the seal. If the pressure gauge does not go into the 20s, press down on the flask with tongs. Melt metal in a pouring crucible, flux and pour into mouth of the flask with a smooth even flow. (Imagine that it's honey.)
The flask is cooled and quenched as usual.

Machine Supports

Casting machines must be solidly mounted and surrounded by a splash screen.
A wash tub bolted to a bench.

The caster can be set into the bench to save space.
Hinged lid is plywood.

A garbage can filled 2/3 full of rocks and cement is stable, safe and can be moved around the shop. Set bolts into wood to insure their proper location, then set the wood into cement.

Casting

Hollow Core

In order to cast a hollow object, a core of investment material is first created to occupy what will be the interior space of the final casting.

Using Cores

A core is a lump of mold material (investment) that is anchored within the mold where it creates a cavity or hollow in the finished casting.

1. With coarse files or knives, carve a block of hardened investment to the shape of the desired interior.

2. Cover this core with wax either by painting hot wax or by dipping the core into melted wax to build up successive layers.

3. File and model the wax as usual.

4. To anchor the core into the mold, drill holes into the core and push wires of metal to be cast (*chaplets*) as shown. See the next page, "Providing a Grip."

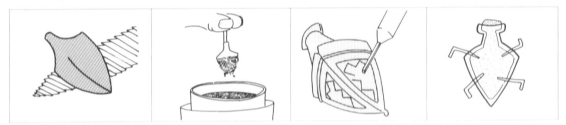

Traditional Two Part Mold

Make a model in clay, plasticene or wax. Work on a base made of wood and wire.

Make a wall of thin brass or aluminum shims, pushed into the model. This will be the parting line, so avoid undercuts.

Drip plaster or investment onto the model, trying not to trap air bubbles. Build up several layers, ending with cloth strips pressed into the plaster.

When the plaster is thoroughly dry, pry the mold pieces apart and remove the model. Wash thoroughly. If air bubbles are visible in the plaster, they can be filled with fresh plaster.

After lubricating the mold with liquid soap or Vaseline, paint melted wax into it. The thickness of the wax will be the thickness of the metal when you're done.

When the wax is hard, pull it out, make repairs, sprue, join halves with hot needle and model the seam. Invest and cast as usual, making certain that the investment fills the interior.

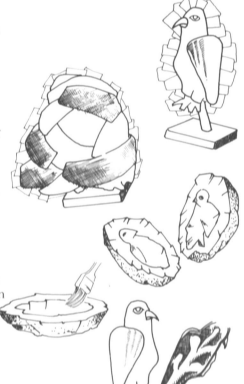

99

Implants

In lost wax casting it is sometimes helpful to "implant" a stone or finished piece of metal in the wax model. If proper precautions are taken the object can remain in position throughout the burnout and casting operations.

Providing a Grip

When a model is made and pieces are set into it, they are of course held in place by wax. Keep in mind that during burnout the wax will be removed. If precautions are not taken the small pieces may become loose and drop into the mold cavity, ruining the casting. Investment has an adhesive quality and will probably grip small pieces as long as sufficient surface area is available. A slightly rough surface will hold better than a smooth one. Each situation will require its own solution. In some cases a design may be modified to provide a "finger" of investment to grip the implanted piece on each side and hold it in place. Sometimes an extension may be soldered to a small piece to lock it in position. This can later be sawn off the finished casting.

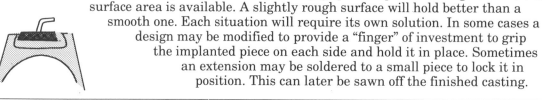

Bezels

Unless you have a delicate touch it can be difficult to accurately shape bezels in wax. A neater job is likely to result when a bezel is made of thin metal strip. To make a subtle transition between the bezel and the work, the metal bezel may be set into the wax. As shown, wax can then be modeled around the bezel. Any metals with a melting point above burnout temperature (670°C/1250°F) are safe to use in this way. Sometimes the molten metal will fuse onto the bezel but usually the oxides accumulated in the flask during burnout prevent a strong bond. It is a good practice to solder the bezel in place immediately after pickling the casting, before the perfect fit gets distorted.

Metal Implants

Metals of contrasting color may also be cast together as described above. If a small piece is to be inlaid it may be sawn out and worked as desired. A bevel must be filed on the edge of these pieces to lock them in place. Soft wax is then dripped or pushed like putty over the piece. As described above, a grip must be provided.

When a large piece of metal is being used its weight can cause the sprue to bend over. To prevent this a secondary support is used. Because this connects outside the funnel area of the flask no metal will enter this cavity even though its wax has burned out.

Stones

Some stones will withstand burnout temperatures and the thermal shock of inrushing molten metal. Such stones may be "set" in the wax and cast in place. This process especially lends itself to irregular stones and crystals. Implanted stones are handled as above and in the preceding pages except that after casting the flask should be air-cooled rather than quenched. Gem materials that are likely to withstand this method:

DIAMOND
SAPPHIRE
RUBY
TOURMALINE
TRANSPARENT SYNTHETICS

Remember that impurities may cause a tough stone to crack.

Shortlife Molds

When only a small number of duplicates are needed it is possible to use an inexpensive mold. These will yield from 1 to 10 impressions depending on the complexity of the form being cast.

Clay Impressions

Probably the simplest way to duplicate an existing shape is to take an impression by pressing it into clay. This technique is ideal for a flat one-sided object in low relief. Either plasticene or earthen clay may be used, but note the former is more sensitive to high temperatures. Roll or pat the clay to a smooth pancake and dust the top surface lightly with talcum or corn starch. Press the object into the clay and lift it cleanly away. Melted wax can then be poured or dripped into the cavity. Try to lay down a smooth even layer of wax so as to avoid trapping air bubbles. Brushing will enable you to control the thickness of the model you are creating. Allow the wax to harden competely, then lift it out and wash it under cold running water, using a toothbrush to remove excess clay. Pits in the wax can be filled with soft wax, but if a great deal of repair is necessary you should probably just try again.

Alginate

This material will be familiar to all jewelers who had orthodontia. This is the "mashed potato stuff" that is used to take dental impressions. It can be purchased through dental supply companies, but is usually cheaper through a jewelers supply. It comes as a light powder (often flavored!) and is mixed with water. A paper cup makes a handy mixing jar. Add just enough water to make a thick batter consistency and pat it into place over the material being molded. You must work quickly because alginate has a very fast setting time, which is both a blessing and a curse depending on how well prepared you are. It will become firm in under two minutes, but allow it to set for another 5 minutes to insure full curing. The mold has some flexibility but will tear if stressed too far. Alginate will dry out and become too rigid to use within 12 hours. Its life can be extended slightly by storing the mold under water, but the best results will be achieved within the first couple hours after taking the impression.

Room Temperature Vulcanizing (RTV)

(also called Cold Mold Casting, CMC)

The past decade has seen the development of scores of synthetic rubber compounds that are changed from a liquid to an elastic solid state when two components are mixed together. As the name implies, this reaction occurs at room temperature but yield a rubber whose strength and flexibility approaches that of a vulcanized rubber.

In general these molds are sulfur-based compounds that require a small amount of catalyst to harden, the reaction usually taking overnight. The mixed compound can be spread onto an object or poured into a dish over the piece. Of the three options on this page this is certainly the most expensive, but still a little cheaper than the commercial options described next.

For more information contact The Perma-Flex Mold Company, 1919 E. Livingston Ave. Columbus, OH 43209, (614) 252-8034.

Rubber Molds

Because conventional casting of precious metals requires that the investment mold be destroyed to retrieve the finished casting, a supplementary step is needed to produce wax models. These can be made by injecting molten wax into a rubber mold that will flex sufficiently to allow the model to be removed.

Vulcanized Molds

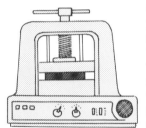

Slabs of raw uncured rubber are laid into a sturdy rectangular mold frame made of steel or aluminum. When roughly half the depth is filled, the object to be reproduced is laid into place. Because of the temperatures and pressures involved, this model must be of a hard material. Metal is usually used but wood or a hard plastic such as nylon or Delrin will work. The mold frame is then packed with more rubber and set into a vulcanizer. This machine will maintain the firm pressure and temperature (164°C/310° F) needed to cure the rubber. Curing takes about 15 minutes per 1/4" of mold, or about an hour and a half for an average piece. The vulcanized mold material will be similar to rubber band rubber. The mold is cooled and cut as shown below. For further information on rubber molds, consult the manufacturer's literature for your equipment.

Rubber Molds without a Vulcanizer

The metalsmith on a budget will be glad to know that it's possible to make the mold described above in a kitchen oven. Use the same rubber, and if possible, buy an aluminum mold frame. If this is too dear, make a frame from aluminum strapping sold in many hardware stores to trim doors. Drill a small hole to allow for excess rubber to squirt out. Pack the mold as above, trapping the model in the middle of a sandwich. The stack should be arranged so that it is about 3 mm (1/8") thicker than the frame. Set the stack between two plates of steel or thick aluminum plate, and close with a C-clamp at firm pressure. Set into a 300° F (150° C) oven. After 15 minutes, open the stove and, wearing gloves, tighten the C clamp a half turn. Repeat this tightening in another 15 minutes and heat until the rubber begins to ooze out of the hole. Remove the mold and allow it to cool completely before cutting it open.

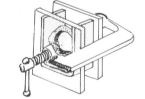

Mold Cutting

For either of the above methods it is necessary to cut the mold so the original model and subsequent wax impressions can be removed. This is a delicate and demanding skill, and only experience can really teach it. The parting line, where the mold pieces meet, might be visible on the finished casting so it should be located either where it can be easily removed or where it won't damage the design. Having a clear idea of the model and the desired location of the parting line will make cutting easier. Use a sharp blade and work with small slices while

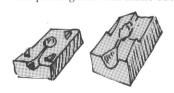

pulling the mold apart. A bent fork or can opener is a convenient third hand. To register the mold sections a zig-zag pattern or a couple of raised buttons are cut near the outside edge. Some shapes require complex mold divisions. For more information on this topic I recommend *Centrifugal or Lost Wax Casting* by Murray Bovin.

Casting

Chapter 6

Stones

Introduction

Lapidary is an art all to itself with its own rich history, language and literature. The following pages cannot be comprehensive but attempt to provide some working knowledge as a foundation for further reading and discovery.

Lapidary, the art of working with gemstones, is a complex field of study all by itself and few metalsmiths can give as much time to it as they would like. Still, there is a need for information because most workers in fine metals use gems sooner or later. The following pages provide an introduction for those who deal with stones as a secondary aspect of their craft. It does not pretend to be complete or academic, but is intended only to lay a foundation for further investigation.

There are over 2000 minerals in the earth's crust. Trying to organize this material has proven difficult. Color and hardness, for instance, aren't appropriate because a stone may occur in several shades and kinds of crystals. Chemical and mineralogical divisions similarly confuse rather than simplify the matter. I turned finally to the alphabet. What follows is an alphabetical list of fifty popular stones with some information, history or tips for each one. Where possible, I have included folklore for each gem. I don't mean to imply a proven relationship between the stone and magical qualities ascribed to it. But then, I don't want to discount the possibility either.

Birthstones

Today the commercial jewelry industry has effectively blunted any charm or seriousness concerning the relationship between earth materials and the season of one's birth. There was a time when such relationships, often involving astrological movements, played an important part in daily life. The list below is borrowed from George Frederick Kunz whose book *The Curious Lore of Precious Stones* (Dover 1971) is recommended for further investigation.

January	garnet, hyacinth
February	amethyst, hyacinth, pearl
March	bloodstone, jasper
April	diamond, sapphire
May	agate, emerald, chalcedony, carnelian
June	emerald, agate, pearl, chalcedony, turquoise
July	ruby, carnelian, onyx, sardonyx, turquoise
August	carnelian, moonstone, topaz, alexandrite, sardonyx
September	sapphire, lapis lazuli, coral
October	opal, aquamarine, beryl
November	topaz, pearl
December	turquoise, ruby, bloodstone

Wedding Anniversary Tokens

1	rose beryl	paper
2	crystal	cotton
3	chrysoprase	leather
4	moonstone	silk
5	carnelian	wood
6	peridot	sugar
7	coral	wool
8	opal	clay
9	citrine	willow
10	turquoise	tin
11	garnet	
12	amethyst	linen
13	agate	
14	ivory	lace
15	topaz	
25	silver	
30	pearl	
35	jade	
40	ruby	
45	sapphire	
50	golden	
55	emerald	
60	diamond	

Cut

In addition to the intrinsic properties of a material, value and beauty are dependent on the skill and imagination of the cutter. Some cuts, such as the traditional brilliant with its 57 facets are mathematically designed. Others are intuitively shaped by the lapidary.

From the metalsmith's point of view, gem materials may be considered in terms of:

- **Color** — In many cases, like agates, color is entirely a matter of taste. In others, such as emerald, a deep color is a major factor in value.
- **Cut** — The planes or curves should be symmetrical, well polished, and arranged to complement the material.
- **Hardness** — A gem that will not retain its polish is of limited value. In setting, it is important to know the hardness of the material being used. Soft stones should be set in a way that will protect them.
- **Luster** — This refers to the brightness of the shine. Some stones have a lesser value because they will not polish well.
- **Purity** — (absence of inclusions) Some stones are valued for their inclusions, such as rutilated quartz or moss agate. In other stones, such as amethyst, inclusions lower the value.
- **Special Effects** — Cat's eye and iridescence are examples of this.

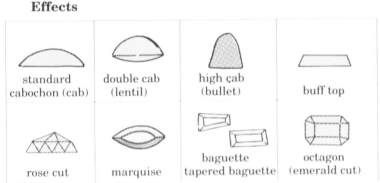

standard cabochon (cab)   double cab (lentil)   high cab (bullet)   buff top

rose cut   marquise   baguette / tapered baguette   octagon (emerald cut)

To evaluate the quality of a cutting job, look for regular symmetry on a faceted stone and a smooth and even curvature on a cab. Here are examples of poor cutting:

Moh's Scale

Each material will scratch those with a lower number and be scratched by those with a higher number. The steps along the scale are not regular. #2 and #3, for example, are close in hardness while #10, diamond, is 80 times harder than #9.

1. talc
2. gypsum
3. calcite
4. fluorite
5. apatite
6. orthoclase
7. quartz
8. topaz
9. corundum
10. diamond

Moh's Hardness of studio materials

2.5	fingernail, fine gold, fine silver, lead
3	copper
4	sterling
5.5	window glass
6	knife blade
6.5	file
9	silicon carbide (sandpaper)

105

Summary Chart

Fifty popular gem materials are briefly described in the following pages. They are summarized below but remember that these materials can exhibit wide differences from one specimen to another.

Name	Colors	Hard	Op/Trns*	Sensitivity	Facet	Cab	
agate	many	7	o	yes		✔	often banded
alexandrite	purple-blue	8-9	t		✔		changes color
amber	yellow	2	both	very		✔	organic
aquamarine	light blue	8	t	very	✔		
amethyst	purple	7	t	yes	✔	✔	
aventurine	green-brown	7	o	yes		✔	sparkles
beryl	many	8	t	very	✔		possible cat's eye
carnelian	red	7	o	yes		✔	
chalcedony	blue	7	o	yes		✔	
chiastolite	patterned		o				
chrysoberyl	many	8	both		✔	✔	cat's eye
chrysocolla	blue-green	6	o	yes		✔	also called Elat
chrysoprase	light green	6	o	yes	✔		
citrine	yellow	7	t	yes	✔	✔	
coral	red,pink,black	3	o	very		✔	organic
corundum	many	9	t		✔	✔	
diamond	clear	10	t		✔		
emerald	green	8	both	yes	✔	✔	cleaves easily
garnet	many	7	t	yes	✔	✔	
hematite	black	6	o			✔	
ivory	white	2	o	very			organic
jade	many	6	o	yes		✔	greasy luster
jasper	red-green	7	o			✔	
jet	black	4	o	very		✔	organic
labradorite	blue-black	6	o	very		✔	iridescent
lapis lazuli	deep blue	6	o	yes		✔	
malachite	green	5	o	very		✔	
magnetite	dark grey	7	o				magnetic
moonstone	many	6	t	yes		✔	adularescent
onyx	many	7	o	yes		✔	
opal	mixed	6	t	very		✔	interior colors
pearl	many	3	o	very			
peridot	green	7	t	yes	✔	✔	
quartz	many	7	both		✔	✔	
rock crystal	clear	7	t	yes	✔	✔	
ruby	red	9	both		✔	✔	star or cat's eye
rutile	red	7	both		✔	✔	common inclusion
sapphire	many	9	both		✔	✔	star or cat's eye
sardonyx	brown	7	o	yes		✔	
serpentine	green	2-6	o			✔	dust has asbestos
sodalite	blue	6	o			✔	
spinel	many	8	t		✔	✔	
tiger's eye	blue-brown	7	o	yes		✔	silky interior
topaz	yellow	8	t	yes	✔	✔	cleaves easily
tourmaline	green-pink	7	t	yes	✔	✔	dichroic
turquoise	blue	6	o	yes		✔	
zircon	many	7	t		✔	✔	cleaves easily
zirconia, cubic	many	9	t		✔		recent synthetic

* Opaque/ Transluscent

Stones

Agate

• A type of chalcedony;
a crypto-crystalline quartz.
• The name comes from an ancient, now untraceable Sicilian river, *Achates*.
• Worn by a farmer on the upper arm to insure a good harvest
• placed on right horn of oxen to protect them.

Red - protection from spiders and scorpions.
Green - relief from eye trouble.
Green with stripes - A woman who drinks water in which such a ring has been washed will never be sterile.
Grey - worn on the neck to prevent a stiff neck.
Moss agate - also called dendritic (Greek, "dendron," tree)

Alexandrite

• This natural stone is a type of chryso-beryl that shows a range of transparent colors, from blue in daylight to reddish-yellow in artificial light.
• More widely available is a synthetic stone, actually a treated corundum, H9.

• The stone was named for Czar Alexander II who, according to legend, came of legal age on the day the stone was discovered.

Amber

• This is not a stone but the naturally hardened resin of *pinus succinifera,* the amber pine.
• Transparent amber is 120-180 million years old. Opaque amber, called *copal*, is 60 million years old.
• The name comes from the Arabic *anbar*. The Greeks called it *elektrum* from the Phoenician word for sun or golden. Because amber will hold a charge this gave us our word *electric*.
• To test a sample, brush it with methyl alcohol or ethylacetate. Nonfossil resin such as plastic will dissolve.
• Another test is to set into brine: real amber will float but artificial will sink.
• Amber can also be tested by touching with a hot needle. The smoke thus caused will either smell like a pine woods or a plastics factory.
• Some amber contains thousands of tiny air bubbles. This is called bone amber and can be cleared by heating in oil.

Magical Uses
• Amber dust mixed with honey or water was used to treat ears, eyes, stomach, liver, and kidneys.
• The smell of burning amber helps a woman in labor.
• Holding an amber ball will keep one cool on a hot day. It was used to treat fever victims.
• Amber beads preserve the wearer against rheumatism, toothache, rickets and jaundice.

Caution: Amber will dissolve in solvents like acetone or nail polish remover. It will be worn down by mechanical buffing with compounds like tripoli.

Aquamarine

• The name comes from the Latin, "beryllus aquamarinus," *beryl resembling seawater*.
• It is traditionally a sailor's talisman.

• This gem increased in popularity around 1920 when heat treatment was developed to turn pale stones into deeper blue shades.

Stones

Amethyst

• A form of quartz. The top grade is a deep purple and has no flaws or inclusions.
• From the Greek for *not drunken*. The gem was believed to protect from the effects of wine, especially if held under the tongue while drinking.
• When heated to 550-560° C amethysts turn dark yellow or reddish-brown and are called citrines. They are more richly colored and more expensive than natural citrines.
• The color can fade if the stone is left in strong sunlight for a long time.
• Placed under the pillow, amethysts insure pleasant dreams, improve memory, and provide immunity from poison.
• Some people believe that a wearer of this stone will become gentle and amiable.

Aventurine

Hardness 7

• A fine-grained quartz with many flake inclusions, occuring in many colors, mainly green, brown, and gray.
• The ubiquitous sparkle of this stone is called *aventurescence*.

Beryl

Hardness 7.5 to 8

• This stone occurs in a wide color range including pink, orange, yellow, green, blue-green and blue.
• It is also found colorless (called *goshenite*). This resembles rock crystal and was used for lenses and crystal balls.
• Pink beryl is known as morganite, after the banker and gem collector J.P. Morgan.
• Beryls can show some chatoyancy when cut as cabochons.
• This stone is said to protect the wearer from helplessness caused by fascination. It was also used to treat diseases of the eye, jaundice and liver disease.

Carnelian

Hardness 6.5 to 7

• A red chalcedony, its color being due to the presence of iron.
• The opaque variety is called *sard*. When in brown and white layers it is called *sardonyx*.
• Carnelian was said to stop nosebleeds and to prevent blood from rising to the head.
• It is a strong protection from the evil eye.

Chalcedony

Hardness 6.5 to 7

• Pronounced *kal-SED-ne*.
• cryptocrystalline quartz; that is, quartz with very tiny crystals. Carnelian, onyx, agates and chrysoprase are all kinds of chalcedony.
• In the world of jewelry the word refers to a solid color, translucent, light blue stone. These may be made by dying agates but the naturally occurring variety is more desirable.

Chiastolite

• This is an opaque form of andalusite that grows in cigar-shaped crystals. When sliced, these show a light-colored cross or shamrock against a dark green background.
• Found near the Shrine of St. James in Santiago de Compostella in Spain where religious power is often attributed to the stone.

Chrysoberyl

• Pronounced *KRIS-o-ber-l*.
• This stone occurs in both a transparent and a cloudy variety and can be yellow, green or brown. Clear stones are usually faceted while the cloudy are cut as cabochons.

• Chrysoberyl has one of the most attractive cat's eyes of all stones. This occurs as a bright silvery line that travels across the curved surface of a polished gem as it is moved. The effect is called *chatoyancy* from the French word for cat, *chat*.

Chrysocolla

• A hydrous silicate formed by the decomposition of copper ore near the surface.
• From the Greek, **chrysos**, *gold* and **kolla**, *glue*. In ancient usage the term included malachite. Both were used as a flux for soldering and fusing gold.
• Occurs in variable shades of blue and green and can resemble turquoise.

• Chrysocolla from the site of King Solomon's Mines in Eilat, Israel is called eilat (elat) stone.
• Because this is a copper-bearing ore it will be damaged by pickles, like Sparex, which attack copper oxides.

Chrysoprase

• From the Greek words for "gold" and "leek," referring to its golden-green color, which is caused by nickel salts.

• A light green translucent chalcedony, the most valuable of the chalcedony family.

Citrine

• This yellow quartz can be found naturally or may be made by heating amethyst (purple quartz) to around 550° C (1050° F). Treated citrines have a deeper color and are more expensive than the natural.

• Yellow-brown variety is called *cairngorn* after their place of origin in Scotland.
• Dark reddish-brown quartz is called "sang de boeuf," French for *ox blood*.

Coral

• This is not a stone in the usual sense, but a rock-like material formed from the underwater deposit of many tiny skeletons of invertebrate animals.
• From the Greek *korallion*, originally derived from the word for pebble.
• Coral can occur in many shades of reddish-pink, white, and black which is called *akabar*.
• Coral was thought to stop bleeding, guard against poison, and protect dogs from rabies.
• This is a soft material and should be treated gently. It will not tolerate harsh cleansers, abrasion or heat.

Corundum

• Until the Middle Ages, corundum was called hyacinth and thought to exist only as a blue stone. When it was discovered that other colors of corundum existed, the name of sapphire was used for the blue variety.

• Corundums of other colors are usually identified by a color name, such as yellow sapphire, green sapphire, etc. except for red corundum which is called *ruby*.
• Corundum occurs in yellow, green, reddish-yellow, pink, mauve, brown and black.

Stones

Diamond
Hardness 10

- From the Greek "adamas," *unbreakable, indomitable* .

- Diamonds were believed to render all poisons harmless and to drive away madness, night spirits and evil dreams.

Emerald
Hardness 7.5 to 8

- A bright green beryl, very valuable if free of inclusions and of strong color.
- Emeralds are notoriously brittle and need great care in setting. For this reason a thick girdle on a faceted stone is preferred.
- Do not clean emeralds in an ultrasonic machine. The solution may penetrate the stone and cause it to shatter.

- Inclusions are called the "jardin" (French, *garden*) of the stone.
- Linked to fertility and the Earth Goddess, it is a birthstone of spring.
- Sacred to the Goddess Venus, worn by women to ease childbirth.
- Said to stifle an epileptic fit.

Garnet
Hardness 6.5 to 7.5

- From the Latin "granum," *grain or pip*, which in turn came from the Phoenician word for pomegranate, "punica granatum."
- When on the body, garnets are said to prevent skin diseases.
- Garnet assures the wearer of love, faithfulness and safety from wounds.
- When danger approaches, the stone loses its brilliance.
- For obvious reasons red garnets have been associated with blood. As recently as 1892 native soldiers in the Kashmir fought the British with bullets made of garnet, in the belief that these would find their way magically to their targets.
- Garnets will protect the wearer from evil and from terrifying dreams.

Types of garnets:
1. pyrope - A deep red color. Its name in The Greek means *"fiery eye."*
2. almadine - Dark red with a tinge of mauve. Purple variety is called rhodolite.
3. Spessartite - Red-orange or orange-brown. Shows internal wavy veil of fluid contained in the stone. Rare and expensive.
4. Grossular (Grossularite) - A speckled green stone resembling jade. Hessonite is a sub-species.
5. Uvarovite - Rare, intensely green stone.
6. Andradite - This contains iron. It is rarely cut.

Hematite
Hardness 5.5 to 6.5

- A lustrous black stone often cut with facets or carved with a warrior's head.
- Though the stone is black, it will leave a red streak when scratched along a rough surface. The stone appears to "bleed" and so takes its name from the the Latin word for blood, "haima."
- Hematite (also spelled "*haematite*") is the world's most important iron ore.

- Powdered hematite is known as red ochre when used as a pigment and as crocus when used as a polishing compound or abrasive.
- Hematite can form naturally as a cluster of thin plates and in this configuration is known as an *alpine rose* or *iron rose*.

Ivory

• Ivory comes from the tusks of elephants and is becoming increasingly rare as the elephant approaches extinction. In many parts of the world it is illegal to use ivory.
• Other similar materials should be identified with an adjective, as *whale ivory*. True ivory is made up of many translucent layers and has a soft sheen caused by the partial penetration of light.
• Ivory can be identified by a characteristic grain pattern. This becomes more obvious with age.

Jade

• The term jade refers to two distinct minerals not differentiated until 1863. These are properly called *jadeite* and *nephrite*.
• Spanish conquistadors found many objects of carved jade and, believing it to ease kidney pains, called it "piedra de ijada" (*loin stone*). European doctors called it "palis nephriticus" from the Greek "nephros," *kidney*.
• Because of its waxy lustre, the Chinese called it *wet stone* and believed it could slake thirst.
• Jade occurs in white (mutton fat), yellow, lavender, earthy brown and black as well as the familiar greens.
• Jade can be confused with californite, grossularite, sausserite, pectolite, chrysoprase and aventurine.
• This stone was believed to protect from lightning, to aid in battle, to bring rain, to drive away beasts and evil spirits and to aid in childbirth.

Jasper

• From the Hebrew *yashpeh* and Assyrian *yashpu* referred to in Cuneiform writings of 1500 BC. Originally the word meant any green stone.
• Jasper occurs in many colors and patterns, including stripes and pictures. These are really fossilized algae made when decomposed organic matter was replaced by silicon oxide (i.e. jasper).
• Green chalcedony with flecks of red jasper is called *bloodstone* or *heliotrope*.
• In ancient Egypt, red jasper was associated with the blood of Isis.
• Green jasper was associated with St. Peter by the early Christians.
• Said to drive away night spirits, staunch bleeding, and help during pregnancy.
• Green jasper was used in rainmaking.

Jet

• A dense black coal found in many places around the world. Especially popular in Britain under the reign of Queen Victoria, when most jet came from the town of Whitby.
• Jet nullifies spells and charms.
• Burnt and powdered jet is said to drive away snakes and reptiles and to heal toothaches and headaches.
• Traditionally Irish housewives burned jet during their husband's absence to insure his safety.

Labradorite

• This is a blue iridescent feldspar found on the coast of Labrador.
• A similar gem mined in Finland shows a wider range of colors and is called *spectrolite*.
• Black moonstone is usually labradorite from Madagascar.

Stones

Lapis Lazuli
Hardness 5 to 6

• From the Latin "lapis," *stone* and Arabic "lazuli," *blue*.
• Known for its deep blue color, sometimes found with flecks of gold-colored pyrite or whitish-gray mottlings of calcite.
• Lapis is still being mined in Afghanistan at the oldest mine in the world . When mining began 6000 years ago, the country was called Babylon.
• Lapis was sent to Egypt as tribute. There it was carved to make cylinder seals and ground to a powder for eye makeup.

• In Ur, kings sharpened their swords on lapis in the belief that it would make weapons invincible.
• Sumerians believed that a wearer carried the presence of God with him.
• In ancient Egypt, the stone was symbolic of truth (Ma) and was worn by the chief justice.
• In the Middle Ages, painters mixed oil with powdered lapis to make the color aquamarine.
• The gem is believed to ease eye troubles, asthma, to induce sleep and relieve anxiety.

Malachite
Hardness 5 to 6

• A copper ore made up of deep and pale green stripes or concentric circles. Because it is formed in thin layers, large pieces are somewhat rare.
• Malachite powder was used by the ancients as eye makeup.

• It was commonly held to ease labor, protect infants and children, and soothe their pain when they were cutting teeth.
• Because of its high copper content, malachite will be damaged by jewelers' pickle.

Magnetite
Hardness 6 to 7

• Also called *lodestone*.
• This is a black iron ore that is very magnetic. Although we use little for jewelry today, in ancient times this was an important stone.
• It was believed that the stone was alive. To care for it, the owner set the stone in water once a week and "fed" it iron filings. It was taken to mass to drive the devil out of it.

• Believed to dispel melancholy, ease labor, improve memory when worn on the neck, heal sores, and relieve pains in the hands and feet.
• Magnetite assists sexual activities when one partner is anointed with this stone and the other with iron filings.

Moonstone
Hardness 6 to 6.5

• A feldspar of orthoclase with thin layers of albite. This yields a play of light called *adularescence* as light is spread by the fine particles or layers. The effect is a cool frosty glow that accounts for the name of this gem.
• Occurs in white, gray, pink, green, blue, chocolate and an almost clear variety that looks like a water droplet.

• When worn around the neck, moonstone protects against epilepsy and sunstroke. It is used to treat headaches and nosebleeds.
• When hung on fruit trees it produces abundant crops and generally assists all vegetation.

I am afoot with my vision.

Walt Whitman

Onyx

• A chalcedony composed of black and white bands. In usage the term often refers to an agate dyed uniformly black.
• Onyx with brown and white bands is called *sardonyx*.
• When cut to show concentric circles, onyx forms an eye-like amulet that was worn by the Sumerians, Greeks, Egyptians, and Romans to ward off evil.

• This stone was widely disfavored except when cut as a protective eye. It was said to incite contention between friends, give the wearer broken sleep and terrifying dreams and cool the fires of love when worn around the neck.
• The Arabic name for this stone, "el jaza," means *sadness*.

Opal

• From the Sanskrit "upala," *gem*.
• Opal is hydrated silicon dioxide that shows a range of color flashes, usually including red, blue, green and violet. The play of colors is the result of water trapped in the stone (1-15% by weight). Care should be taken that opals do not dry out. A periodic coating of baby oil is recommended.
• Opals from Mexico & Brazil contain more water and are less stable than Australian opals.
• Opals are thought to possess the virtues of all the stones whose colors appear there. The Roman Senator Nonius, for instance, so valued a large opal that he chose exile rather than surrendering the gem to Mark Antony.

Types of Opal:
Harrlequin - a mosaic of iridescent color.
Pinpoint - Multitude of minute specks of many colors.
Flash - as above when showing red.
Flame - Bright orange-red; translucent to transparent.
Fire - bright orange-red; translucent to transparent.
Matrix - stone cut so as to leave the opal attached to the rock in which it was formed. This is done to add strength to an otherwise dangerously thin specimen.
Doublet - opal glued to a backing of obsidian or onyx to increase color play.
Triplet - doublet with rock crystal glued on top to increase lustre and strength.

Pearl

• A lustrous deposit formed inside a living bivalve mollusk, often in response to an irritation felt by the animal. Though many mollusks form such deposits, most species do not have attractive surfaces.
• Pearls are formed in saltwater and freshwater clams. They are identified by their place of origin, eg. Mississippi River pearls.
• The largest source of pearls is Lake Biwa in Japan where extensive pearl farming is done.
• Pearls sometimes grow attached to the shell of the animal. These are called *blister pearls.*
• Cultured or cultivated pearls are made inside a mollusk but have human help to get started. A bit of tissue or a glass or plastic bead is inserted in the animal and allowed to collect nacreous secretions for about 4 years.
• Imitation pearls are much less valuable. They are made by repeated dipping of a plastic bead into a coating made of glue and ground sardine scales. When lightly rubbed on the front of a tooth, the imitation pearl will feel smooth. The genuine (Orient) and cultured pearls will feel slightly rough.
• Pearls are attributed to the Goddess Venus as the symbol of innocence.
• Care should be taken that pearls are not subjected to sudden temperature changes. Wash them in lukewarm soapy water and restring as old cord becomes worn. Knots should be tied between pearls to keep them from rubbing against one another.

Stones

Peridot

• A transparent gem, sometimes called chrysolite, occuring as pale-to-deep yellow-green.
• Peridot is associated with the astrological sign of Libra and is assigned to the sun.
• In ancient Hebrew writings this stone is linked with the Tribe of Simeon.
• Peridot is believed to cure liver disease and dropsy, to free the mind from envious thoughts, and to dispel terrors of the night. For full magical power, set in gold.

Quartz
Hardness 7

• Quartz is the most common of all minerals.
• Included in this family are amethyst, citrine, flint, onyx, aventurine, jasper, carnelian, rock crystal, agate and crysoprase.

Rock Crystal
Hardness 7

• From the Greek "krystallos," *ice.*
• It was once believed to be hardened ice, and to have the ability to slake thirst.
• Romans drank from crystal goblets and physicians used the stone as an ice pack to ease inflammation of the gall bladder.
• Indians thought it was the glass of heaven and carved prayer beads from it.
• Crystal has been used throughout history as a reflective surface to concentrate a viewer's consciousness, especially in the form of spheres; i.e. crystal balls. The activity of staring into crystal until the mind becomes receptive to supernatural influences is called *scrying.*

Ruby
Hardness 9

• A corundum that occurs as a deep red transparent stone and as an opaque reddish-gray material. In this form it may exhibit a star (*asterism*) or a single line *chatoyancy.*
• When flawless, a ruby is more valuable than a diamond.
• Synthetic rubies are produced for jewelry, watch bearings and laser equipment.
• Historically, ruby is associated with royalty and the power of life and death.
• Rubies were attributed the power to prevent loss of blood and strengthen the heart.

Rutile
Hardness 6.5 to 7

• From the Latin *rutilus* meaning reddish.
• A brownish or red stone, occasionally transparent but more commonly opaque.
• It is best known as an inclusion in other minerals. In quartz, rutile appears as needles of a golden color. These have been given the romantic name of "Cupid's darts." In rubies, needles of rutile are called silk and create star effects.

Sapphire
Hardness 9

• From the Hebrew *sappir.*
• This form of corundum can occur as blue, yellow, pink, brown, black, lilac and green, both as transparent and opaque, the latter sometimes showing a star (*asterism*) or cat's eye (*chatoyancy*).
• Until the Middle Ages, sapphires were called hyacinths because of their pale blue color. When it was realized that the mineral occurred in other colors, the term sapphire was adopted for the blue variety while others use a color description; eg. yellow sapphire.
• Sapphires are traditionally connected with the eye and the sky, and therefore with vision and the ability to read the future.
• Sapphires render black magic harmless and help the wearer discern falsehood and guile.

Stones

Sardonyx

• A kind of chalcedony made brown by the presence of iron. Specifically the name refers to specimens that include bands of white.

• Sardonyx was a popular stone in ancient times and was credited with many powers. The stone was thought to make warriors victorious, protect against poisonous snakes, make a suitor more appealing, neutralize the malign influence of black onyx, increase intelligence and make the wearer fearless and happy, and to protect against witchcraft, sorcery, and incantation.

Serpentine

• An opaque green stone with mottled reddish-brown or milky patches. This with its waxy appearance makes it look like snakeskin, hence the name.

• Serpentine is common and occurs in many color and hardness variations. It is used architecturally and to carve objects like bowls and sculptures.

• This stone was believed to protect against snakebite and other poisons and was thought to be most effective if kept in the natural, uncut state.

• Medicine drunk from a serpentine vessel is thought to be more beneficial.

Sodalite

• A popular opaque stone most widely known for its blue color, which somewhat resembles lapiz lazuli. It also occurs in lavender, mauve, yellow- green, green, and pink. Purple shades can fade in sunlight.

• White and grayish-white mottlings are often found in sodalite; in poor grade material these will be obvious.

• The name of this mineral comes from its sodium content.

Spinel

• A transparent stone of red (the most valuable), pink, green, blue-green and purple.

• Synthetic spinel is produced in large quantities and is associated with inexpensive jewelry in imitation of diamonds, aquamarine, sapphires, and others. Air bubbles inside the stone often betray these synthetics.

Tiger's Eye

• Blue, violet, and golden brown translucent stones showing a silky interior that often iridesces as the stone is rotated. It can sometimes be cut to show a cat's eye.

• The effect is the result of asbestos fibers that have been partially replaced by quartz.

• When the fibers are coarse, the stone may be called a *hawk's eye*.

Topaz

• A transparent stone usually of golden yellow but also occurring as pink, red, blue, green and colorless specimens. From Sanskrit "tapas," *to glow*.

• Topaz cleaves easily and therefore requires care in cutting and setting.

• Some varieties can fade in sunlight.

• In ancient times, the word topaz referred to several other stones and today it is often mistakenly used for smoky quartz and citrine.

• Rubbing or gentle heating of topaz electrifies it causing it to attract small particles like bits of paper or hair.

Stones

Tourmaline

• A transparent stone of many colors, most notably green, blue-green and pink.
• Often several colors appear side by side. Crystals cut to reveal a pink semicircle with a green rim are called *watermelon tourmaline.*

• Name comes from the Sanskrit *"turamali."*
• Tourmaline is dichromatic; it shows a bright color from one direction but will look almost black when seen from the side. Like topaz, this stone will hold static electricity if it is rubbed or gently heated. Together these two tests provide identification.

Turquoise

Hardness 5 to 6

• A blue or blue-green stone, usually opaque but occasionally translucent.
• From French "Pierre Turquoise" which means *Turkish stone*, a reference to its popular use in Turkey. Arabs call it "fayruz" or "firuzaj," *the lucky stone.*
• Blue material will turn green when it absorbs oil from the skin. After polishing, most turquoise is sealed with a plastic that soaks into the stone and closes the pores.
• Reconstituted material (bits of turquoise compressed with adhesive) is sometimes used in cheap jewelry. To test a sample, lay a hot needle against the stone. If it contains adhesive, the resulting smell of plastic will give it away.

• Some pieces of turquoise are cut so as to contain some of the rock in which they were formed. This is called *matrix* turquoise. Some varieties show fine dark lines running throughout the stone; this is called *spiderweb* turquoise.
• Turquoise is thought to protect the wearer from poison, bites of reptiles, and diseases of the eye.
• Some people think these powers are in force only if the stone was received as a gift.
• Giving a turquoise is also said to improve its color.
• Since the thirteenth century this stone was held to give sure-footedness to a horse. The idea was later enlarged to protect against all falling.

Zircon

Hardness 7 to 7.5

• A transparent brittle stone occurring as brownish or green material, usually heated to turn pale yellow and blue. It can be found naturally colored as orange-red (most valuable), purple, reddish-brown and brownish-yellow.

• Because its brittleness makes it difficult to cut, stones of more than a couple carats are rarely seen.
• Zircon is said to drive away evil spirits and bad dreams, banish grief and melancholy restore appetite, induce sleep, and protect against lightning.

Zirconium (cubic)

Hardness 8.5

• A transparent singly refractive, manmade gem produced from the element zirconium.
• It is available in many colors, as well as a bright white that resembles diamond.

Because of its "fire" and low cost, CZ has replaced yag (synthetic garnet), spinel, and strontium titanate as a diamond substitute.

I am simply impressed by the unexpected insights that shower down on me when the job is to imagine, as contrasted with the woodenly familiar ideas which clutter my desk when my job is to tell the truth.

Kurt Vonnegut, Jr.

Setting Tips

Some jewelry pieces call for highly specialized techniques, but there are a few concepts and tricks that apply to almost all settings.

Setting Procedures

Hold work securely.

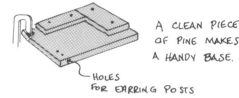

A CLEAN PIECE OF PINE MAKES A HANDY BASE.

HOLES FOR EARRING POSTS

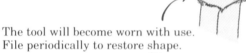

Always work from alternate sides.

When trying a stone in place, it may be lifted in and out with beeswax.

Tools

The face of a bezel pusher should not be polished, since that might make it slip. To provide a little grip, sand the face with medium grit paper.

On soft or delicate materials (shell, enamels, etc.) a plastic pusher is recommended.

This can be made from a toothbrush as shown.

The tool will become worn with use. File periodically to restore shape.

To use a hammer... grip the workpiece securely and tap with a smooth punch.

Bezel Rocker

To make a bezel rocker, saw this shape from 12 or 14 gauge brass, file the edges smooth and mount it in a file handle.

ACTUAL SIZE TEMPLATE

Avoid these errors:

With a bezel, be sure the metal lays down on stone.

To use, hold the rocker like a pencil and rock vertically at several points around the stone. Then turn tool face to horizontal and swing back and forth to smooth the bezel.

When setting a buff top, don't go over the top.

Stones

More Setting Tips

Though many settings have been in use for centuries, there are still opportunities to invent a new style. Each stone and jewelry design provides an opportunity for a unique solution.

It's impossible to give a rigid formula for the events of stone setting but here is a typical progression.

1. Complete all soldering.

2. Pickle and neutralize the piece by soaking it in a baking soda/water solution. File, sand and buff to the desired finish. Wash and dry it well.

3. Oxidize or patina, if desired.

4. Lay the stone into position and check to be certain it is level and seated.

5. Push the bezel or prongs over the stone. Work your way around the stone, taking several courses to achieve the setting.

6. Use a pumice and rubber wheel to smooth irregularities. Do not use sandpaper, even the finest grit.

7. Burnish the bezel or prongs to polish and toughen the metal.

8. Polish a bezel with a leather coated stick. For prongs, use a bristle brush with a small amount of compound. Light thrumming may be desired in some settings.

Designing the Setting

As you select a setting for a particular design, consider these factors.
- The size, regularity and toughness of the stone.
- Which is its best side?
- How dominant should it be in the whole design?
- Consider the ways in which stones can be secured.

		Examples
Pressed over rim		Bezel Gypsy
Pinched above and below the stone		Prong Channel
Wrapped or tied		Beach Stones
Rivets or Pins		Fraternal Rings
Posts		Pearls Gem Beads

Stones

Box Bezel

The bezel is a thin band of metal that surrounds a stone and is pressed over its edge to hold it in place. It is probably the oldest and most widely used setting in the world.

1

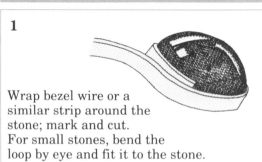

Wrap bezel wire or a similar strip around the stone; mark and cut. For small stones, bend the loop by eye and fit it to the stone.

2

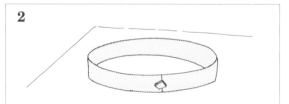

Clean the ends to make a tight fit. Use as little solder as possible because it is stiff and hard to push over a stone.

3

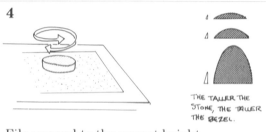

Check the fit. If the bezel is too small, stretch as shown or by planishing with a steel hammer. If too loose, remove a piece of bezel and resolder.

4

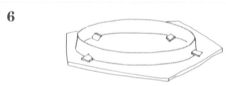

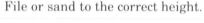

THE TALLER THE STONE, THE TALLER THE BEZEL.

File or sand to the correct height.

5

File or sand a knife edge around the top of the bezel. Stop just before the rim disappears. If this is lost, it's easy to go too far.

6

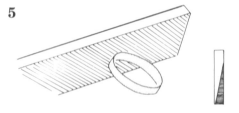

Rub the bezel on sandpaper to true and clean bottom edge, then recheck the fit. After soldering to flat sheet, pickle and check the joint. It's important that the bezel is attached all the way around.

7

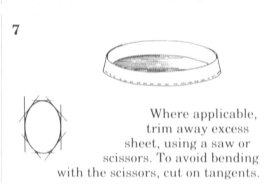

Where applicable, trim away excess sheet, using a saw or scissors. To avoid bending with the scissors, cut on tangents.

8

Solder the bezel into position on the workpiece.

Step Bezel

This variation of the bezel on the preceding page has a delicate ridge running around the interior that supports the edge of the stone. Step bezel material can be purchased or fabricated as neeeded.

Advantages
- It uses less material, saving cost and reducing weight.
- It can be faster than a box bezel to make, depending on the type used.
- It can allow light to show through the stone, depending on the design.

Styles

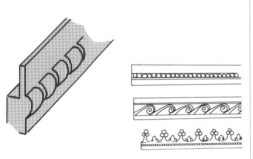

Step bezel may be bought. It is generally available only in fine silver and 14K yellow gold. Some distributors will also have a fancy style called *gallery step bezel*.

Another method is to create the step before bending the bezel around the stone. To avoid an excess of solder, file the angle shown.

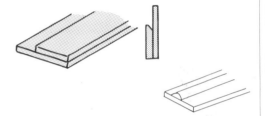

A variation uses wire to make a bearing. Provide a flat surface for a neat solder joint.

After completing a bezel ring that fits the stone, make a second ring (bearing) that fits snugly inside the first. If a base is used on the bezel, this ring does not need to be soldered in.

For faceted stones, file a bevel on the inner ring before putting the two pieces together.

A bearing may also be cut. Make the bezel of heavy stock such as 16 or 18 gauge. Flex shaft tools or gravers may be used.

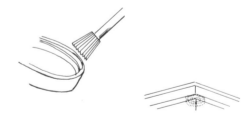

To reduce pressure on the corners of rectilinear stones, cut away the bearing under the corner (shaded) with a graver or flex shaft bur.

I realize it's the things you pass up that torment you, not the things you do.

John Dos Passos

Stones

Fancy Bezels

This family of bezels uses stamping, applied wire and a range of other details to give a bezel a greater impact in a design.

Gallery Wire

This is a decorated strip of wire used as molding or as a bezel and can be bought in many ornate patterns. The decorations shown here are made by filing, stamping, drilling and engraving. Some patterns can only be made when the strip of metal is flat (such as stamping) but most are easier after the bezel has been made.

| round needle file | triangular file & drill bit | half-round file & saw | stamped line, filed edge, engraved ▲ | barrette file, & scribe point |

After a bezel has been made and soldered onto a base, it can be made more delicate by cutting with a saw.

Collar

Construct a bezel as you would for box bezel or ledge bezel, but use a thicker wall. I recommend 18 gauge for a stone under 5 mm and 16 gauge for a larger one.

Setting is done with a planishing punch with rounded corners and a polished face. The chasing hammer is used with repeated light taps.

The object must be firmly anchored. Use a pitch pot, engravers' ball, shellac or sealing wax on a board, or a vise. Support rings on a soft-wood wedge.

The stone is "locked" in place with four sharp blows evenly spaced around the bezel. In successive courses around the stone, the angle of the tool is raised until it is vertical. The bezel is planished with the tool so very few marks are made. The shape may be defined with a file or pumice wheel. No sandpaper! The collar is then buffed either by machine or with a polishing stick.

Tooled Edge

This setting is similar to the collar bezel but has a rougher look because of the texture left by the tools used.

Start with a bezel made of thick material, usually 20 to 14 gauge. The object is securely gripped as before and the bezel is pushed in as shown at the left. Push the bezel at four equidistant points to anchor the stone into position. When the stone is securely held and the bezel is uniformly laid over, use a tool with a point that resembles a screwdriver.

The edges of the tool should be rounded over, and it should be polished to add luster to the texture. The tool is held nearly vertical and moved around the stone with many light taps, creating the decorative effect.

Raised Settings

This style of setting is used to elevate the bezel above the body of the jewelry piece.

For a Round or Oval Cabochon

1. Make a bezel of the usual shape having most of the back open. This may be done by soldering the bezel to a sheet and then cutting out the interior space, or by soldering a ring of square or rectangular wire inside the bezel.

2. Make a small section of cone whose larger diameter is the same as that of the bezel. This may be done by bending an arc or by soldering a loop closed and forming it in a dapping block.

3. Solder spacers (wire or, as shown, short lengths of tubing) onto the back at regular intervals.

4. Rub the tubing lightly on sandpaper to make sure each one has a flat face. Solder the cone into place, then cut and file the tubing flush with the bezel. The cone may be cut to accommodate a ring shape.

For a Square or Rectangular Stone

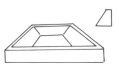

1. Make a rectangular frame of heavy square wire. The outside of the frame should equal the dimensions of the stone. File a bevel on the inside edge.

2. Make another frame, a little smaller than the first. It is not necessary to file the inside edge.

3. Cut a spacer block from sheet or wire. The size will depend on the depth of the stone. Don't let the stone protrude through the back, particularly for a ring. Saw a groove in each spacer to hold it in position and solder. 2 or 4 spacers can be used.

4. Keeping careful alignment, solder the frames together.

5. Cut prongs from 22 gauge sheet, score a groove down the center, bend and file the edges smooth.

6. Solder the prongs into position, then solder the head to the workpiece. In setting, press against the corner first. It's possible that the prongs might need to be cut slightly at the top so they will bend over the stone neatly. Burnish to close this.

Prongs

Prongs are fingers of metal that support a stone with a simple elegance that allows the stone to dominate a design. It is possible to make prongs that almost disappear, creating the effect of a stone simply laid into position.

Whether simple or complex, a successful prong setting must follow these guidelines:

- Prongs must reach over the stone's girdle to hold it securely.
- Prongs must be located so the stone cannot slip out in any direction.
- The stone must be supported from beneath.
- The prongs must not cover so much of the stone that the result is cumbersome.
- Prongs must not snag on fabric.

Wire

All these styles are simply laid out flat and soldered. The shaded areas indicate their size in relation to the stone they would hold. Often the tips of the prongs are planished to make them thinner and more graceful.

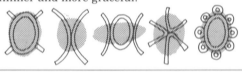

Turtle

This is cut from sheet metal and gets its name from the animal it resembles. Many variations are possible.

Arc Bending Jig

This piece of equipment is not essential but it's handy if many cone-shaped settings are to be made.

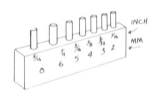

It can be made of wood, but will wear better if made of metal. To use it, cut a strip of sheet as wide as the cone must be. Slide this snugly between two posts and bend in a series of short tugs.

Basket Setting

1. Bend two V-shapes of wire and prop them up on the soldering block. Solder at the point of contact. To make a 6 prong head, use three V-shapes.

2. Make a ring to hold the prongs together. This can go on the inside (subtle) or outside, (decorative). In either case, start by soldering the ring closed so it can be made round and stretched to the right size if necessary. The inside ring is a little smaller than the stone's diameter; the outside ring would be made to fit around the stone (as if it were a bezel). When the size is right, solder this in place.

3. The head is then attached to the workpiece, which is pickled and polished. A bearing is cut, the prongs are cut to the correct height and shape, and the stone is set as usual.

123

Crown

This is a time honored and reliable setting for a faceted stone. Crowns can be purchased or made to accommodate a particular setting. The collet head below is a variation on it.

Crown Setting

The basic unit of this setting is a cone. These can be made from tubing with the use of a tool called a *bezel block*. This steel tool consists of a heavy plate with a series of conical holes and corresponding tapered punches. Select a tube whose diameter equals that at about mid-height of the desired cone and be sure it is annealed. It is then set into the die and struck with the punch, usually forming the cone in a single blow.

- To fabricate a cone from sheet, layout and saw an arc to make a cone that will enclose the stone (see page 176).
- Bend the cone with pliers and by tapping it with a mallet. True the seam by running a sawblade along the joint. Solder.
- After truing the cone on a mandrel, mark out prongs, first from a top view and then on the sides. Use dividers to mark a line parallel to the base. With a saw, cut away the area between the prongs. To hold while cutting, the cone is mounted on a dowel with sealing wax or shellac, or held in pliers that have been specially shaped for this. Use a round file or a bud-shaped bur to make the prongs neat and even.
- Invert the head and repeat, cutting away the area between the prongs. This is not necessary for small stones. Many variations of shape are possible.
- Bend and solder a ring to become the base of the setting. Either use square wire or flatten the ring so it will make positive contact with the base of the crown. In large settings a variation is to saw off the lower section of the cone, putting it carefully aside. After cutting decorative sections below the prongs, the lower section is soldered back into place.
- Solder the crown to the workpiece, then pickle and file as necessary to perfect the shape. Cut a bearing with a bur, graver or file. Cut prongs to the correct height, file to shape, and set the stone.

MODIFIED
ROUND NOSE
PLIERS

Collet Prong Head

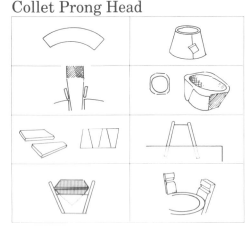

1. Lay out arc; see page 176. For small stones accuracy by eye is sufficient.
2. Bend into a loop and close with Hard solder.
3. True up on a small mandrel, often a scribe or centerpunch. Set across open vise jaws to stretch.
4. File a flat surface for each prong. Keep the spacing even.
5. Cut tapered prongs from 18-22 gauge sheet.
6. Solder the prongs in place. They may be poked into the soldering block if needed.
7. Pickle, rinse and check the fit. Stone should not rest on the collet. If it does the collet is too big or the angle of the cone is too steep.
8. Solder to the piece, polish, and cut bearings in each prong.

Gypsy

This somewhat specialized setting uses a ridge of metal that is pulled up from a surface to hold a stone. Its simple look doesn't indicate how technically demanding it is to make.

As shown for a ring

1. Make a ring shank, allowing for the stone's diameter and if faceted, for its height.

2. Drill a hole about half the size of the stone's diameter.

3. With a setting bur or graver, enlarge the hole to hold the stone. When correct, the stone's girdle should be just below the surface.

4. For a cabochon the hole would look like this. Use a flat graver or cylinder bur to carve it out.

5. File away a small bit of metal just around the setting. This will create a tiny rim that will be pushed over the stone.

6. With the stone in place, set four "corners" with a bezel pusher or a chasing hammer and a small planishing tool. Check to see that the stone is level and that there is a consistent rim to cover the stone. If so, continue with the setting and follow with a burnisher, pulling the metal up onto the stone.

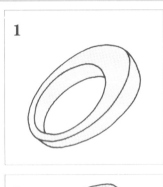

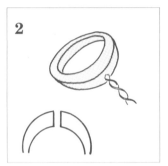

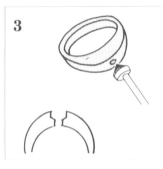

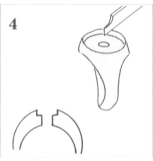

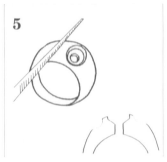

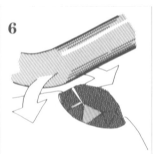

Roman (a variation)

When a bearing has been made, the stone is set into place and a burnisher is used concentrically around the setting to wear down a groove. As a trench is formed, pressure is increased, pushing the metal onto the stone. In effect, this is a combination of steps 5 and 6 above.

Though many have practiced the art without making drawings, those who made their drawings first did the best work.

Benvenuto Cellini

Stones

125

Pavé

In this traditional setting many stones are set so close together that little metal can be seen. The object is "paved" with stones. The technique requires precision and patience, but is within the grasp of any goldsmith.

1. Set stones into plasticene and take measurements from center to center of each stone with dividers. Transfer these measurements to the metal; drill holes slightly smaller than the stones.

2. With a tapered bur, enlarge each hole to be just as large as the stone. At this point the stone should not fit into the hole, but rest with its girdle just flush with the surface of the metal.

3. With a graver or bur, cut a bearing for each stone. Now the stone should drop into the hole so that its girdle is just below the surface.

4. Use a round graver to pull up a curl of metal from the area around the hole. This can be started with the stone removed, but don't delay too long before inserting it. Note the alternate method below.

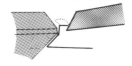

5. With a blunt round graver, lift each triangle up by cutting part way under it. Stones should be in place by this time because the pressure inward will start to grip them.

6. With a beading tool, give a clean hemispherical shape to each prong. This is used in a wiggling motion and may be lubricated with spit.

Alternate for Step #4.
With a flat graver, cut away the area around the holes, leaving 3 or 4 triangles of metal evenly spaced around each.

Box Setting
1. Use a sheet thicker than the height of the stone. Mark the center and drill a small hole.

2. Cut a bearing with a graver or bur. Note the depth; it is important.

3. Carve a groove with a round graver. The little triangles will become prongs.

4. Cut away the shaded area with a flat graver and shape the prongs with beading tools. A decorative millgrain line is often cut around the square.

Gravers
If you plan on doing a lot of this, buy 3 identical round gravers and prepare them with varying slopes.

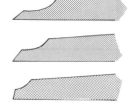

The pointiest will cut a clean curl, the middle will cut and push and the blunt one is primarily a pushing tool.

Stones

126

Channel

In this family of settings, a stone or stones are laid into a trench and held as the rim is pressed over. This setting requires very careful measuring and fitting.

Rectangular Stones

Depending on the location of the mounting and the toughness of the stone, it is sometimes possible to simply cut a pair of parallel grooves and slide the stone into place. Of course it is important that the metal be rigid, that the grooves be uniform and level and that the pressure on the stone be sufficient to grip the stone without crushing it. The grooves may be cut with gravers, a hart bur or a needle file. Use close magnification to insure that the angles of the cuts perfectly match the angles of the stone. After the stone is slid into position, a small tab of metal is pressed up at either end of the setting to prevent the stone from slipping out.

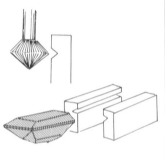

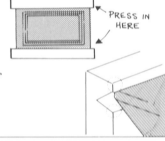

PRESS IN HERE

An alternate method for setting square or rectangular stones is a variation on the gypsy setting shown earlier. A recess is carved into the metal with gravers, burs

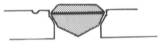

or by piercing, so the stone's girdle lays just below the surface of the metal. With the stone in place, a lip of metal is raised from the surface to form a rim that will press down on the stone. This bulge can be created on soft metals such as silver and high karat gold by pressing with a burnisher. In tougher metals, use a round graver to cut a groove about a millimeter outside the stone. This will provide a shallow rim that will help start the setting process.

Round Stones

To prevent round stones from pivoting on their culets during setting, each stone should have its own bearing.

1. Lay out the stones by gluing them into position on a thin film of wax. Mark the lines between each stone.
2. Locate the center of each segment with a criss-cross and drill a small hole here. In a ring, these should all be perpendicular to the surface.
3. Enlarge the holes with a bud bur, then cut a seat with a setting bur. The stone should rest slightly on the surface of the metal.
4. Cut a channel with gravers and files to a depth a little greater than the height of the crown. The walls of this cut should be vertical and the groove should be smooth and polished.
5. Angle a hart bur into each hole to undercut a notch for each stone. The slowly rotating bur will undercut a crescent-shaped groove into one wall and then be swung down to cut into the opposite wall. Repeat this for each hole.
6. Tilt the stone into position and use pliers to press the walls of the channel onto the stones. Small flat punches are then used to press the metal flat onto the stones. Final shaping is done with a pumice wheel and a leather-coated polishing stick.

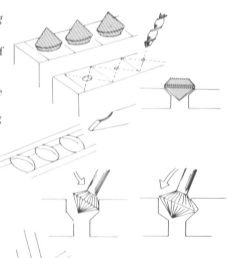

127

Assorted Settings

The hand craftsman is uniquely qualified to deal with one-of-a-kind stones and the unusual settings they often require. A good designer makes even conventional stones exciting through inventive mountings.

Setting From Behind

1. Make a bezel to surround the stone, slightly higher than usual. Turn in the top edge with a burnisher or solder a rim or pierced sheet in place.
2. Make a collar to fit inside the bezel. Square or rectangular wire is handy for this. A snug fit is important.
3. When the piece is polished and cleaned, the stone is set into place and the collar is pushed in against it from the back.
4. Small curls of metal are cut in the bezel wall with a square or round graver and pressed down onto the collar.

A variation on the above is to hold the collar in place with screws or rivets. Note how well these techniques lend themselves to a 2-sided image.

Millegriffe

1. Make a collet (tube) with an inside diameter smaller than the stone. A thick wall is important.
2. Mark a line around the base and file a bevel to this line.
3. Cut a bearing with a bur or graver. File off the inside corner at arrow. BEADING
4. Solder to piece, finish, set stone. Note the shape here.
5. Make a series of beads with punch. Use a graver &/or file to cut notches between beads.

Making a Square or Rectangular Frame

Many settings require a frame that is a perfect fit for the stone. Lack of precision at this early stage will almost always make subsequent steps difficult or impossible. The following method is a standard approach, whether making a tiny setting or a large container. It seems long in the telling, but after a few tries, you'll see the logic of the steps.

1. Cut off a piece of flattened wire or strip, a little longer than two adjacent sides. File a notch with a square file and bend into an L shape. After checking with a square to be sure the corner is exactly 90° solder the corner. Make two of these shapes.
2. Measure and cut the small side so that its length will equal the desired interior dimension of the box. Repeat this with the other unit.
3. Slide the 2 Ls together and mark the place at which they make a frame that is exactly the desired length. Place the solder as shown.

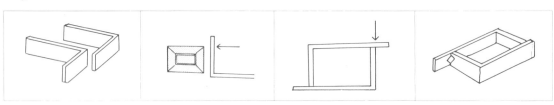

Stones

Assorted Settings

These pages offer a glimpse at the kinds of alternate solutions to traditional settings. Use these to get started but don't be limited by them.

Pedestal Prong

This setting is built on a pedestal or column exactly the same width as the stone's girdle. It can can be short or tall, plain or decorated. The setting is among the most versatile, and can be made with 3, 4, 5 or 6 prongs and can be used with both cabs and faceted stones.

1. Make a ring of 16-20 ga. sheet. The outside diameter is the diameter of the stone.
2. For a faceted stone, file a bevel around the inside edge of this ring.
3. Cut oversized lengths of square or half-round wire for prongs. File a point on each one.
4. Push the prong wires into charcoal around the ring (pedestal). Solder.
5. After completing this piece, prongs are trimmed, shaped, and pushed over stone.

Lamination

Carefully saw and file a sheet to match the size and slope of a stone. This sheet is then set over the stone and held in place with rivets or screws. The edge adjacent to the stone can be burnished for a tight fit.

RIVET

Cut Down Setting

1. Make a collar (tube) as tall as the desired setting and slightly too small for the stone to fit inside. The walls must be thick.

2. Cut a bearing (seat) with burs or gravers.

3. File the lower portion to visually lighten the form.

4. Lay out prongs with a scribe.

5. Cut away the metal between prongs with a flat graver, so prongs are the original thickness at the top and blend into tube at the lower line. Collar may be held on shellac-covered dowel while cutting.

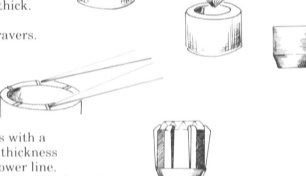

The universe is full of magical things patiently waiting for our wits to grow sharper.

Eden Philpots

Stones

Stringing

Though a little practice might be called for, stringing is really just as easy as it seems. It requires little space and few tools and yet can produce dazzling results.

Equipment

• Tweezers are often used to hold the beads and may be protected from making scratches with a couple layers of nail polish.
• A needle tool is handy for guiding the location of knots and poking old bits of string out of bead holes.
• A biology needle works well, or a sewing needle can be taped to a pencil.
• To hold the beads, use a piece of velvet taped to a board or a piece of stiff paper folded into ridges. If much stringing is to be done, you might invest in a plastic bead tray.

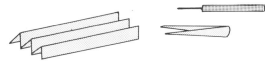

String

Whatever string you use, be certain that it fills the bead hole or the resulting strand will be sloppy and insecure. Ordinary sewing thread can be used, but it is generally too thin for most beads. Likewise dental floss can be used, but because it is flattened it isn't the best choice. Beading cord is produced in nylon threads of about a dozen sizes and many colors. These are often sold on small cards in short lengths that have a needle permanently afixed to one end. The traditional and still probably the best choice is silk cord. It resists stretching and is sold in many bright colors and a wide range of sizes. The thinnest cord is called #00 and sizes move up the alphabet through A, B and C as they get bigger. From F the series goes to FF and then FFF which is the thickest silk available.

Bead Tips

After stringing, the cord is generally tied off and attached to a hook of some sort. These findings can of course be bought readymade or fabricated at the bench. A typical ending is a small device called a bead tip that consists of a small cup with an attached finger. The knot of the cord is settled into the cup and the tip is bent over to hide it as it clutches the finding. An alternate method uses a simple piece of tubing to crimp onto the cord. This can be done with round nose pliers or a dull snips. In either case a dab of glue or nail lacquer should be laid on the knot.

Ending with a French Wire

This process is a little more involved but yields a more finished looking end. A French wire is a coil of extremely fine wire (usually brass) that can be made or purchased from a beading supplier. Slide about a half inch onto a threaded needle and move it 2 or 3 inches onto the cord. Slide on the first bead and tie a knot. Repeat this for several beads, then tie off the short thread and cut it. Dab on a little glue and continue threading on a single strand. At the other end, leave the last three beads unknotted, slide the French wire into position and thread the cord back through the first bead where you will tie a knot. Proceed through the second and third beads, tying as you go. Apply glue to the last couple of knots of the strand.

Pearls may be drilled with conventional bits. Go slow to allow the pearl to cool. When drilling through, put masking tape on the bottom to protect the nacre from chipping off.

Don't put pearls or soft stones in prongs without cementing them too. Rotation will cause scratches like these.

For very thick beads of fashion quality, a plastic coated stainless steel cord called Tiger Tail is often used. This is a strong cord, but it cannot be knotted and does not have the suppleness of silk. Never use it with fine beads or pearls.

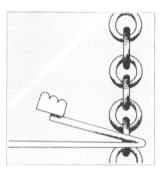

Mechanisms

Ends & Bails

No matter how simple a pendant, it will involve a bail and a terminal on the chain or cord. These often provide an opportunity for decoration or design that can become the focus of a piece.

End Caps

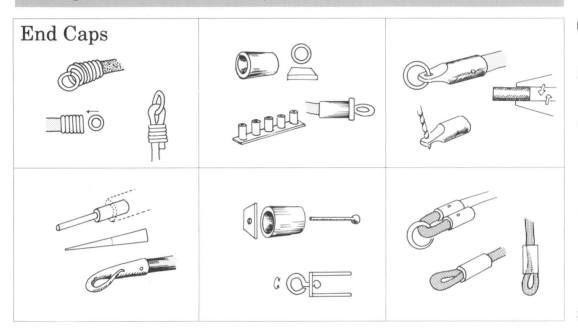

Bail

This term refers to the point at which a chain or cord connects with a pendant. From Old Norse *beygla*, meaning hook or ring, semicircular handle of a pail, kettle or cannon.

Fold Down Bail

For a pin that is also worn as a pendant.

1. Wire is beaded, flattened, and drilled.

2. Sheet is cut & folded as shown.

3. Loop is formed and riveted onto A. Bend the loop to one side to do this.

4. The holder is soldered into place and the unit is assembled.

Pins

Commercial pin findings are not always appropriate to the scale or sophistication of a piece of fine jewelry. Findings made for a particular piece can bring a special elegance.

- The pin mechanism must be located above the central axis to prevent the brooch from tipping forward.
- At rest, the pinstem should be slightly above the catch. This will create a tension that will help keep the pin closed. A similar tension is put on the elevation of the stem by the "foot" of the pinstem.
- The end of the pin should not extend beyond the catch.
- The point of the pin must be sharp and smooth to penetrate fabric. Snip to size, file, sand, burnish and polish.
- The catch is positioned with its opening downward.
- Pinholder & catch are sweat soldered carefully, using a tiny piece of Easy solder. Melt the solder onto the brooch and set the pin pieces into the solder puddle.

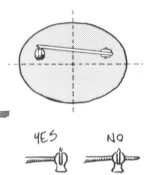

YES   NO

Tube-in-a-Tube Pin Catch

This catch is held closed by the friction of a small pin against the end of the larger tube. To open, rotate the small tube until the tab engages slot. The tab keeps the smaller tube from coming all the way out.

1. Make telescoping tubing. The smaller inside diameter must fit pinstem.

2. Solder a strip of sheet onto the larger tube to act as a pedestal.

3. Cut slot in larger tube with saw.

CUT AWAY THIS PIECE

4. Draw wire to match slot; solder at right angle to end of smaller tube.

5. Slide tubes together and with the small pin tight against the end, saw the other end off flush. Slide tubes open and file about 1/2 mm more off the end of the smaller diameter tube.

6. With tubes in open position, solder a knob on the end of smaller tube. Knob is sheet, bead or bezel.

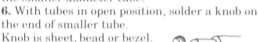

Simple Pins

1. Solder a generous loop of wire onto the back of a piece.
2. Snip the wire.

CUT HERE

3. Twist the wire to harden it.
4. Curl as shown with round nose pliers.

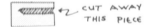

1. The pinstem is made by soldering wire to piece of sheet.
2. The catch can be as simple as an L-shaped piece of sheet. An alternative is a small two-sided box that traps the pin. A similar structure can also be fabricated from wire.

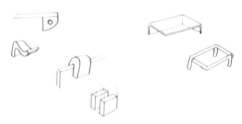

3. The pinholder is made from sheet, bent over a piece of the same sheet that was used to make pin end. After soldering this unit onto the workpiece, the curve is sawn off and holes are drilled.

Mechanisms

Buckles

Buckles require more strength and durability than most other jewelry closures and offer a challenge to the inventive handcrafter.

Prong Style Buckles

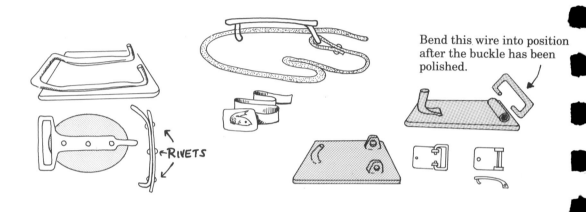

Bend this wire into position after the buckle has been polished.

←RIVETS

Military Style

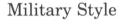

This device clamps onto a web belt to lock it into the buckle.

TONGUE IN HERE

BAR PINCHES BELT HERE

Tongue Styles

The bar across the middle is shaped in one of these ways to keep the tongue centered.

FORGED

Cuff Link Styles

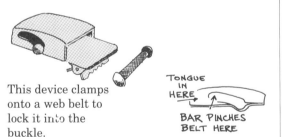

← SPRING

This commercial finding allows the holder to be silver soldered into place. The cuff bar is held by a rivet.

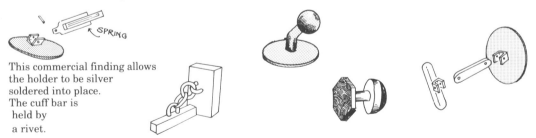

The principal mark of genius is not perfection but originality.
Arthur Koestler

Mechanisms

Clasps

Closures on bracelets and necklaces must be reliable, comfortable and easy to operate. And they shouldn't be ugly.

Box Catches

This universal and standard clasp is a staple of jewelry design. Box claps can be purchased but are often more effective when made to go along with a design.

Three Basic Models

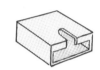

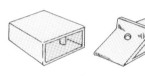

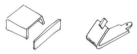

The advantage of this style is that the location of the hole can wait until the clasp is completed. Paint the tongue and slide it into place. Drill at the end of the scratch.

Safety Mechanism

Tube Box Catch

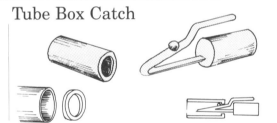

This short cut clasp is made by drilling a hole, piercing a U-shaped line, and soldering a peg into the drilled hole. Lift the tongue while soldering.

Fish Hook Clasp
Made from 14, 16, or 18 gauge half-round wire.

• In all these clasps it's very important to measure carefully. It is often helpful to make the receiving side first and then make a test piece in copper or brass to check the fit.
• The tongue should slide snugly into its bay, with no sloppiness side to side.
• The tongue is usually 24 gauge metal. After folding and checking the fit, planish on the fold to harden.
• The amount of squeeze needed to release should be slight. This is made by having a long tongue; 10 mm would be average. Too short a tongue requires more push to release and is therefore more likely to break.

I hear and I forget. I see and I remember. I do and I understand.
Chinese Proverb

Mechanisms

Spring Clasps

This articulated mechanism can provide a sophisticated movement as well as a dependable closure. Though commercially available, they can be made at the bench to add a special flair.

Spring Plunger Clasp

1. To make the dividing partition in the tube, saw off a thin slice of the wire and stretch it slightly by hammering. Push it into the tube and solder it.

2. Forge or file, solder, bend into a curl. Be sure that the end of the curl is "tucked under,"

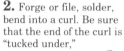

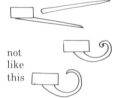

not
like
this

3. Make a nailhead on the wire; see page 80.

4. Make a tiny spring by tightly wrapping hard-drawn 30 ga. brass wire. Found springs from clocks, toys or pens can also be used.

5. After polishing, bend the curl to the side to allow the spring and plunger to be slid into place. Bend the wire back to hold them.

6. To clasp, push the rectangular tab straight in; the plunger will slide into the tube. To unclasp, just pull straight out.

Tension Spring Catch

For pins, barrettes, earrings, etc.

1. Solder a bar of 14 or 16 gauge sheet onto the back of the piece. File a groove on the top edge.

2. Solder a tube in the center of this piece, resting in the groove.

3. Solder heavy square wire onto top back edge of tube. After soldering file to this shape:

4. Cut another piece of sheet as thick and wide as the bar (#1) but slightly longer. Solder pins on the sides.

5. Saw two lines in from the top edge, centered, and the same distance apart as the length of the tube in #2.

6. Bend up center tab and cut away about 2 mm of the side flaps.

7. File a groove into the shortened ends.

8. Solder a piece of the same tube used before across the short tabs. Saw out the center section of the tube.

9. Harden pins by twisting; taper and sharpen them. After polishing, assemble with a pin as you would for a hinge. This might require pushing down on the spring unit (piece with pins). Adjust center tab by bending with pliers to create the correct amount of tension.

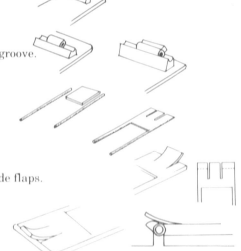

Jump Rings

These simple rings are the building blocks of chains and many other forms. They can be purchased but are far more commonly made as needed. It is usually as easy to make 10 as 2, so common practice is to build up a supply as extras are made.

Making Jump Rings

Wrap a wire around a rod of the chosen size. Some handy mandrels are file handles, nails, dowels, wire, knitting needles.

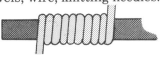

Slide the coil off and saw or cut with a separating disk.

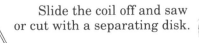

Wire wrapped around a square or rectangular mandrel is difficult to slide off. To provide clearance, wrap the form with masking tape. After wrapping, burn the tape away. The wire will then slide off.

NEVER POLISH CHAINS ON THE BUFFING WHEEL

unless you have an over supply of fingers...

Instead, pull the chain taut as shown and rub it with steel wool, Scotchbrite, a scratchbrush or a cloth impregnated with polishing compound. Note how a wire or string handle is used at each end.

Assembly Sequence

1. Make as many rings as you think will be needed. Bend half closed and join with Hard solder.

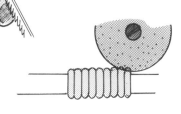

2. Thread a pair of closed rings onto an open ring. Close it and solder with Medium.

3. Connect two of the 3-piece units with a new ring and solder it with Easy. Continue joining units of 7, 15, 31, etc.

Should This Ring Be Soldered?

It's a good question and one that comes up often. Where it is possible, the answer is probably yes. Unsoldered jump rings can look messy and weaken a chain. Where you do not want to solder the proper question is: How thick a wire and small a ring do I need to provide enough strength? Remember that jump rings can be made of work-hardened wire.

Mechanisms

Chains

There is something especially exciting about making a flexible object from a rigid material. Chainmaking offers technical challenges and an enormous range of design possibilities.

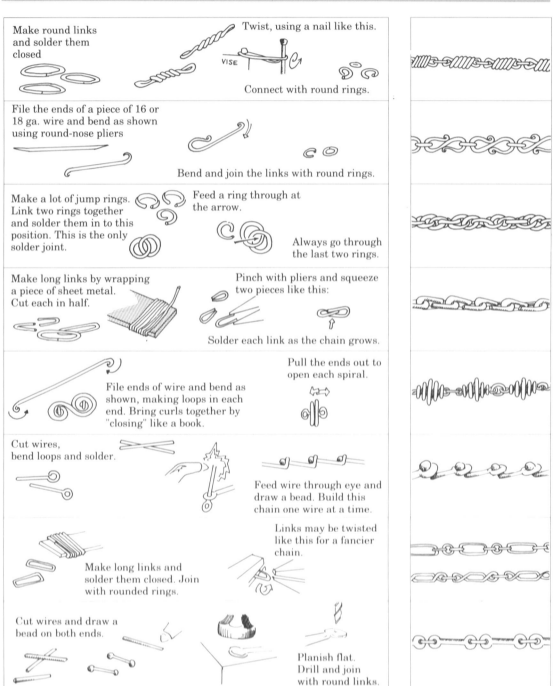

Make round links and solder them closed

Twist, using a nail like this.

VISE

Connect with round rings.

File the ends of a piece of 16 or 18 ga. wire and bend as shown using round-nose pliers

Bend and join the links with round rings.

Make a lot of jump rings. Link two rings together and solder them in to this position. This is the only solder joint.

Feed a ring through at the arrow.

Always go through the last two rings.

Make long links by wrapping a piece of sheet metal. Cut each in half.

Pinch with pliers and squeeze two pieces like this:

Solder each link as the chain grows.

File ends of wire and bend as shown, making loops in each end. Bring curls together by "closing" like a book.

Pull the ends out to open each spiral.

Cut wires, bend loops and solder.

Feed wire through eye and draw a bead. Build this chain one wire at a time.

Links may be twisted like this for a fancier chain.

Make long links and solder them closed. Join with rounded rings.

Cut wires and draw a bead on both ends.

Planish flat. Drill and join with round links.

Mechanisms

139

Miscellaneous Chains

Chains can be delicate or dramatic, precious or funky, symmetrical or irregular. In every case invention is encouraged. Experiment not only with linkages, but with proportions and materials as well.

Gimbals

Variations on this idea of combining pivots in two planes are endless. As shown, the joint unit of a multi-link chain can combine both directions. Another approach is to allow each link to alternate the direction of the movement.

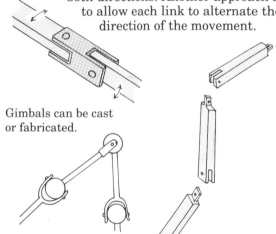

Gimbals can be cast or fabricated.

Egyptian Spiral

After experimenting to get the desired size, cut off pieces of wire, file the ends to a taper and bend.

Begin the bend like this.

Make a coil on each end and bend in the middle like this:

Connect links by sliding each one here.

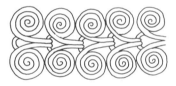

Figure 8

After winding a coil around a rod, pull down four rings and cut. Open the rings in the middle as you would open a book. Curl out each end and form a small loop at each tip. Hook these links together, each one holding the link ahead and behind.

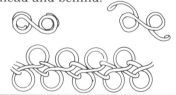

Coil Links

Wrap wire to make a coil and pull down any number of rings (here five). Cut. With pliers, pull out and open the end links. After connecting the links, the rings are made symmetrical and closed.

Clove Hitch Links

Start by soldering up a number of loops of relatively fine gauge wire. Experiment to determine the size you like best.

Make the first link over a nail, then build the rest of the chain link by link. You can practice this process with rubber bands.

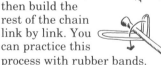

Perhaps some day it will be pleasant to remember even this.

Virgil 50 B.C.

Miscellaneous Chains

Examples of chains are all around us. From hardware stores to heavy machinery, design possibilities will present themselves if you keep your eyes open.

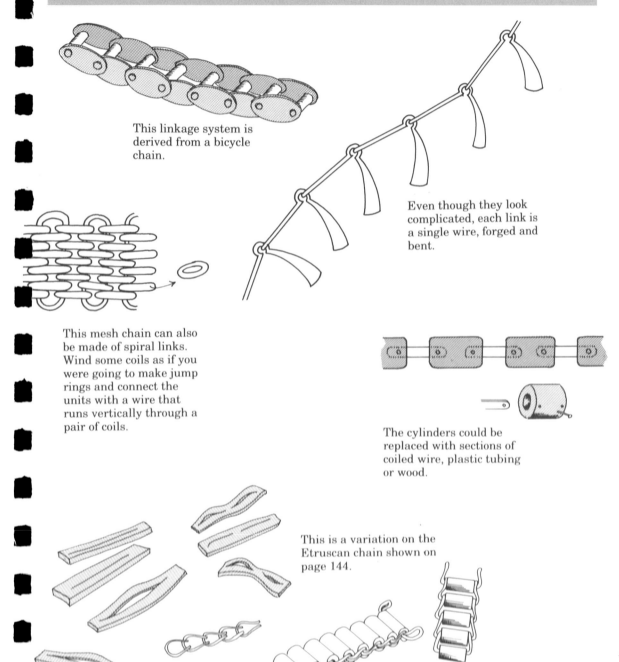

This linkage system is derived from a bicycle chain.

Even though they look complicated, each link is a single wire, forged and bent.

This mesh chain can also be made of spiral links. Wind some coils as if you were going to make jump rings and connect the units with a wire that runs vertically through a pair of coils.

The cylinders could be replaced with sections of coiled wire, plastic tubing or wood.

This is a variation on the Etruscan chain shown on page 144.

141

Woven Chain

This traditional chain uses a simple weaving technique to create a cordlike structure that provides reasonable flexibility with an intricate pattern.

• This chain may be made with 3, 4, 5 or more loops. This description uses a 3-loop chain to illustrate, but the process is identical throughout except for Step 1, where you form the number of loops you want to use. Chains with more than 5 loops have a hollow center and can therefore be crimped.
• Grab the end of the wire with pliers to pull each new loop snug on the scribe.

• Try to keep the loops uniform in size. Having a scribe with a point that tapers to the correct size cylinder will make this easy. A filed piece of coat hanger in a pin vise is a handy solution.
• Wires of various metals may be mixed for color effects. See the next page for information about splicing two pieces together.

---

1. Begin with this bend in small (22-28 B&S) gauge wire. Use a piece of annealed wire no longer than two feet.

2. Fold the short end across the loops like this.

3. Gather in the loops and wrap them with the short end. Using pliers, pull the loops into a symmetrical arrangement, like this.

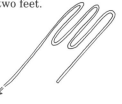

TOP VIEW

4. Feed the supply (long) end through any loop, going from inside the bunch outward.

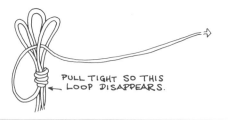

PULL TIGHT SO THIS LOOP DISAPPEARS.

5. Slide the end into the loop it just came out of and out through the adjacent loop. Put a scribe in the new loop and pull it tight.

6. Repeat this process, folding new loops upward (i.e. along the chain's axis) as you go. Pull each loop tight on the scribe.

For splicing, finishing and variations, see the next page.

Woven Chain

As is often the case with chains, the learning of a single linkage, or in this case a single stitch, can lead to dozens of varieties of chain. By altering the wire size and the number of loops, a wide range of chains can be made with this single technique.

Splicing

The woven chain is made from roughly two foot pieces of wire. Anything much longer than this tends to kink and work harden. The chain shown on the preceeding page uses about a foot of wire for each inch of chain, so an 18" chain will probably have about 9 sections of wire or 8 splices.

Add a new length of wire when the stub of the preceding piece is about an inch long. The new wire continues on the same path as the old one would have, out the adjacent loop. Twist the old and new ends together. It's important that you keep the twist inside the chain.

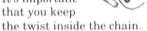

THE TWIST

Flexing the Chain

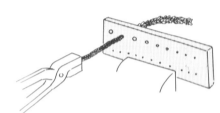

To compress and elongate, pull the chain through a drawplate after annealing.

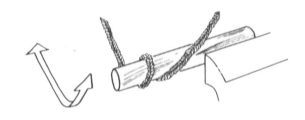

To make the chain flexible, anneal and wrap around a dowel held in a vise. Pull back and forth vigorously. Anneal and repeat.

Variations

• The 3 loop chain shown will take on a triangular shape as it is woven. A 4 loop chain will naturally become square. Either of these shapes may be exaggerated by using a drawplate.

• Increasing the number of loops and decreasing the size of each loop will make the chain appear increasingly complex.

• You can make a tapered chain by adding a loop every once in a while. Simply curl the wire to make a new loop and continue. To taper down, periodically fold one of the loops into the center and bypass it. Of course this version cannot be passed through the drawplate. Roll along the bench top under a piece of wood to make it uniform.

Basic Etruscan Chain

This classic chain combines extreme flexibility with strength and beauty. This page illustrates the simplest version and the following page describes some of the many variations that have made this chain so popular for so long.

Though I have called this chain by the name of a specific culture it has in fact a wide and ancient history. Virtually identical constructions are found in Egyptian, Hellenistic, Etruscan, Roman, Chinese, Indian and South American cultures. In museums you'll see examples so delicate they make your eyes hurt just to look at them. Go into an Armory and you'll find much larger versions used in equestrian tack. In Medieval times large silver links were made up into chains worn around the waist. As times got hard (and waists got thinner) the end link could be removed and bartered. This explains why some people know this as the *Money Chain*. It is also known by the accurate but clumsy "Loop-in-Loop".

Making Loops

All the chains shown on this and the next page have their basic building block in common. Each is made with an elongated loop which has been fused, soldered or cut from sheet. Because uniformity here will show up as a more supple and attractive chain, it is important to avoid bumps at the joint. For this reason fusing is preferred when possible. An alternate solution, especially good for sterling, is to use extremely small pieces of solder. I make this by rolling sheet solder as thin as the rolling mill will allow and then cutting it into very small pieces. As a soldering probe I use a clay needle with a very fine tip. Though a small torch tip is helpful, any normal soldering tool can be used.

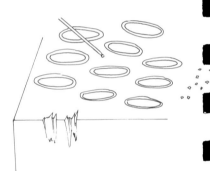

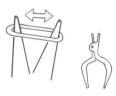

With round-nose pliers, pull each loop into an elongated oval. These should be about the same shape, which can usually be achieved by eye. An alternative is to file a small groove into the back of the pliers jaw. You can also use a commercially available tool called a ring pliers, which opens the links with a squeeze rather than a pull. These are sold in hardware stores to open hose clamps.

Assembly

Note that for the basic chain any size loop and wire thickness will give a handsome effect. In the complex versions on the next page you will need to pay close attention to this proportion.

Bend a ring in half and slide it into a twist of wire as a handle. Slide the next loop through here and bend it up to receive the next and so on. Some people prefer to bend the loops before inserting them.

After the chain is assembled, set a sharp scribe into a vise and press each link down on it four times. This sounds more time consuming than it is. The result is a well shaped and flexible chain. It may be annealed and pulled through the drawplate if desired.

Mechanisms

Complex Etruscan Chains

These variations on the basic chain shown at the left are all based on long oval links that have been soldered or fused before assembly. They require a little patience, but, oh, what a result!

Alternate Axis Double

This variation is simply a matter of making two "basic " chains, one inside the other.

1. Make a pile of oval links as described earlier. To start a double-link chain, solder two of these crosswise. You may also want to solder on a length of wire to act as a handle.

2. The ends of the *lower* oval are bent up and a new loop is fed through. Bend it a little to hold it in place.

3. New loops are added this way, always going through the lowest loop possible. It might be necessary to straighten or enlarge loops with a scribe as you go along.

Loop Proportions
For a double-link chain

Wire (B&S)	Loop Inside Diameter	Finished Chain Diameter	Links per Inch
22	10 mm	5 mm	13
24	7	4 mm	18
26	6	3.5 mm	20
28	5	3 mm	24

BiColor
The double chain shown above makes an interesting effect when made with contrasting metals. Alternate either every other link, or every two links.

Single Axis Double

Set 2 bent loops together and thread a third loop through the lower of these. Pull it up and thread another new loop through the lower of the two available loops. Continue in this fashion. The result will be a dense chain with a pronounced herringbone pattern. This chain is also known as *foxtail*.

This dense structure can be applied to the double axis version shown above, or to a triple or quadruple axis.

The Sailors Knot

Each link is given its shape individu- ally as the chain is made. Grip a scribe vertically in a vise, push onto this and a second scribe and pinch at arrows with a round nose pliers.

A variation is to shape each end of the link separately and then flatten the loop by planishing. The link is then "folded" or bent upwards, shaped as above, and the next link is inserted.

Idiot's Delight

Some people think this chain got its name from the fact that it is so easy to make. Others maintain that the name refers to the mental degeneration caused by trying to figure it out.

• Links are left unsoldered and should be work-hardened by drawing the wire down or twisting before coiling.

• The proportion of wire size to loop size is important for a compact chain in either style.

Wire Size	Inside Diameter		Links per Inch
16 B&S	3/16"	4.8 mm	20
18	5/32	4.0	24
20	1/8	3.2	28
22	3/32	2.5	33

Parallel Link

1. Make rings. Open about half, close the other half. Always open by twisting sideways.

2. Feed open ring through four closed rings and close it.

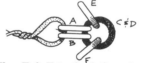

3. Feed a second open ring through the four and close it. Shading indicates two rings, side by side.

4. Flop two rings back and put a wire or paperclip through to serve as a handle.

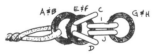

5. Flop E & F to the left and right. Flop C & D forward and backward to expose shaded area of E & F. Slide a needle through here.

6. Slip two closed rings (G & H) on an open ring (I) and feed it through where the needle is. Let needle drop out, close ring. Add a second link beside I and close it. (J)

7. Let the chain droop to allow each link to fall into place. When you lay it out it should look like this.

8. Fold G forward and H backward to expose the lower portion of I and J. Slide the needle through here. This is a repeat of 6.

9. Continue as before, adding an open ring that already has two closed rings on it. And so on... Do not buff on the machine.

Sequential Link

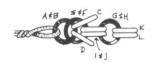

Follow 1-7 above. At this point add two more rings through G & H and close them. These are marked K & L.

Repeat the flopping operation: K & L to either side, G & H laid apart to expose the bottom section of K & L. Insert needle here to mark the spot.

As above, add an open ring that has two closed rings on it. Double this joint by adding a second ring in the same place. Now add two more (like K & L) and continue.

Mechanisms

Basic Hinge

This simple hinge uses lengths of tubing that are soldered in alignment to allow a piece to swing or to open. Though daunting at first, hinges are worth mastering because of the possibilities they present.

If the material is too thin to take the stress of a hinge, *bearers* should be soldered on, inside or out. This is especially important for round or oval containers.

Prepare a seat (trough) in which the *knuckles*, or hinge sections, will lie. Care in this step is important. A straight round file is better than a tapered one. A joint file is made for this. A scraper may be made by grinding off drill bit.

Measure and cut knuckles, keeping the ends square. If only three knuckles are used, the single piece goes on the lid and may be slightly longer than the other two.

File a bevel at each end just at the seam to make a solder-stop. Cut nicks in the seam to help locate it during soldering. If the tube has no open seam, skip the notches.

Flux the groove and the knuckles and lay them into position. Some jewelers slide the knuckles onto a snug-fitting oiled steel pin (nail, binding wire, etc.) to guaranty that they stay in a straight line. Tie with binding wire if necessary. Position seams to contact the box and place solder as shown.

Heat only until solder flows, then quickly remove the torch. Quench in water. Remove the binding wire and steel pin, then pickle. After polishing and washing, a tight fitting pin (see below) is slid into place and slightly flared on each end with a riveting hammer to hold it in place.

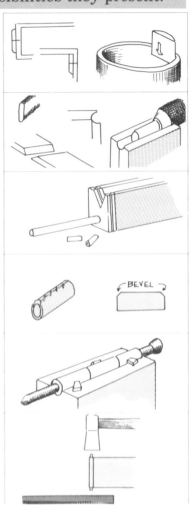

The Use of the Cutting Broach

Even well made hinges will probably have knuckles that are slightly out of alignment. This will result in a small amount of play or sloppiness in the hinge. One solution uses a gradually tapered five-sided steel rod shown here. These are usually sold in sets of a dozen in a progression of sizes. With the hinge together, the broach (held in a pin vise) is rotated gently to scrape away bits of metal inside the hinge. It is pulled out and wiped off often as work progresses. When contact is made with each knuckle (lid will hold itself open), file a wire to a similar taper and tap it lightly into place.

Unusual Hinges

These are only a few of the hundreds of variations on the simple hinge shown on the preceding page.

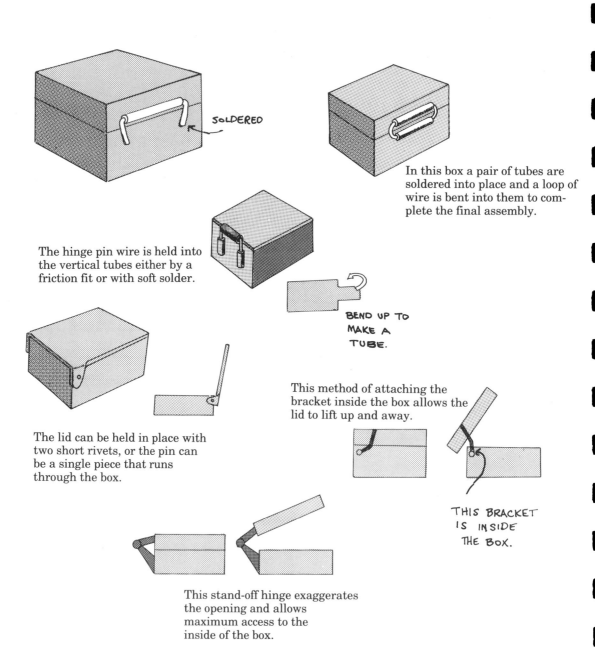

SOLDERED

In this box a pair of tubes are soldered into place and a loop of wire is bent into them to complete the final assembly.

The hinge pin wire is held into the vertical tubes either by a friction fit or with soft solder.

BEND UP TO MAKE A TUBE.

The lid can be held in place with two short rivets, or the pin can be a single piece that runs through the box.

This method of attaching the bracket inside the box allows the lid to lift up and away.

THIS BRACKET IS INSIDE THE BOX.

This stand-off hinge exaggerates the opening and allows maximum access to the inside of the box.

Cradle Hinge

This traditional hinge is shown here on a rectangular box, but it also lends iself to curved structures, such as lockets and watchcases. It is simple to make and elegant in use.

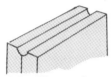

1. Prepare a trough by filing and scraping.

2. Buy or make two tubes that telescope together. Remember that soldered tubing may be drawn like wire, so it's pretty easy to get a good fit.

3. With a saw, cut a slot in the larger tube, trying to make it run straight down the tube.

4. Set this tube in position with the sawn slot located as shown, where the box and lid come together. Solder both sides.

5. Cut the entire length as shown. The lid should come free.

6. Repeat the process, removing the top third.

7. Measure and cut hinge knuckles using a jig or flex shaft. This example is showing three knuckles but any number may be used. An uneven number is customary.

8. Set a knuckle into the cradle and join with Easy solder.

 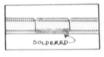

9. Set box and lid together and mark the location of first knuckle with file notches on cradle.

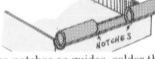

10. Using the notches as guides, solder the other knuckles into their cradle. Check the placement. If it is incorrect, reheat and slide the knuckles as needed.

11. Pickle, polish, wash and set the hinge by first reaming with a broach. This is not essential but makes a tighter hinge.

12. The cradle, besides holding the knuckles for soldering, makes a "stop" to limit the swing. This may be adjusted as shown.

Mechanisms

149

Hidden Hinges

This hinge along with its many variations is used when an obvious hinge would interfere with a design. Surface patterns such as engraved lines can make these hinges almost invisible.

Made With Tubing

1. Tabs are laid out and cut. To be effective the fit must be exact.

2. With the pieces held together, a groove is scribed and filed in both sections.

3. With the two pieces separated, a length of tubing is soldered into each groove. After soldering, excess tube is cut away with a saw.

4. To provide a stop to keep the lid from falling all the way open, solder a length of square wire along one side just in front of the tubing: don't cut any away. The height of this piece and distance from the tube will control the swing. Higher and/or closer will limit the swing.

5. File a bevel on the underside of each cove in both pieces. Be careful not to file away the top edge, thus ruining the accuracy of #1.

6. One section (with the stop) is soldered to the piece. A hole is drilled in the side of the object for the pin and the hinge is assembled.

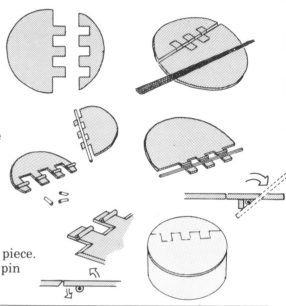

Made With Sheet

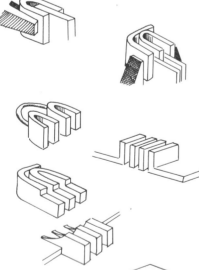

1. Knuckle units are made of heavy sheet: 14-18 gauge. A strip is cut and bent around another piece of the same gauge. Squeeze with parallel jaw pliers.

2. To make the third knuckle of this unit, a piece of strip is temporarily soldered in place and squeezed in the same way.

3. A similar device is used to make the other half of the hinge, this one having four knuckles. Two units like #1 are made and soldered temporarily to a piece of wire to hold them the correct distance apart (i.e. one thickness again).

4. This unit is then soldered onto the top of the container as shown. When soldering is complete, cut away excess including the sheet between the knuckles.

5. The first unit must overhang its edge to reach into the 4- knuckle unit. To keep the top of the finished hinge flush, file as shown. After checking the spacing between the knuckles, solder this unit to the lid.

6. The two units are put together and a hole is drilled through all. The top is then soldered to the container, the pin being set before or after soldering depending on accessibility.

Spring Hinges

These tensioned hinges can hold a box closed or make it spring open. They can also be used in findings and to allow pieces to come apart into several sections.

Coil Spring

• The spring is provided by a coil of hard drawn wire. Depending on the weight of the lid and the fineness of the piece this can be gold, sterling, brass, nickel silver, or steel. The steel may be salvaged from a pen spring.

• The hinge is made in the usual way except that a space is left to be occupied by the spring. This may be made by cutting away one of the knuckles but it will be neater if you plan ahead and leave a space when soldering on the knuckles.

• In assembling, the spring is cocked into position and the pin is run through it. This can be a ticklish operation and is easier with two people. The tails of the coil must protrude to make this spring work. Depending on where you put these you can make the lid spring open or closed.

• The spring can be made less obvious if the knuckles are made of coiled wire.

Depression Spring

This is best used where only a small push is needed. It is common on the covers of pocket watches, for instance. This spring is not in the hinge at all. Somewhere near the hinge is a piece of metal that is pushed down when the lid is closed. When the clasp is released the little tab pushes upward.

Each application will need its own design but here are a few examples:

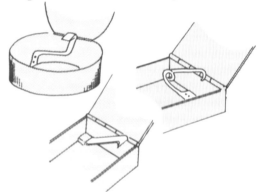

Spring Hinge Pin

This is the most subtle of the bunch. It does not lend itself to short or slender hinges.

1. Make a hinge that is conventional in every way except that it has an even number of knuckles. This means that one end knuckle will be on the base and the other on the lid.

2. After polishing, slide a tight fitting tube through the hinge, keeping it a little shorter than the hinge proper. This will provide strength and smooth operation.

3. You will need several strips of flat springy metal. Watch mainsprings are best but in a pinch, hard-drawn brass or nickel silver can be flattened out and used. Cut 2 or 3 pieces about an inch longer than the hinge. Slide these through and lock them with a wedge, tapped into place.

4. With pliers, grip the extending spring pieces and give them a twist or two. Lock in place with a similar wedge and check the action. If slack, give another twist. Depending on the direction of the twist, the spring will open or close. When correct, tap the wedge and trim off excess.

Threaded Closures

Screw type mechanisms can be made without the use of dies and lend themselves to containers as well as jewelry findings.

Partial Thread

This example uses a cylinder shaped jar, but by observing the process you'll see that it can be modified for hundreds of applications. In this case I'm showing the thread on the container and the catch on the lid, but the reverse would work equally well.

1. This top view of the container shows equal divisions. The two "threads" must be carefully positioned directly opposite each other.

2. Scribe delicate guidelines around the container to locate the threads.

3. Bend a piece of wire to match the curvature of the container. Square or half round wire is referred because its flat surfce will make a solid contact.

4. Locate these pieces along the guides and solder into place. Steel or nickel clips might help in this.

5. Solder a pair of small projections on the inside of the lid, again making certain that they are directly opposite each other. The height should equate with the center of the thread.

6. If the closure is stiff even after pickling, mix some abrasive grit with oil to make a paste and coat the thread. Open and close the unit until any irregularities have been ground away. To make the grit, set a piece of sandpaper into a can and burn away the paper with a torch.

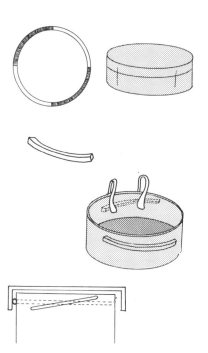

Full Thread

1. Make the tube that will become the neck of the closure, let's say a bottle. Using a rod very slightly smaller, wrap wire to make a coil. The direction of wrapping will determine the direction of the screwing/unscrewing motion. Slide the coil off and pull it so the spaces equal the thickness of the wire. It is important that the stretching be symmetrical.

2. File a slight flat onto the inside of this coil and force it onto the neck tubing. When you are sure the spaces have remained even, solder it down.

3. With another piece of the same wire, wrap another coil inside the threads. File this while in position to achieve a flat outer surface.

4. Make a tube or collar to fit snugly onto this coil, then unscrew it gently and slide it into the outer tube. Solder into position.

5. If the fit is too snug, refer to #6 above for a remedy.

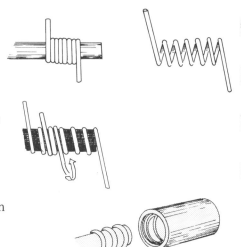

Chapter 8

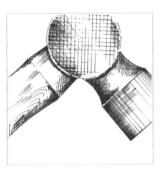

Tools

Studiowares

You can't keep house without housewares, and a studio has similar needs. A lot of petty frustration can be avoided by planning ahead. Keep yourself well supplied and organized.

Studio Chemicals / Their Uses

Studio Chemicals	Their Uses
Ammonia	Cleaning, patinas, neutralize ferric chloride.
Baking soda	Neutralize acids & pickle.
Organic solvents (alcohol, thinner, etc.)	Cleaning metals, lamp fuel.
Hydrogen peroxide	Cleaning, pickle additive.
Detergent	Cleaning, scratchbrushing.
Pumice handsoap	Cleaning.
Waterless cleaner	Degreasing, cleaning.
Nail polish	Masking off.
Light oils (WD 40, Marvel Mystery)	Lubrication, honing, and rust removal.
Motor oil	Tool hardening, cooling.
Ferric chloride	Etchant.
Nitric acid	Etchant, gold testing.
Liver of Sulfur	Patina solution.
Trisodium Phosphate	Flux ingredient, anodizing.
Gold darkener	Patina solution.

Miscellaneous Supplies

Various glues
- fast & slow epoxy
- white glue (*Elmer's*)
- cyanoacrylate (*Super Glue*)

Assorted tapes
- masking tape
- duct tape
- electricians'
- good music

Odds and ends
- pencils & pens
- string
- matches
- aspirin.

Medical Supplies

- Bandaids, including knuckle and fingertip shapes.
- Burn ointment (aloe plant)
- Chemical icepack
- Bottled eyewash
- Hydrogen peroxide

Storage

Never store chemicals in a container that could be confused with food. Wherever possible, use the manufacturer's container.

Always mark all containers clearly, often on both the lid and the jar. If it is a solution you've mixed, always include the recipe and the date.

Even simple chemicals can be harmful to children and pets. Keep all chemicals in a locked or childproofed cabinet.

When an idea is wanting, a word can always be found to take its place.

Goethe

Measuring Tools

It is hard to underestimate the importance of proper measuring when working with the fine tolerances of jewelry. To be effective, tools must be accurate and accurately used.

Rulers

A ruler, like any other tool, requires some care in use to do its job well.
• When measuring or drawing a line, use a sharp pencil or scribe that can slide evenly along the ruler's edge.
• Work in lighting that does not cast shadows.
• Steel rulers are more precise than plastic ones.
• Do not take measurements from the end of a ruler since it could be worn and therefore inaccurate.
• The smallest division of any ruler is printed near one end. In this case the smallest calibration is tenths of a millimeter.

Degree Gauge

Also called a douzieme gauge or 72 gauge from the French watchmakers' measurement. 12 douziemes = 1 ligne = 2.25 mm = .0888 inch.

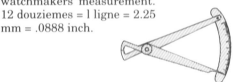

In this spring-activated tool the size of the opening at the top is indicated by the scale at the bottom.

Gauge Plate

This is a thick piece of steel cut with slots of specific size. It measures both sheet and wire in the Brown and Sharpe system (also called American Standard and American Wire Gauge, A.W.G.). The other side often shows thousandths of an inch. To use, find the slot that makes a snug fit, but won't distort the metal by jamming it in. Be careful not to measure where the edge has been thinned by planishing, or where a bur raised by snips will affect accuracy.

Vernier (VUR nē r)

This is a secondary gauge used to subdivide the smallest units on a primary gauge. It is most often found on a sliding caliper.

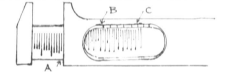

A vernier is read by adding three separate units. This example uses inches but the logic is the same for metric. First read the full inches at **A**. Then read 16ths at the first line on the vernier scale (**B**). Next, count the spaces on the vernier scale from left to right until the first place where lines coincide (**C**). This reflects the number of the smallest unit, here 128ths. Convert all these fractions to a common denominator (128) and add them.

Micrometer

This is a precise and accurate tool used for measuring thickness, usually in thousandths of an inch. The barrel unscrews along the shank, rotating through the digits 1-25 at A. Marks on the shank indicate units of 25 thousandths each. The small numbers on the shank demark hundredths (i.e. four units of 25.)

In the example, the space at B is .3035 inches.

Dividers

In addition to making circles like a compass, the dividers can be used to hold a measurement for quick reference. Another use is to lay out parallel lines by dragging one leg of the tool along the edge of a piece of metal.

Hand Tools

There is a special pleasure in making or remaking a tool so it does exactly what you want it to do. A willingness to devote attention to this aspect of the craft can deepen your pleasure and often facilitate your work methods as well.

Sweeps Drawer

Cut a small hole in a back corner of the sweeps drawer and cover it with a piece of window screen. Below this, attach a shallow box that can be removed. The box and track that holds it can be made of brass, tinplate, wood, or plastic. By sweeping scraps over this, larger pieces can be quickly sorted from filings.

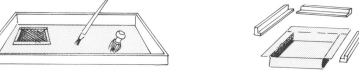

Small Vise

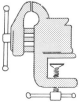

These small vises can be bought new or often found at used tool shops. Be sure that the jaws meet evenly and completely. They can often double as a bench block for riveting.

Bench Brush & Dust Pan

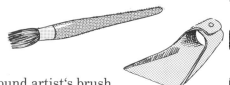

Buy a round artist's brush or a shaving brush and make a small pan from thin brass to wrap around it. Use it daily to pick up sweeps.

Magnetized Tool Holder

These holders can be bought from tool suppliers and are handy for pliers.

Bench Block

A small block of steel with a polished surface and crisp edges will prove invaluable for riveting, centerpunching and similar light hammering. Visit a machine shop for a scrap or end cut. Protect with a wooden or plastic cover.

Attached Apron

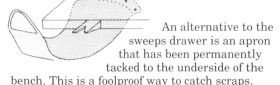

An alternative to the sweeps drawer is an apron that has been permanently tacked to the underside of the bench. This is a foolproof way to catch scraps.

Slab of Rubber for Setting

A piece of dense foam rubber is a useful pad for filing and to support work when setting stones. Keep a dirty one for filing and a clean one for finish work.

Hand Tools

I'm convinced that one of the things that draws people to make jewelry is the pleasure of the hand tools we get to use. Many of these can be made from scratch or modified from other tools.

Bench Pin

Any hardwood can be used. These shapes are common starting places. In practice the pin is filed, drilled and carved to meet specific needs. You might find you want different interchangeable pins to meet a variety of specific needs.

Squares

A small square can be made from steel or brass rod. One side is thicker than the other to allow the square to rest against the item being marked. File and solder carefully.

Pliers Rack

This can be made from a piece of coat hanger wire or a 1/2" strip of steel or brass.

Saw Blade Holder

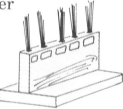

Bench Knife

A knife can be improvised by grinding and resharpening a used kitchen paring knife. These can often be bought at a flea market.

Chuck Keys

Small tools can be more easily located if they are fitted into a file handle or soldered into a broken screwdriver handle.

Sanding Boards

Make up these boards by gluing papers of various grits to panels of Masonite or Plexiglas. Both sides may be used, so three boards will provide a thorough range of grits. These are especially handy for truing up flat areas. A hole in the corner will allow them to hang up.

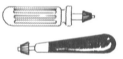

Scraper

A scraper can be made by breaking off an old

triangular file and grinding a point. Faces should be ground smooth and polished.

You wouldn't say an axe handle has style to it. It has beauty, and an appropriateness of form, and a "this-is-how-it-should-be-ness." But it has no style because it has no mistakes. Style reflects one's idiosyncrasies.
Charles Eames

Tools

Abrasive Paper

The wide range of papers available indicates how complicated the technology of abrasive papers has become. A clear understanding of the uses and options of abrasive papers will save a metalsmith wasted time and money.

The use of abrasives is ancient and can be seen in Egyptian drawings of jewelers using powders to polish goldwork. Even before written history we can surmise that hard stones were used to shape and polish tools and weapons. Through most of history natural minerals were used as abrasives, the most common being flint and sand, both in the quartz family and having a Mohs hardness of 7. To a lesser extent garnet, corundum, emery and pumice were used as well. In the last hundred years a number of synthetic abrasives have become possible because of the high temperatures of induction furnaces. These have the advantage of uniformity and toughness over natural materials and today account for most abrasives. They are pressed into wheels or glued onto paper or cloth and are heavily used in industry. Perhaps the most common industrial abrasive, and the one of most interest to jewelers is silicon carbide. This tough particle has a Mohs hardness of 9.5, making it harder than all stones except diamond. Each grain of silicon carbide is tough and will last a long time and when it breaks it will expose a sharp jagged edge. Many people underestimate the lifespan of silicon carbide and discard it when a simple shakeout or water rinse would be sufficient. Silicon Carbide is sold under several trade names including *Carborundum, Crystolon* and *Carbolon.*

Grit Numbers

Abrasive particles are sorted by sifting them through screens that are identified by the number of holes per inch. This is the number that is then given to the abrasive paper, which is why a 400 paper is a finer grit than an 80 paper. It is important to note the difference between grit (particle size) and the hardness of the material. A 500 silicon carbide paper for instance will seem very mild but it will scratch most stones because the particles are so tough. A 120 grit emery paper will seem coarse but it will quickly wear away to nothing on a hard surface such as hardened steel.

Leverage

In order to get the most from your abrasive papers, wrap them on a flat stick (lattice) like this. Use a scribe to score each corner so the folds will be crisp. By wrapping a stick in several layers you will be able to simply discard the top surface as it wears and continue working. Wrap several sticks so you have a full range of grits and keep them clearly marked. Commercial devices are available for this purpose. For delicate work glue paper onto paint stirrers or popsicle sticks. Spray adhesive makes this easy.

Micro Finishing Films

A recent development in the abrasive industry is the use of extremely precise sizing technology to create papers with uniform particle size. These are adhered to plastic film and yield a brighter finish than conventional papers. Micro films are produced with aluminum oxide, silicon carbide and diamond particles.

Nylon Fibers

Most of us are familiar with the red or green scouring pads, sometimes called Scotch-Brite, sold in grocery stores. This nylon web is handy in the studio to clean away oils and oxides. Another version of this pad has particles of abrasive distributed throughout the mesh. Because the plastic is yielding, this pad follows contours as it is dragged across a workpiece. The particles do not bite into the surface and therefore do not remove any metal but leave a network of shiny grooves similar to scratchbrushing.

Tools

Files

Files are a powerful tool for creating form and for refining the finish that is so important to the final result of a piece. Care and practice in their use will always be repaid.

Hand Files

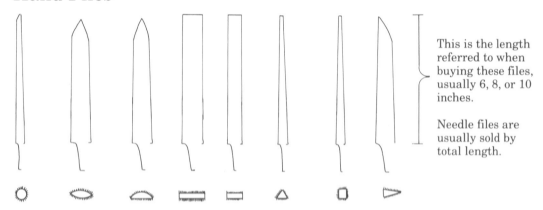

This is the length referred to when buying these files, usually 6, 8, or 10 inches.

Needle files are usually sold by total length.

Round Crossing Half Round Flat Pillar Triangular Square Knife

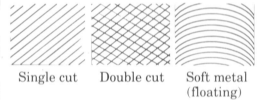

Single cut   Double cut   Soft metal (floating)

A single cut is generally finer and will cut slower than a double cut, but the coarseness of the file must be considered since various degrees of coarseness are available in each style.

Foreign made files are often incorrectly called "Swiss" files. They are usually graded by number from 00 (coarsest) to 8. American made files usually use the names shown. An exception is called Swiss Pattern, which indicates American made files emulating the Swiss precision.

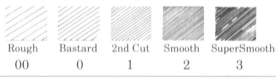

| Rough | Bastard | 2nd Cut | Smooth | SuperSmooth |
| 00 | 0 | 1 | 2 | 3 |

Files should be equipped with handles to provide increased leverage and to protect the hand from the tang. Handles are usually held on by friction, though some have a threading mechanism inside the ferrule.

Tips

The teeth on all files point away from the handle and therefore cut on the push stroke. Lift the file or ease pressure on the return stroke to prevent bending over the teeth and shortening the life of the file.

Hold the index finger like this to press down while filing. It is important that the work be stable. Cut notches in the bench pin as needed. Don't file while walking around.

Keep files clean with a file card (a wire brush) or by scraping with a thin piece of brass. As it is used, the brass will develop serrations that reach into the file's grooves.

159

Mallets

A mallet is a hammer-like tool that is made of a material that is softer than the work metals of the jeweler. Familiar mallet materials are rawhide, wood, paper and plastic.

Alternate Shapes

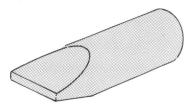

Like hammers, mallets
lend themselves to a wide range of shapes.
Here are a few basics, but be open to the idea of
designing or modifying mallet heads as a particular need arises.

Mounting Handles

These methods are appropriate for hammers as well.

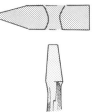

The handle is filed to a taper that snugly fits the eye, which has its larger opening upward.

Make a saw cut in the top of the handle equal to the short axis of the eye. Tap the handle into place and check alignment.

Slide a wooden wedge into place, dab some white glue on it, and tap it into position. Trim off excess.

Ultra High Molecular Weight (UHMW)

This recently developed plastic is rigid and relatively inexpensive, making it a perfect choice for mallets. It can be cut with a bandsaw, drilled with standard wood bits and shaped with a rasp. A power sander can be used, but avoid friction heat.

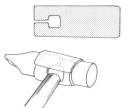

If more weight is desired, use lead to wrap or fill the mallet.

By the hammer and hand, all the arts do stand.
Old Proverb

Hammers

The heart of the metalsmith's shop is in the hammers. In fact the word *smith* is derived from the verb *"to smite"* or to hit. Metalworking hammers can be bought new, but many smiths alter old hammer heads to suit their needs.

Common Shapes

Planishing

Forging, Cross Peen

Collet

Embossing

Goldsmiths

Ball Peen

Raising

Chasing

Cast vs. Forged

The advantages of cast hammerheads are in their ability to be reshaped easily by grinding. Forged hammers are able to withstand harder use, because the crystals of the steel have been more densely packed during manufacture. These are made in a power hammer called a drop forge and so are called "drop forged hammers."

Care

Faces that will contact a workpiece should be free of pits and scale. Many smiths keep a piece of crocus cloth at hand to rub the face of each hammer before using it. A muslin buff (preferably stiff) with a tough abrasive compound like white diamond, Simichrome, or Lea compound will give a good polish. For long term storage the face can be protected with a layer of Vaseline, wax, or oil.

Handles

• These must be strong without being bulky or heavy. Fibrous woods such as hickory and ash are commonly used. Any dense wood can be used as long as the grain is not convoluted.

• A long-handled hammer delivers more power but is more difficult to control than a short-handled one. A length that provides a comfortable mix of power and control is correct. A rounded end on the handle will usually be more comfortable than a squared off shape.

• A cross section that is oval or faceted generally provides a more efficient and comfortable grip than a round handle. Rubberized coatings are available but many people prefer the feel and grip of smooth untreated wood. It will acquire a hand rubbed oil finish during use.

• The European style chasing hammer is most effective with a springy handle. A fruit wood like apple is good for this, since it can be made thin enough for flexibility without impairing strength.

This old anvil laughs at many a broken hammer.
Carl Sandburg

Flex Shaft

This versatile tool, properly called the *flexible shaft machine*, has become a standard benchside friend to most jewelers. It is simple to operate and maintain and deserves all the care you can give it.

Motors

A glance at a catalog can make the choices seem bewildering, but take heart. It's not as difficult as it appears. The principal difference in the motors is their horsepower and speed. While there are a few unusual sizes, most companies stock a 1/15, 1/10 and 1/8 horse power motor. The lighter models produce speeds of 14,000 RPM and the larger one go up tp 20,000 RPM. For occasional use, the midsize model is probably fine. Production shops or schools will be better served with the larger motor. From the motor hangs the element that gives this tool its name. It is a bronze coil surrounded by a steel spring for support and encased in a black rubber sheath. This is the part of the tool most likely to wear out unless you keep it well lubricated.

Handpieces

This is the part of the tool that grips the burs and attachments that actually do the work. Again the selection is large. The most popular handpiece consists of an aluminum cylinder mounted with a Jacobs cuck. This is the familiar three-prong affair surrounded by a toothed collar. It has the advantage of versatility in that it will grip any size shank up to the limits of its largest opening. This allows the use of toothpicks, cotton swabs and similar improvised tools.

Another type of handpiece allows for a quick change from one bur to another, sometimes even while the machine is still turning. This can be important to production shops. Some handpieces have a slimmer body than others and some are jointed with a section of steel spring. These comfort features are obviously related to how many hours a day you hold the tool. *Hammer handpieces* convert the rotational movement of the motor into a back and forth stroke. This can be used for stone setting, texturing or carving. Better models of these handpieces will allow you to control the depth of the stroke. The speed is controlled through the foot rheostat.

Foot Rheostat

The third piece of the package is the foot pedal that controls the speed of the machine. The traditional pedal presses on a carbon rod that slides into a housing to control the amount of power sent to the machine. These are the cheapest and they wear out after a couple of years. The new development is a solid state electronic rheostat. These are often set into a heavier casing, which gives them the added advantage of remaining stationary.

Maintenance

Most flex shafts need to be lubricated about every 100 hours of use. Use the grease sold for this purpose to coat the inner workings of the shaft itself. Simply pull off the handpiece with a stiff tug, then loosen the set screw that holds the shaft onto the motor. Slide the coil out and coat it with grease. Some handpieces are sealed, but those that aren't need a few drops of light oil to keep them running cool and true. Apply this in all the openings you can reach.

On either side of the motor you'll find a broad screw, often of plastic. Beneath this is a 1/4" carbon rod attached to a screw. These are called the *brushes.* They will eventually wear down and need to be replaced. Buy a new set from a distributor, slide them into place and replace the screws.

Jigs

These can be bought or often made in the shop. With some ingenuity you can alter and improve on these to suit your needs.

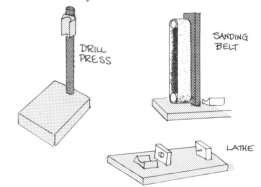

DRILL PRESS

SANDING BELT

LATHE

Tools

Motors

While many metalsmithing techniques are pre-industrial, there are times when a small motor will speed up a process or yield a better result. Motors can often be scavenged from a defunct machine or re-configured to better suit a particular need.

Beware of the danger of electrical shock. Because electricity is so much a part of our everyday lives we run the risk of forgetting its danger. Only a licensed electrician should work on wires that carry voltage through your studio. The following comments pertain only to pieces of equipment, and of course these must be unplugged when you work on them.

All electrical motors will have an information plate clearly attached on the outside of the housing. This will tell you the speed (in revolutions per minute, rpm) the voltage, and the type of current used. Household current is called alternating current (AC) and is probably what you want. The only other kind you're likely to run across is direct current (DC) which is created by batteries. Though it is possible to convert a motor from one to the other, the cost is prohibitive. A very common motor is a quarter horse 1725 rpm single phase motor. These are used in most washing machines, dryers, refrigerators and household heating systems. Fortunately for us, this is also a good size for the jewelry studio.

Setting Up a Buffing Motor

Use a threaded tapered spindle to allow buffs to be quickly interchanged. These can be bought at most jewelry supply companies but you'll need to know the diameter of the motor's shaft and the direction of rotation. The first is a simple measurement taken with a ruler across the rounded part of the shaft. To determine the latter, wire up the motor temporarily and note the direction of rotation. The buffing wheel must rotate downward, so this will determine the position of a one-spindle machine. If you want the spindle to be on a particular side, the direction of rotation might be alterable: see below. In a two-spindle machine this doesn't matter. Just buy one right and one left-handed spindle.

Attach the tapered spindle with its set screw and measure the height of the spindle. Be sure to allow enough room to accommodate the buffing wheel and still have a couple of inches of working room beneath it. It might be necessary to mount the bracket on a piece of wood to give it the correct height.

Remove the plate attached to the side of the motor housing and you'll see a couple of screw terminals. Strip the plastic sheath from the last inch of the power cord and connect the copper wires to these. If there are three terminals, attach one strand to the center screw and the other to either of the other heads. If the rotation is incorrect, leave the center alone and move the other strand to the opposite screw.

An alternate hook up that I prefer is to include a light fixture into the arrangement. In this way when you turn on the motor the light comes on as well. Follow the diagram. A further enhancement (and a good idea) is to build in a plug for your dust collector. This can also be connected to the same switch, as shown in the last drawing.

When the assembly is complete, be certain that there is no possibility of exposed wires touching each other and put the cover back into position. Everything should be safe, but just to be cautious, be certain that you are not in contact with the machine and flip the switch. If the power goes out in your neighborhood, you goofed.

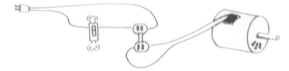

THE SWITCH AND PLUG ARE MOUNTED IN A SQUARE ELECTRICAL BOX LIKE THIS.

163

Anvils

Few objects have a more immediate connotation with a trade than the anvil. It is the time honored symbol of the value and strength of work made in metal.

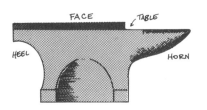

There was a time when every farm had an anvil, and most cities had a supplier, but nowadays they are increasingly difficult to find. Used anvils occasionally turn up at auctions and scrap dealers. For an anvil in decent condition you can expect to pay about a dollar a pound.

The face of an anvil can be ground smooth by a machine shop. Attempts to weld on a new face or fill recesses with welding rod are generally unsuccessful or prohibitively expensive. In grinding the face, take care not to cut away the

hardened steel plate that makes up the top 1/2" of the face (shaded above). A good anvil can be made from a piece of railroad track. Find these at a junk yard or foundry. The surface should be ground smooth, either by a machine shop or with a belt sander. A point can be cut with an oxy-acetylene torch but that is not usually necessary. Other flat pieces of steel may be used as anvils. Though it helps to have hardened steel it is not essential. Keep it heavy, smooth and well-anchored, and it will work.

Anvil Stands

Mandrels

It would seem impossible to have too many mandrels. The most common varieties are the tapered mandrels named for their uses; bezel, ring and bracelet. Any hard object that will lend you its shape will work. Here are some economical substitutes for conventional tools.

drift pin (hardware store)

drive pin (auto parts store)

machine shop rejects

chair or table leg (junk yard)

machine parts (junk yard)

baseball bat (local team)

Also, if an area vocational or technical school has a machine shop, you might find that they will custom make mandrels to your specifications.

Stakes

Since most stakes must suit a special need, it is less likely that you will turn up a piece of scrap steel with the right shape. Some smiths forge their own stakes or make patterns in wood to be cast by a foundry. Either way is time consuming and expensive, but sometimes necessary.

Hardwoods such as maple can be used in many cases and have the advantage of not marring the work piece; see page 59 for a wooden side stake for crimping and raising. A new generation of stakes is being made of hard plastic, with Ultra High Molecular Weight (UHMW) being preferred. Thermoplastics that can be shaped when warm open many possibilities.

Ingot Molds

Ingot molds offer the metalsmith the possibility of making useful sheet and wire from scrap metal, and of mixing alloys as needed.

Heavy castings like this may be bought, or sheet steel and square steel rod can be used to make one like this:

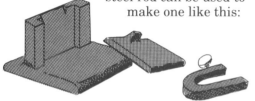

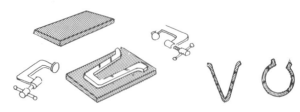

Small C clamps or spring clamps are used to hold the mold together; note the air vents.

1. Lubricate the mold with Vaseline, oil or soot.

2. Heat the mold until the lubricant (if oil) starts to smoke. The mold may be set into a pan of sand or an empty cast iron skillet.

3. Heat the metal in a pouring crucible, adding flux a couple of times.

4. Pour the metal through the flame in a single even flow. Allow the red color to fade before removing and quenching the ingot.

Investment

• Mix up some investment, remove bubbles, and pour into an empty milk carton. When the block has hardened, tear off the carton and carve the desired shapes.

• Pour a slab of investment to make the other side of the mold by laying pieces of wood on a sheet of glass. Sand both units as necessary to insure a tight fit between the two pieces.

• Before the first use, both mold pieces should be cured by heating them in a kiln to around 1000° F (538° C). To use, grip the two halves lightly with C-clamps, set the assembly into a dish of sand and preheat before pouring. There is no need to lubricate. The mold is fragile but reusable.

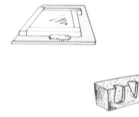

When you need a short piece of heavy wire, an ingot may be improvised by drilling a hole of the desired size in a charcoal block. Use a pouring crucible or carve a melting recess in the block and tilt to pour.

Firebrick may be used as above for an ingot mold. The surface will not be as smooth but these bumps will come out in subsequent rolling, forging or drawing.

Simple Jeweler's Bench

For those with some woodworking ability, these plans will get you started with a simple bench made from conventional lumberyard materials.

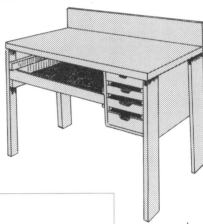

COST: $50-60

MATERIALS:

1	4x4 x 3/4" plywood CDX, one side surfaced
1	4x8 x 1/4" tempered Masonite
2	2x4 x 8' (straight ones)
41'	1x3 random lengths
18'	1x2 random lengths
6'	1x6 random lengths
4 lb.	1 1/2" plaster nails
4	3" flat head wood screws

This bench has been designed to accommodate standard lumberyard materials and to require only basic tools. Those with access to power equipment might want to consider modifying these plans for better wood, fancier joinery, or a "breakdown" possibility to allow the bench to be taken apart for easier transport.

The dimensions shown here are given as whole numbers and do not account for the thickness of a sawblade. This is usually 1/8 inch on a table saw and should be calculated into your plans. The height of the bench will depend on your own height and on the height of the chair you'll be using. A typical finished height is 36".

Plywood

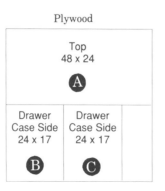

Masonite

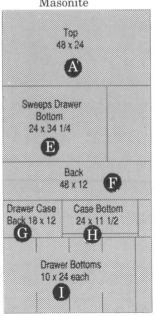

Simple Jeweler's Bench

1. Cut pieces. These dimensions do not allow for a saw kerf. If using a table saw, plan ahead and allow for this.

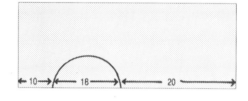

2. The top is made by gluing pieces A and A' together. Use a wood glue (eg. Elmer's) and clamp or weight the pieces while the glue dries. The optional cutout bay ("belly hole") is made with a bandsaw or sabre saw after the glue has dried.

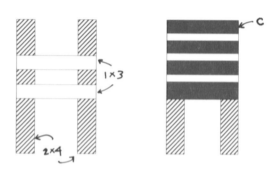

3. Assemble the leg units. Use a square to be sure all pieces are perpendicular.

4. Assemble left side of the drawer case. These dimensions will duplicate those on the leg units.

The shaded cleats are 1x3; the others on this piece are 1x2.

Assembly

5. Stand up the leg units and join them with a 48" piece of 1x3, 20" down from the top.

6. Set the top into position and secure it with the 3" screws. Countersink these so the top will be flush. Set the Masonite Back (F) into position so about half of it projects above the bench top.

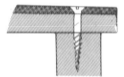

7. The left side of the drawer case is fastened into position by the cleat that attaches to the underside of the top, and by the Masonite panel (H) that spans the bottom edges of the plywood drawer case.

Drawers

The bottom drawer uses 1x6 and the 3 top drawers use 1x2.

The sweeps drawer uses 1x3 on sides and back, 1x2 on front.

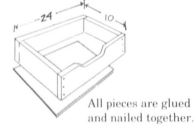

All pieces are glued and nailed together.

Hardwood Bench

The plans on these two pages describe a professional bench that is a little more expensive and complicated than the one shown on the preceding page. If you have woodworking skills or a friend who does, this is an excellent workspace.

This bench is made of maple or a similar hardwood. Its construction requires a table saw and an understanding of cabinetmaking skills. The sizes given are for a typical bench, but they can be altered to suit your needs. An advantage of this bench is the fact that it breaks down for travel and can be fit into the trunk of a car. I can pack all my equipment into the large center drawer and make a self-contained (though heavy) unit, which I can reassemble in about 5 minutes.

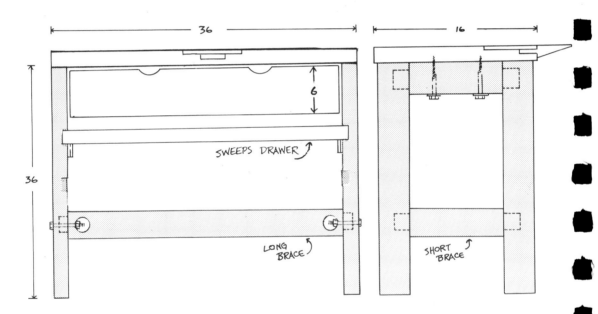

(All measurements are in inches)

HARDWOOD

	pieces	
Top	1	1 1/2 x 36 x 16
Legs	4	1 1/2 x 3 x 36
Short Braces	4	1 1/2 x 3 x 11 1/2
Long Braces	2	1 1/2 x 3 x 35
Large Drawer		
Sides	2	3/4 x 6 x 16
Back	1	3/4 x 6 x 31 1/2
Front	1	3/4 x 6 x 34
Sweeps Drawer		
Sides	2	3/4 x 3 x 16
Back	1	3/4 x 3 x 31 1/2
Front	1	3/4 x 1 1/2 x 34

OTHER

	pieces	
Drawer Bottoms	2	1/4 x 31 3/4 x 15
(Masonite or plywood)		
Drawer Divider	1	1 1/2 x 3 x 14 1/2
Side Bearings	2	1/2 x 3 x 14 1/2
Bolts	4	3/8 x 3
Lag Bolts	5	3/8 x 4
Drawer Glides	2 prs	15"

Hardwood Bench

1. The wood is first glued, thicknessed and sawn to nominal size. The top can be made of several pieces glued up for the purpose or from commercial butcher block.

2. The two side units are made with mortise and tenon joints. They are permanently glued up, with care taken to insure that all the angles are square. Drill 3/8" holes in the top braces before assembling the leg units. These holes are used to connect the top to the legs.

3/8" HOLES

3. After the glue has dried, mortise slots are cut into each of the leg units. Corresponding tenons are cut on the ends of the two long braces, which are drilled with a 1 1/2 or 2" hole as shown.

3/8" HOLES IN TOP BRACE

4. The braces are dry-fitted into place and a 3/8" hole is drilled through the tenon on a center line with the large hole. Bolts through this hole will hold the leg units together.

5. The top is set into place and secured with lag bolts that are set through the braces and into the underside of the top.

6. The drawers are made with a dado on the front piece and a lap joint on the back as shown. The sweeps drawer is shorter at the front than the back and its sides slope to accommodate this, but otherwise the two drawers are identical. The bottom is fitted into a 1/4 " groove cut for this purpose. The drawers are held together with glue and small finishing nails.

7. Install the drawer glides according to the instructions that come with them. It is important that the large drawer use a glide rated for at least 30 pounds, but the lower unit can be a lighter duty model.

8. Options:
The large drawer can be divided by inserting a brace down the middle. An extra piece of the "leg" material is handy for this. Cut a tongue as shown. With the addition of a couple of slim pieces on either side of the drawer you will have created a bearing to support a couple of trays. Make these of any handy wood and of a dimension that is the correct width and equal to about half the depth of the drawer. Paraffin rubbed along the lower surface will allow these to slide easily.

The top section can be routed out to accomodate a 6 x 6 x 1/4" steel plate, which is drilled in the corners to accept countersunk screws. Before securing this plate, rout out a smaller area to accept the tongue of a bench pin. Drill a hole and add a T-nut to take a thumbscrew. This arrangement provides a flat surface and a cooling plate in the center of the bench and a secure pin that is flush with the benchtop.

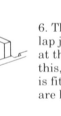

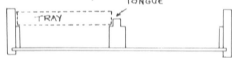

TONGUE
TRAY

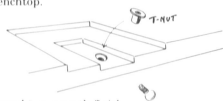

T-NUT

9. Hand plane all the corners to remove their sharpness and sand to a smooth finish. Protect the wood with oil or varnish.

169

Hardening Steel

The ability to harden and temper steel gives the studio metalsmith the ability to create or modify tools as required for each job. This element of control is an important ingredient in developing confidence as a craftsperson. See page 12 for further information.

1. Tool steel is sold in its annealed state, but if you are recycling a worn tool the first step is to anneal it. Heat to bright red and **cool as slowly as possible.** Bury the hot steel in sand or ashes to achieve a slow cooling. Another method is to heat in a kiln then leave the steel in place to cool slowly.

2. Shape the tool by forging, sawing, grinding and filing. Forging must be done while the steel is red hot. Do not strike after the color has gone or the steel may crack. When making a patterned tool such as a stamp, the image is checked by pressing it into clay.

3. The tool is hardened by heating it to glowing red-orange and quenching immediately in oil or brine. Small tools may be held in tweezers. Large pieces are set on a brick or may be heated in a forge or furnace. Punches are usually hardened only

for the inch or two up from the stamping end. The goal here is to convert the pearlite stage into martensite. Because this phase is not magnetic, a magnet can be used to confirm a high enough temperature. At proper temperature, a magnet will not stick.

4. Check for hardness by stroking a file across the tool. It should not cut in and should make a glassy sound.

5. Remove the gray oxide scale with fine sandpaper. This will allow for better perception of colors in the next step.

6. Reduce brittleness by heating in a step called *drawing the temper* (drawing; tempering). This can be done with a torch or, for small pieces, on a hot plate. Go slowly, letting heat travel from a thick section to a thinner one. The higher the temperature (longer heat) the softer, more flexible the steel will become.

Testing Steel

Mild steel (also called low carbon steel) contains .15-.3% carbon. This amount is insufficient to cause hardening. To test an unknown piece of material, hold it against a grinding wheel. Tool steel throws bright white star-like sparks. Mild gives dull, round orange sparks.

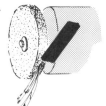 

Low Carbon   Medium Carbon   High Carbon

Tempering Colors

	°C	°F	Color	Properties	Uses
	200-225	400-445	pale yellow	hard, little flexibility	drill bits
	225-265	445-490	yellow	hard, less brittle	punches
	265-300	490-535	golden yellow	hard, increased flexibility	chisels
	300-325	535-580	brown-purple	holds edge but is flexible	thick knife blades
	325-350	580-650	purple	medium hard, flexible	thin knife blades
	350-500	650-900	blue	not hard	springs

Tools

170

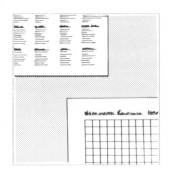

Reference

General Safety

Metalsmithing is not a killer craft. The attention given in this book to safety precautions should not discourage anyone from pursuing this ancient and fulfilling field. As craftspeople we all know that "If it's worth doing, it's worth doing well." We must also remember that "If it's worth doing, it's worth doing safely."

In order to clearly mark those areas that deserve special safety care, this book uses a system of safety alert logos. Their meanings are simple; it is up to you to heed the warnings and protect yourself.

Ventilation

As used in this book, "ventilation" refers to a powered movement of air. Opening a window is a pleasant thing to do on a sunny day, but it does not constitute ventilation.

The size of your studio and the type and volume of fumes being produced will determine the scale of the blowers needed. In a small shop, a vented stove hood may be adequate. These can be bought from lumberyards or kitchen remodeling companies, who sometimes have used or scratched units at a reduced price.

A much better form of ventilation uses a vacuum system working at the level of the bench top. These pick up fumes before they have a chance to rise to the height of the operator's face.

Respirators

Respirators filter air before it enters your system. They are generally considered less effective than active ventilation since they can be a little uncomfortable.

A worthwhile respirator will have a canister or cartridge filter to chemically remove impurities. It will cost $20-30.
1. Look for the NIOSH seal of approval.
2. Choose a filter made for the danger to which you are exposed.
3. Your mask must make a tight and comfortable fit.
4. Change filters as needed. This is indicated by odors entering the mask, or difficulty in pulling air.
5. If you have trouble breathing or a history of respiratory illness, consult your doctor.

Common Sense

This is your best protection. Even safe procedures can be dangerous if abused. Remember that accidents don't happen only to the "other guy." If you feel uncertain about a tool, get help. If you feel ill or dizzy, stop doing what you're doing. If illness persists, contact your state hospital system, Department of Occupational Safety, or

**The Center for
Occupational Hazards, Inc.**
5 Beekman Street
New York, NY 10038
(212) 227-6220

While most of the information in this book can apply to metalsmithing on any scale, keep in mind that it is written primarily for work of jewelry size. It is not intended as a resource for larger studios or industry, where other safety requirements may very well exist. For help in this area, contact your state's Office for Occupational Safety and Health Administration (OSHA) or the industrial safety division of your state labor department.

Safety

Compound | Effect | Precaution

Compound	Effect	Precaution
Acetone	Headache, drowsiness, skin irritation. One of the least toxic solvents.	Adequate ventilation.
Acetylene	Mild narcotic (intoxicant) in small doses. Large doses can cut off oxygen.	Use caution. Check equipment regularly for leaks. Have professionally repaired if found.
Ammonia	Irritant to eyes, caustic to lungs. Serious when in strong solution.	Use diluted with soap and water.
Aqua Regia 1 part nitric acid 3 parts hydrochloric acid	Most caustic of all acids.	Mix carefully, with strong ventilation. Keep in glass, not tightly stoppered. Do not store in a small space. To dispose, return to distributor.
Asbestos	Made up of fibers the body cannot dissolve. A carcinogen whose effects take 20-30 years to develop.	Avoid it. Avoid it. Avoid it. Avoid it. Use substitutes.
Benzene solvent for plastics	Intoxication, coma, respiratory failure.	Use alternative solvent. Avoid it!
Cadmium solder ingredient	Affects brain, nervous system, lungs, kidneys.	Avoid if possible; use very good ventilation.
Chlorinated Hydrocarbons epoxy solvent	Dissolves fatty layer of skin. Causes liver and kidney damage.	Avoid if possible; ventilate, wear neoprene rubber gloves.
Copper Compounds	Oxides can irritate lungs, intestines, eyes and skin.	Ventilate when heating. Wear gloves when handling a lot, like when raising.
Cyanides Used in plating	Mists inhaled or falling on skin are poisonous.	Ventilate well, wear protective clothing. No nude plating.
Flourides Flux Base	Can form hydrofluoric acid in the lungs.	Ventilate. Avoid breathing the fumes.
Lead	Damages brain, central nervous system, red blood cells, marrow, liver, kidneys. Fumes are especially dangerous.	Avoid if possible. Ventilate well. Minimize handling, wash hands after touching.
Ketones Acetone, lacquer thinner, etc.	Skin, eye, and respiratory tract irritants. Can cause peripheral nerve damage.	Ventilate, wear appropriate respirator. Wear gloves.

Reference

173

Safety

Compound	Effect	Precaution
Liver of Sulphur (Potassium Sulfide)	When heated to decomposition, it releases sulphur oxide fumes that react with moisture to form hydrogen sulfide. In high concentration this can cause brain damage and suffocation.	Do not allow mixture to come to a boil. All coloring benefits can be obtained from a warm, not hot, solution.
Mercury	Damages brain, nervous system and kidneys.	Avoid fumes and skin contact. Ventilate and wear gloves.
Pitch	Skin irritant when hot.	Wear gloves, avoid heating to a boil.
Platinum	Metal is safe but fumes when melting can cause lung and skin irritation.	Ventilate.
Polyester Resins	Skin irritants. Some release toxic fumes on mixing with binders. Some are explosive.	Wear gloves and ventilate. Store according to directions.
Silver Compounds Silver Chloride Silver Nitrate	Absorbed into skin as vapor or dust, these can cause a disease called *argyria*. Silver dust in eyes can cause blindness.	Wear goggles, gloves and a respirator.
Sulfuric Acid & Sparex (Sodium Bisulphate)	Irritates skin and respiratory tract. Damages clothing.	Ventilate. Keep container covered. Do not mix stronger concentration than necessary. Neutralize with baking soda and water mixture.
Tellurium	Fumes generated in refining gold, silver, copper, and in welding. Irritates skin and gastrointestinal system.	Ventilate. Early symptom is "garlic breath" and a metallic taste in the mouth.
Toluene Toluol Substitute for Benzine	Causes hallucination, intoxication, lung, brain, and red blood cell damage.	Avoid if possible. Ventilate well.
Turpentine	Skin irritant. Brain and lung damage possible.	Ventilate. Wear gloves.
Zinc Compounds	Dust and fumes attack the central nervous system, skin, and lungs.	Ventilate and wear respirator.

Alloys

Symbol		Au	Ag	Cu	Zn	Other	Melting Point °C	°F	Specific Gravity
Al	Aluminum					100 Al	660	1220	2.7
Sb	Antimony					100 Sb	631	1168	6.6
Bi	Bismuth					100 Bi	271	520	9.8
260	Brass, cartridge			70	30		954	1749	8.5
226	Jewelers Bronze			88	12		1030	1886	8.7
220	Red Brass			90	10		1044	1910	8.8
511	Bronze			96		4 Sn	1060	1945	8.8
Cd	Cadmium					100 Cd	321	610	8.7
Cr	Chromium					100 Cr	1890	3434	6.9
Cu	Copper			100			1083	1981	8.9
Au	Gold (fine)	100					1063	1945	19.3
920	22K Yellow	92	4	4			977	1790	17.3
900	22K Coinage	90	10				940	1724	17.2
750	18K Yellow	75	15	10			882	1620	15.5
750	18K Yellow	75	12.5	12.5			904	1660	15.5
750	18K Green	75	25				966	1770	15.6
750	18K Rose	75	5	20			932	1710	15.5
750	18K White	75				25 Pd	904	1660	15.7
580	14K Yellow	58	25	17			802	1476	13.4
580	14K Green	58	35	7			835	1535	13.6
580	14K Rose	58	10	32			827	1520	13.4
580	14K White	58				42 Pd	927	1700	13.7
420	10K Yellow	42	12	41	5		786	1447	11.6
420	10K Yellow	42	7	48	3		876	1609	11.6
420	10K Green	42	58				804	1480	11.7
420	10K Rose	42	10	48			810	1490	11.6
420	10K White	42				58 Pd	927	1760	11.8
Fe	Iron					100 Fe	1535	2793	7.9
Pb	Lead					100 Pb	327	621	11.3
Mg	Magnesium					100 Mg	651	1204	1.7
	Monel Metals			33		60 Ni, 7 Fe	1360	2480	8.9
Ni	Nickel					100 Ni	1455	2651	8.8
752	Nickel Silver			65	17	18 Ni	1110	2030	8.8
Pd	Palladium					100 Pd	1549	2820	12.2
	Old Pewter					80 Pb,20 Sn	304	580	9.5
Pt	Platinum					100 Pt	1774	3225	21.4
Ag	Silver (fine)		100				961	1762	10.6
925	Sterling		92.5	7.5			920	1640	10.4
800	Coin Silver		80	20			890	1634	10.3
	Mild Steel					99 Fe, 1 C	1511	2750	7.9
	Stainless Steel					91 Fe, 9 Cr	1371	2500	7.8
Sn	Tin					100 Sn	232	450	7.3
Ti	Titanium					100 Ti	1800	3272	4.5
Zn	Zinc				100		419	786	7.1

Circle Divider

Circle Divider

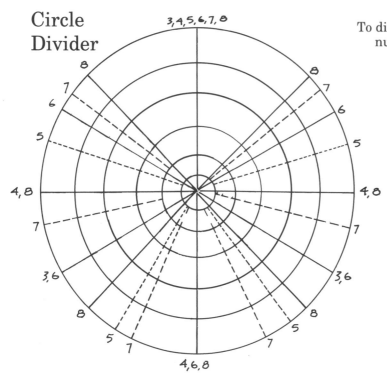

3, 4, 5, 6, 7, 8

To divide a circle into a given number of parts, connect all points marked with that number. For instance, to divide a bowl into 5 segments, center it on the template and mark at every line that has a 5.

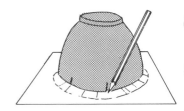

It might be helpful to enlarge this by photocopying it.

To Divide a Circle into a Number of Equal Parts

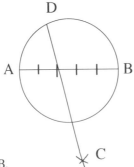

1. Draw diameter AB.
2. With A as center and AB as radius, describe an arc. With B as the center and the same radius, describe another arc crossing at C.
3. With a ruler, divide AB into as many parts as you wish to make, in this case five.
4. Draw a line from C through the second division, regardless of the number of parts being divided.
5. Step the distance AD around the circle with a compass to determine equidistant points.

Making a Cone Pattern

1. Draw the side view of the cone exactly as you want it.
2. If making a frustrum (shaded), extend lines to meet at **o**.
3. Set compass with radius **ob** and draw arc.
4. Multiply **ab** times pi (3.14). Mark this distance on the arc with a wire or string to find **c**.
5. Connect **oc**. The striped area is the pattern.

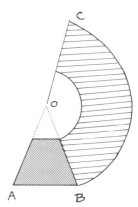

Reference

History of Metalsmithing*

* slightly condensed

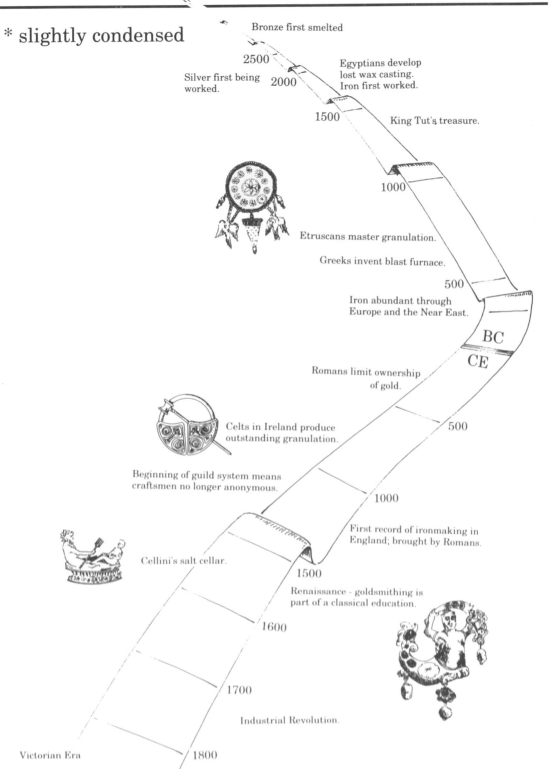

Bronze first smelted

2500

Silver first being worked.

2000

Egyptians develop lost wax casting. Iron first worked.

1500

King Tut's treasure.

1000

Etruscans master granulation.

Greeks invent blast furnace.

500

Iron abundant through Europe and the Near East.

BC
CE

Romans limit ownership of gold.

Celts in Ireland produce outstanding granulation.

500

Beginning of guild system means craftsmen no longer anonymous.

1000

First record of ironmaking in England; brought by Romans.

Cellini's salt cellar.

1500

Renaissance - goldsmithing is part of a classical education.

1600

1700

Industrial Revolution.

177

Victorian Era

1800

Photography Summary

Photography is complex, both as an art and a science. To deal with it comprehensively requires much more space than this. Experimentation and professional help will complement these basic hints.

Photographing small reflective objects presents two problems. Because the camera is close to the work, depth of field becomes critical. To keep both the foreground and background in focus, it is necessary to keep the lens opening (f-stop) small, like 16. To allow enough light to reach the film through such a small opening, a long exposure time is needed. Since it is impossible to keep the camera steady for the length of time required a tripod must be used. To reduce the risk of jiggling the camera, use a cable release. Work may be shot in daylight (with the appropriate film) but greater consistency is possible when using lights. These must be matched to the film being used and are usually mounted in aluminum reflectors. To properly illuminate the work and avoid shadows, light should come from both sides and sometimes from above and below. To avoid hot spots (bright reflections) the light should be diffused and/or reflected.

Checklist

1. Set the object in place and arrange for the best angle and proper framing.
2. Add close up rings or lenses to allow focusing.
3. Turn on the lights; correct shadows and hot spots.
4. Look for reflections. Figure out what they are and how to get rid of them.
5. Set a gray card (available from a photo dealer) into the field and take a reading on a light meter, either as a separate tool or the one built into the camera. Set the aperture at the highest number on your camera and adjust the shutter speed as required.
6. Double check the image. If it's good, make the exposure.

Attention to relative sizes is important in translating an object into a photograph. In rare cases, a common object like a coin can be set beside the piece, but this usually creates a distraction. Instead, the relationship between the object and the picture area is used to provide a sense of scale.

Light Bouncing

Very reflective objects are difficult to photograph because they mirror the objects around them. Make a white enclosure to solve this. To avoid the reflection of the camera and photographer, use a piece of white cardboard or sheet with a hole cut out for the lens. A small piece of cardboard can be hand-held to "catch" reflections.

Background Material

It's easy to forget that a close-up photo is like a magnifying glass. Materials that look good to the naked eye become a jungle of lint and flaws when viewed close up. Medium values of colored paper make good background surfaces. *Color-aid* paper (available at an art supply store) is especially rich looking.

Photo Booths

WHITE FABRIC, PAPER OR PLASTIC

Conversions

Multiply the known unit by the figure to the right of the measurement you desire. For instance, how many grains are in 3 carats?

known	x	# from chart	=	answer
3	x	3.0865	=	9.2595

carats	to grains	x 3.0865		pennyweights (dwt)		
	to grams	x .2			to grains	x 24
	to milligrams	x 200			to grams	x 1.5551
grains	to carats	x .324			to oz, avoir.	x .05486
	to grams	x .0648		lb. avoirdupois		
	to milligrams	x 64.799			to grains	x 7000
	to oz, avoir.	x .002286			to grams	x 453.59
	to oz, troy	x .00208			to kilogram	x .4536
	to pennywght	x .04167			to oz, troy	x 14.5833
grams	to carat	x 5		lb troy	to gram	x 373.242
	to grains	x 15.4324			to kilogram	x .3732
	to oz, avoir.	x .03527			to oz, avoir.	x 13.165
	to oz, troy	x .03215			to lb, avoir.	x .82286
	to pennywght	x .64301		feet	to centimeters	x 30.48
kilograms					to meters	x .3048
	to oz, avoir.	x 35.274		meters	to feet	x 3.2808
	to oz, troy	x 32.1507			to inches	x 29.37
	to pennywght	x 643.015			to yards	x 1.0936
	to lb, avoir	x 2.2046		millimeters		
	to lb, troy	x 2.6792			to feet	x .00328
oz, avoirdupois					to inches	x .03937
	to grains	x 437.5		inches	to centimeters	x 2.54
	to grams	x 28.3495			to meters	x .0254
	to oz, troy	x .91146			to millimeters	x 25.4
	to pennywght	x 18.2291		cu cm	to cubic inches	x .061
	to lb, troy	x .07595			to US fl. oz.	x .0338
oz, troy				cu. in	to cu cm	x 16.387
	to grains	x 480			to liters	x .01639
	to grams	x 31.1035			to US fl.oz.	x .554
	to oz, avoir	x 1.0971		US gallons		
	to pennywght	x 20			to liter	x 3.785
	to lb, avoir.	x .06857			to cubic inches	x 231
US fl. oz.					to cubic feet	x .1337
	to cu cm	x 29.5737		liters	to US gallon	x .2642
	to cu inches	x 1.80469			to US quart	x 1.0567
	to liters	x .02957				

There's always an easy solution to every problem - neat, plausible and wrong. H.L. Mencken

Temperature Comparisons

To convert Centigrade to Fahrenheit
- Multiply °C by 9.
- Divide by 5.
- Add 32

To convert Fahrenheit to Centigrade
- Subtract 32 from °F.
- Multiply by 5.
- Divide by 9.

°C	°F	°C	°F	°F	°C	°F	°C
0	32	650	1202	32	0	1300	704
50	122	675	1247	100	38	1350	732
75	167	700	1292	150	66	1400	788
100	212	725	1337	200	93	1450	788
125	**257**	**750**	**1382**	**250**	**121**	**1500**	**816**
150	302	775	1427	300	149	1550	843
175	347	800	1472	350	177	1600	871
200	392	825	1517	400	204	1650	899
225	437	850	1562	450	232	1700	927
250	**482**	**875**	**1607**	**500**	**260**	**1750**	**954**
275	527	900	1652	550	288	1800	982
300	572	925	1697	600	316	1850	1010
325	617	950	1742	650	343	1900	1038
350	662	975	1787	700	371	1950	1066
375	**707**	**1000**	**1832**	**750**	**399**	**2000**	**1093**
400	752	1025	1877	800	427	2050	1121
425	797	1050	1922	850	454	2100	1149
450	842	1075	1967	900	482	2150	1177
475	887	1100	2012	950	510	2200	1204
500	**932**	**1125**	**2057**	**1000**	**538**	**2250**	**1232**
525	977	1150	2102	1050	566	2300	1260
550	1022	1175	2147	1100	593	2350	1288
575	1067	1200	2192	1150	621	2400	1316
600	1112	1225	2237	1200	649	2450	1343
625	1157	1250	2282	1250	677	2500	1371

Relative Characteristics of Common Metals

Electrical Conduction	Heat Conduction	Malleability	Ductility
1. silver	1. silver	1. gold	1. gold
2. copper	2. copper	2. silver	2. silver
3. gold	3. gold	3. aluminum	3. platinum
4. aluminum	4. aluminum	4. copper	4. iron
5. zinc	5. nickel	5. tin	5. copper
6. nickel	6. iron & platinum	6. platinum	6. aluminum
7. iron	7. tin	7. lead	7. nickel
8. platinum	8. lead	8. zinc	8. zinc
9. tin	9. zinc	9. iron	9. tin

Relative Sizes & Weights

B&S	mm	inches thou. / fractions		drill size
0	8.5	.325	21/64	
1	7.35	.289	9/32	
2	6.54	.258	1/4	
3	5.83	.229	7/32	1
4	5.19	.204	13/64	6
5	4.62	.182	3/16	15
6	4.11	.162	5/32	20
7	3.67	.144	9/64	27
8	3.26	.129	1/8	30
10	2.59	.102		38
11	2.30	.090	3/32	43
12	2.05	.080	5/64	46
13	1.83	.072		50
14	1.63	.064	1/16	51
15	1.45	.057		52
16	1.29	.050		54
17	1.15	.045	3/64	55
18	1.02	.040		56
19	.912	.036		60
20	.813	.032	1/32	65
21	.724	.029		67
22	.643	.025		70
23	.574	.023		71
24	.511	.020		74
25	.455	.018		75
26	.404	.016	1/64	77
27	.361	.014		78
28	.330	.013		79
29	.279	.011		80
30	.254	.010		

To find the weight of a given object in a different metal than it is now, multiply by the factors shown. For instance: if I have a sterling ring that weighs 6 dwts (*known*) and I want to know its weight in 18K yellow gold (*query*),

6 x 1.48 = 8.8 dwts.

Query	Known	Factor
18KY Gold	18KW	1.064
	platinum	.723
	brass	1.885
	sterling	1.480
14KY Gold	18KW	.842
	14KW	1.035
	platinum	.609
	brass	1.589
	sterling	1.248
10KY Gold	18KY	.745
	14KW	.884
	platinum	.539
	brass	1.406
	sterling	1.104
Platinum	palladium	1.758
	iridium	.953
	10% irid plat	.995
	15% irid plat	.993
	rhodium	1.717
	ruthenium	1.771
	sterling	2.046
Sterling	fine silver	.984
	coin silver	1.004
	18KY	.675
	14KY	.801
	10KY	.905
	platinum	.488
	brass	1.273

Reference

181

Silver/Copper Phase Diagram

A phase diagram is a graphic representation of the effects of heat on alloys of various proportions. The diagram shown here is for any mixture of silver and copper. Phase diagrams for just about any alloy you can imagine are available in reference books at the library.

The left edge represents 100% silver. The point marked as **A** indicates its melting point as being 960.5°C (1761°F). The right edge represents 100% copper, whose melting point is shown at **B**. Reading across the graph the percentage of copper is increased as the silver is decreased. Halfway across is an alloy of equal parts of the two metals.
The bottom edge of the graph is the lowest temperature shown, in this case 400°C. Each phase diagram will use different temperature ranges, choosing the range that is pertinent to the alloy being displayed.

To fill in the graph, laboratory tests are made for each alloy, 99/1, 98/2, 97/3 to determine the point at which it is no longer solid (*solidus*) and the point at which it is totally liquid (*liquidus*). These are plotted on the graph and yield the melting curve, shown here as a heavy line that dips down to the left of center. This tells us that of all the possible mixtures of these two metals, a combination of 71.9% silver and 28.1% copper has the lowest melting point. Sterling, an alloy of 7.5% copper, is indicated on the diagram by a dotted line. The graph shows that its melting point is 893 °C (1640 °F).

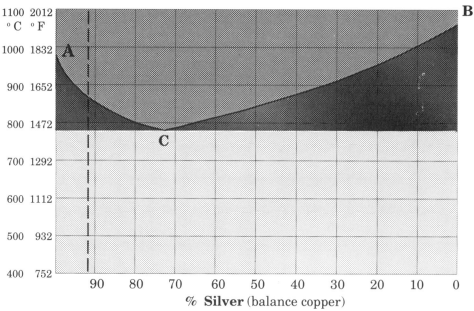

% **Silver** (balance copper)

But there's more. In the light colored lower half of the diagram the alloys are totally solid (called *alpha*). In the medium gray area near the top they're totally liquid (*beta*). In the middle area the metal is in a semi-solid or slushy state. This condition allows metals to be fused and is important in their behavior when cast. You'll notice that in one area the metal passes directly from solid to liquid, at the point marked **C**. This is called the *eutectic point*. If two metals were coated with a eutectic alloy they would easily join as soon as the metal reached this relatively low temperature. This is the principle behind granulation, explained on page 32.

Reference

Stone and Sawblade Sizes

Weight and Size of Some Precious Stones

Diameter	Diamonds	Sapphires	Rubies	Emeralds
1.3 mm	.01 carats	.02 carats	.02 carats	.015 carats
1.5	.015	.025	.025	.02
1.8	.02	.04	.035	.03
2.0	.03	.055	.05	.04
2.2	.04	.07	.06	.05
2.4	.05	.09	.08	.065
2.6	.07	.115	.105	.08
2.8	.085	.14	.13	.10
3.0	.10	.17	.15	.125
3.2	.12	.20	.18	.15
3.4	.15	.24	.22	.17
3.6	.17	.27	.25	.20
3.8	.19	.31	.29	.22
4.0	.22	.36	.33	.25
4.2	.26	.41	.38	.28
4.4	.30	.47	.44	.32
4.6	.35	.53	.50	.37
4.8	.40	.59	.56	.43
5.0	.45	.65	.62	.48
5.5	.59	.88	.85	.61
6.0	.77	1.13	1.07	.75
6.5	1.00	1.38	1.32	.96
7.0	1.25	1.66	1.58	1.22
8.0	1.85	2.50	2.35	1.95
9.0	2.65	3.10	2.95	2.70

Sawblades and Drill Sizes

No.	Thickness	Depth	Drill Equivalent	Recommended for
8/0	.0060	.0130	80	26 B&S gauge
6/0	.0070	.0140	79	24
4/0	.0085	.0170	77	22
2/0	.0100	.0200	75	22
0	.0110	.0230	73	20
1	.0115	.0250	71	20
3	.0140	.0290	68	18
5	.0160	.0340	65	16
7	.0200	.0480	55	12

Weight Charts

Weight per Square Inch of Sheet

mm	inch	B&S	fine silver OUNCES	sterling OUNCES	fine gold DWTS.	10K DWTS.	14K DWTS.	18K DWTS.	platinum OUNCES
6.54	.2576	2	1.42	1.41	52.5	31.4	35.5	42.3	2.91
5.19	.2043	4	1.12	1.12	41.6	24.9	28.1	33.6	2.31
4.11	.1620	6	.894	.884	33.0	19.8	22.3	26.6	1.83
3.26	.1285	8	.709	.701	26.2	15.7	17.7	21.1	1.45
2.59	.1019	10	.562	.556	20.8	12.4	14.0	16.7	1.15
2.05	.0808	12	.446	.441	16.5	9.85	11.1	13.3	.913
1.63	.0641	14	.354	.350	13.1	7.81	8.82	10.5	.724
1.29	.0508	16	.281	.277	10.4	6.21	7.00	8.35	.574
1.02	.0403	18	.223	.220	8.20	4.91	5.55	6.62	.455
.813	.0320	20	.176	.174	6.51	3.90	4.40	5.25	.361
.643	.0253	22	.140	.138	5.16	3.09	3.49	4.216	.286
.511	.0201	24	.111	.110	4.09	2.45	2.77	3.30	.227
.404	.0154	26	.088	.087	3.24	1.94	2.19	2.62	.180
.330	.0126	28	.070	.069	2.58	1.54	1.74	2.08	.143
.254	.0100	30	.055	.055	2.04	1.22	1.38	1.65	.113

Weight per Foot of Wire

mm	inch	B&S	fine silver OUNCES	sterling OUNCES	fine gold DWTS.	10K DWTS.	14K DWTS.	18K DWTS.	platinum OUNCES
6.54	.2576	2	3.45	3.41	128	76.3	86.1	104	7.07
5.19	.2043	4	2.17	2.14	80.1	48.0	54.2	64.6	4.45
4.11	.1620	6	1.36	1.35	50.4	30.2	34.1	40.6	2.80
3.26	.1285	8	.856	.848	31.6	19.0	21.4	25.6	1.76
2.59	.1019	10	.541	.534	20.0	11.9	13.5	16.1	1.11
2.05	.0808	12	.339	.335	12.6	7.50	8.47	10.1	.695
1.63	.0641	14	.214	.211	7.87	4.72	5.33	6.36	.437
1.29	.0508	16	.135	.132	4.96	2.97	3.35	4.00	.275
1.02	.0403	18	.085	.084	3.11	1.87	2.11	2.51	.173
.813	.0320	20	.053	.053	1.96	1.17	1.33	1.58	.109
.643	.0253	22	.034	.033	1.23	.738	.833	.994	.068
.511	.0201	24	.021	.021	.775	.464	.524	.625	.043
.404	.0154	26	.013	.013	.488	.292	.330	.393	.027
.330	.0126	28	.008	.008	.306	.184	.287	.247	.017
.254	.0100	30	.005	.005	.193	.115	.130	.155	.010

Reference

Geometry Formulas

A = area V= volume C = circumference π = 3.1416	
r = radius s = length of side N = number of sides	

Circle

$A = \pi (r^2)$ or
$A = d^2 (.7854)$

$C = \pi d$

Sphere

Area of a Surface = $4 \pi r^2$

$v = \dfrac{4 \pi r^2}{3}$ or $\dfrac{\pi d^2}{6}$

Cone

Area of a Conical Surface=

$\pi r \sqrt{r^2 + h^2}$

$V = \dfrac{\pi r^2 h}{3}$

Circular Segment

$A = .5 [r l - c (r-h)]$
where $l = .01745\, r\, \varnothing$

Cylinder

Area of a Cylindrical Surface =
$2 \pi r l$

$V = \pi r^2 l$

Spherical Segment

Area of Spherical
Surface = $2 \pi r h$

$V = \pi h^2 (r - \dfrac{h}{3})$

Ellipse

$A = \pi d D$
Perimeter (approx)

$\pi \sqrt{\dfrac{2(D^2 + d^2) - (D-d)^2}{2.2}}$

Paraboloid

$V = \dfrac{\pi r^2 l}{2}$

Frustrum of a Cone

Area of a Conical Surface =
$\pi s (R + r)$

$V = \dfrac{\pi h}{3} (R^2 + Rr + r^2)$

Parabola

$A = \dfrac{2 l r}{3}$

Parallelogram

$A = h b$

Triangles
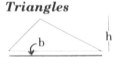

$A = \dfrac{b h}{2}$

Pyramid

A = sum of the areas of triangular sides.

$V = \dfrac{N s r h}{6}$ when the base is a
regular polygon

Trapezium
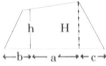

$A = \dfrac{(H+h)\, a + bh + cH}{2}$

Circular Section

$A = \dfrac{r l}{2}$

$l = \dfrac{\pi r \varnothing}{180}$

Trapezoid

$A = \dfrac{h (a + b)}{2}$

185

Periodicals & Organizations

Organization...	*Its publication...*
Society of North American Goldsmiths (SNAG) 5009 Londonderry Drive Tampa, FL 33647 (813) 977-5326 (813) 977-8462 FAX	**Metalsmith** (quarterly) **SNAG Newsletter** (bi-monthly) same address
Artist-Blacksmith Association of North America (ABANA) P.O. Box 1181 RR 5, Box 64 Nashville, IN 47448 (812) 988-6919	**Anvil's Ring** (quarterly) 201 Arts Cottage University Park, PA 16802 (814) 865-6570
American Craft Council 40 West 53rd Street New York, NY 10019 (212) 956-3535	**American Craft** (bi-monthly) same address
Society of American Silversmiths P.O. Box 3599 Cranston, RI 02910 (401) 461-3156	**Journal** (quarterly) same address

Commercial Periodicals

Ornament
P.O. Box 2349
San Marcos, CA 92079

Lapidary Journal
60 Chestnut Avenue
Devon, PA 19333
(215) 293-1962

Jewelers Circular/Keystone
Chilton Way
Radnor, PA 19089
(215) 964-4474

The Crafts Report
Box 1992
Wilmington, DE 19899

Arts Auria
Ebner Verlag gmbH KG
7900 Ulm / Donau
Postfach 3060 Germany

Gold Und Silber
Konradin Verlag
Postfach 100252
7022 Leinfelden - Echterdingen
Germany

Reference

Suggested Reading

Amulets and Superstitions
E.A. Wallis Budge
Dover, NY, 1978 (orig. 1930)

Artists Anodizing Aluminum
David LaPlantz
Press de LaPlantz,
Bayside, CA, 1989

Centrifugal or Lost Wax Casting
Murray Bovin
Bovin, Forest Hills, NY
1971, rev. 1977

Coloring, Bronzing and Patination of Metals
Hughes and Rowe
Watson-Guptill, NY 1982

Contemporary Jewelry
Philip Morton
Holt, Rinehart & Winston,
NY, 1970, rev. 1976

Creative Casting
Sharr Choate
Crown, NY, 1966

Custom Knifemaking
Tim McCreight
Stackpole, Harrisburg, PA, 1985

Design and Creation of Jewelry
Robert vonNeumann
Chilton, Radnor, PA 1961,
rev. 1972

Diamond Setting
Robert Wooding
Dry Ridge School
Erlanger, KY, 1984

Form Emphasis for Metalsmiths
Heikki Seppa
Kent State Univ. Press
Kent, Ohio, 1978

Jewelers Bench Reference
Harold O'Connor
Dunconor Books, Taos NM, 1977

Jewelry Concepts and Technology
Oppi Untracht
Doubleday, NY, 1982

Jewelry: Contemporary Design and Technique
Chuck Evans
Davis, Worcester, MA, 1983

Jewelry of the Ancient World
Jack Ogden
Rizzoli, NY 1982

The Jewelry Engraver's Manual
Hardy & Allen
Van Nostrand Reinhold, NY
1976 (orig. 1954)

Jewelry Making Manual
Sylvia Wicks
Brynmorgen Press,
Cape Elizabeth, ME, 1986

Jewelry Making for Schools Tradesmen and Craftsmen
Murray Bovin
Bovin, Forest Hills, NY,
1971, rev. 1971 & 79

Jewelry Manufacture and Repair
Charles Jarvis
Bonanza, NY, 1978

The Curious Lore of Precious Stones
George Kunz
Dover, NY 1971 (orig. 1913)

The Making of Tools
Alexander Wygers
Van Nostrand Reinhold, NY,
1973

Metalsmith Papers
various authors
SNAG, Tampa, FL, 1981

Metalsmithing for the Artist-Craftsman
Richard Thomas
Chilton, Radnor, PA, 1960

Metalwork and Enameling
Herbert Maryon
Dover, NY, 1971 (orig. 1912)

Metal Techniques for Craftsmen
Oppi Untracht
Doubleday, Garden City, NY
1968

The New Jewelry
Dormer & Turner
Thames & Hudson, London,
1985

Practical Casting
Tim McCreight
Brynmorgen Press
Cape Elizabeth, ME, 1986

Rings for the Finger
George Kunz
Dover, NY, 1973 (orig 1917)

Silversmithing
Finegold & Seitz
Chilton, Radnor, PA 1983

Step-By-Step Knifemaking
David Boye
Rodale, Emmaus, PA 1977

Reference

Suppliers

The companies on this page are full service suppliers. Most will sell tools, chemicals, supplies, books and metal. Of course each is unique and you will need to do your own research.

Allcraft Tool & Supply (800) 645-7124
666 Pacific Street (718) 789-2800
Brooklyn, NY 11217

Anchor Tool & Supply (201) 635-2094
P.O. Box 265
Chatham, NJ 07928

ARE, Inc. (800) 736-4273
Box 8 (802) 533-7007
Greensboro Bend, (802) 533-7008 FAX
VT 05842

Borel & Frei (800) 654-9591
712 South Olive Street (213) 689-4530
Los Angeles, CA 90014 (213) 488-0485 FAX

C.R. Hill Company (800) 521-1221
2734 W. 11 Mile Rd (313) 543-1555
Berkley, MI 48072 (313) 543-9104 FAX

C.W. Somers Co. (800) 322-1003
387 Washington St (617) 426-6880
Boston, MA 02108

E.B. Fitler & Co. (800) 346-2497
RD 2, Box 176B (302) 684-1893
Milton, DE 19968

Forslev's (800) 634-0525
210 South Milwaukee (708) 520-4120
Wheeling, IL 60090 (708) 520-4437 FAX

Frei & Borel (800) 772-3456
119 Third Street (415) 832-0355
Oakland, CA 94607 (415) 834-6217 FAX

Gesswein (800) 243-4466
255 Hancock Avenue (203) 366-5400
Bridgeport, CT 06605 (203) 366-3953 FAX

Greiger's Inc. (800) 423-4181
900 S. Arroyo Prkwy (818) 795-9775
Pasadena, CA 91105 (818) 577-4751 FAX

Jules Borel & Co. (800) 333-4646
1110 Grand Avenue (816) 421-6110
Kansas City, MO 64106 (800) 333-4083 FAX

Norman Thomas Co. (800) 642-7210
742 North Woodward (313) 642-7210
Birmingham, MI 48009

Progress Machine (800) 227-9775
610 South Broadway (213) 489-7262
Los Angeles, CA 90014 (213) 489-2140 FAX

Rio Grande Albuquerque (800) 545-6566
6901 Washington Ave. NE (800) 533-3299 SERVICE
Albuquerque, NM 87109 (505) 344-9671 FAX

Swest, Inc. (800) 527-5057
11090 N. Stemmons Frwy (214) 247-7744
Dallas, TX 75220 (214) 247-3507 FAX

T.B. Hagstoz & Son (800) 922-1006
709 Sansom Street (215) 922-1627
Philadelphia, PA 19106

TSI, Inc. (800) 426-9984
101 Nickerson Street (206) 282-3040
Seattle, WA 98109 (206) 281-8701 FAX

William Dixon Co. (201) 935-0100
750 Washington Avenue
Carlstadt, NJ 07072

Specialty Suppliers

This page lists a few nationally known specialty suppliers. As you expand this list, remember to check the local phone book and magazine advertisements.

Blacksmithing Equipment

Centaur Forge (414) 763-9175
117 North Spring Street
Burlington, WI 53105

Bayshore Metals, Inc. (415) 647-7981
Box 882003 (415) 285-5759 FAX
San Francisco, CA 94188

Anodizing Supplies

East West DyeCom (703) 345-4241
Box 12294
Roanoke, VA 24024

Met-L-Art, Inc. (800) MET-L-ART
Box 4611 (302) 656-8410
Greenville, DE 19807

Metals

Hauser & Miller Co. (800) 462-7447
Box 500700 (314) 487 1311
St. Louis, MO 63150

Hoover & Strong (800) 759-9997
10700 Trade Road (804) 794-3700
Richmond, VA 23236 (804) 794-5687 FAX

Martin Hannum (800) 225-1461
806 South Mateo Street (213) 662-7101
Los Angeles, CA 90021

(base metals)
T. E. Conklin (800) 225-5510
270 Nevin Street (718) 643-6360
Brooklyn, NY 11217 (718) 625-2291 FAX

Miscellaneous

Flux
4S Labs
Box 11819
Phoenix, AZ 85061

Flux
Griffith's Distributors (303) 442-8284
Box 662
Louisville, CO 80027

Niobium, Equipment, Findings
Reactive Metals Studio (800) 876-3434
Box 890 (602) 634-3434
Clarkdale, AZ 86324

Equipment & Supplies
Small Parts (305) 751-0856
Box 381966
Miami, FL 33238-1966

Pitch for Repousse
Northwest Pitchworks (206) 525-4136
5705 26th Avenue NE
Seattle, WA 98105

Rubber Molds
Perma-Flex Mold (614) 252-8034
1919 E. Livingston Ave.
Columbus, OH 43209

Small Screws
T.E. Morris Company (508) 764-4394
394 Elm Street (508) 764-7350 FAX
Southbridge, MA 01550

Patina Chemicals
Bryant Labs, Inc. (800) 367-3141
1101 Fifth Street (415) 526-3141
Berkeley, CA 94710 (415) 528-2948 FAX

Glossary

Alginate	An organic based moldmaking material used to recreate forms in wax for subsequent use in casting.
Amalgamation	The ancient process of mixing a fine metal with mercury to create a paste. The mercury is driven off after the paste is applied, to create a film or inlay of metal. The process has been largely replaced by electroplating, though it is still used in dental inlay.
Annealing	The process of using heat to relieve stresses within a metal. At a heat usually near 2/3rds of the metal's melting point, recrystallization occurs, creating a more flexible alignment among the crystals.
Anodizing	This refers to the use of a current of electricity to affect the surface of a metal. Its most common usage is in aluminum anodizing or the coloring of reactive metals such as niobium or titanium. The term comes from the negative pole of an electrical circuity, the anode.
Anticlastic raising	The effect of stretching the edges of a sheet while compressing its center. Unlike synclastic raising, in which both the x- and y-axis are curved in the same direction, in this process the two axes curve away from each other in opposite directions.
Bezel	A rim of metal that surrounds and secures a stone. They may be of any size and can be either decorated or plain.
Brazing	The joining of metals with solder at a high temperature. The term is often used to refer to the use of brass as a solder for steel.
Burn out	That part of the lost wax casting process in which the mold is evacuated of its model by extreme heat, generally in a kiln.
Chasing	An ancient process in which steel tools and a hammer are used to press recesses into a sheet for decorative purposes. It is also used to refine details on the surface of a cast form.
Depletion Gilding	The process of creating a skin of relatively pure metal by leaching out alloy constituents in an acidic bath.
Die Forming	A versatile process often used in industry, in which a metal sheet is given form by pressing it between two rigid dies.
Diffusion	The gradual mixing of crystals from two pieces of metal. Welding, for instance, is the result of diffusion.
Electroforming	A technical process in which a matrix is suspended in a bath of free metal ions, that are then influenced to attach themselves because of the creation of a flow of electricity, generally provided by a rectifier.
Engraving	An ancient process in which small steel tools are used to carve away bits of metal, either to create a pattern, to form letters, or to create a desired surface texture.
Etching	The process of using acids or strong chemicals to selectively corrode or eat away at a metal object. When etching is used to eat completely through a metal sheet the process is called chemical milling.

Glossary

Eutectic The lowest solidification temperature of an alloy or a metal. Also defined as the point at which the metal goes most directly from liquid to a solid.

Findings Originally the bits and pieces taken from recycled objects by silversmiths (who later "found" a use for them). Today the term includes all manner of attachments that contribute to the function of a jewelry piece, such as earwires, pin backs and so on.

Firescale An oxide of copper that forms within sterling and gold alloys. It is created and enlarged by high temperatures for a protracted time, particularly in the presence of free oxygen. It appears as a purple stain.

Flux Any of a number of chemicals used to prevent the formation on oxides during soldering and melting.

Fusing The semi-controlled melting of a number of pieces to create interesting forms, most successfully done with precious metals.

Granulation Historically this refers to a decorative process of applying thousands of very tiny beads to a metal surface to create patterns or figures. In the studio the term also refers to the joining process developed to create the almost invisible bonds associated with this technique.

Heat hardening The process of fostering crystalline regularity by soaking a metal at a specific heat for an extended time. The absence of vacancies and irregularities render the metal more rigid than it would be otherwise. Though clinically possible for precious metals, the controls required are generally beyond most studios.

Hollow core A casting process used to create hollow forms such as beads or works that would be prohibitively heavy (and costly) otherwise.

Investment soldering The use of a silica-plaster material to secure pieces for soldering. The technique is especially useful when dealing with intricate objects and when many components are being joined at once.

Liver of Sulfur Potassium sulfide, a compound dissolved in water to create a patina on sterling and copper.

Mallets Hammerlike tools of a relatively soft material used to shape a metal without severely thinning it. Typical materials are wood, leather, horn and plastic.

Mandrels Tools used to provide a surface against which a softer metal may be formed. The most common varieties are identified by names related to their sizes, as in bezel mandrel, ring mandrel and bracelet mandrel.

Mokumé A Japanese technique in which layers of metals of contrasting color are fused, distorted and then revealed. The image can be carefully controlled but is most common as a random woodgrain pattern.

Mordants The general term for acids and similar strong chemicals used to etch.

Glossary

Niello	An alloy of silver, copper, lead and sulfur that creates a lustrous black inlay material with a relatively low melting point.
Patinas	Any of hundreds of surface films created on metals to provide a desired color or surface finish.
Phase diagram	A chart that plots the range of melting points for a given alloy, showing the effect of the relative amounts of the various constituent parts.
Photoetching	A technique in which a photographic process is used to create a pattern or image on a surface with an acid resistant medium.
Piercing	The use of a sawframe and blade to create shapes from sheet metal.
Planishing	The use of a hammer or similar impact tool to smooth a metal surface.
Raising	An ancient process in which metal is deformed over a hard surface called a stake to force it into a volumetric shape.
Reactive metals	Any of the six metals in groups 4B or 5B of the Periodic Table. They are characterized by light weight, low malleability and the ability to form a consistent and durable oxide film.
Recrystallization	The process by which molecules within a metal give up alignment with one crystal and regroup with another.
Reducing flame	A torch or kiln flame in which there is more fuel provided than can efficiently combine with the available oxygen.
Repoussé	An ancient process in which hardened tools are struck with a hammer to press metal into a decorative shape.
Resists	Paints, waxes or other coatings used to prevent acids from reaching selected areas during etching.
Reticulation	In metalworking, a process through which a metal sheet is induced to gather itself into ridges and valleys.
Scoring	The process of scratching or carving a recessed line to locate and insure a crisp bend.
Sinking	The compressive process of pressing metal into a form.
Sprues	Channels cut into a mold to allow for the entry of metal. Also the name given to the metal rods that assume this shape in the final casting.
Stakes	Hard forms, usually of steel but sometimes of wood or plastic, over which metal forming such as raising is done.
Stretching	A forming process in which metal is thinned, generally by pinching it between two hard surfaces, such as a hammer and an anvil. This is usually for the purpose of creating a volumetric shape.

Layout Grids

The grids on this and the following pages might
be useful as you sketch out your ideas. Choose
the appropriate scale and lay your sketching
paper directly on the grid.

3 mm

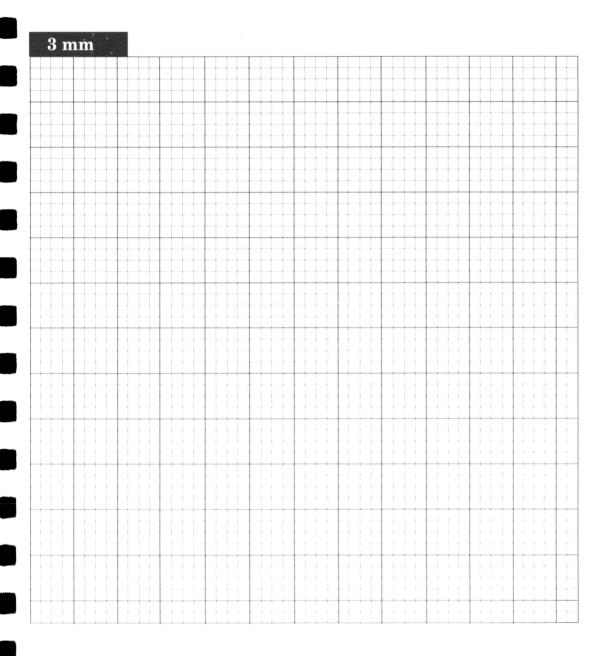

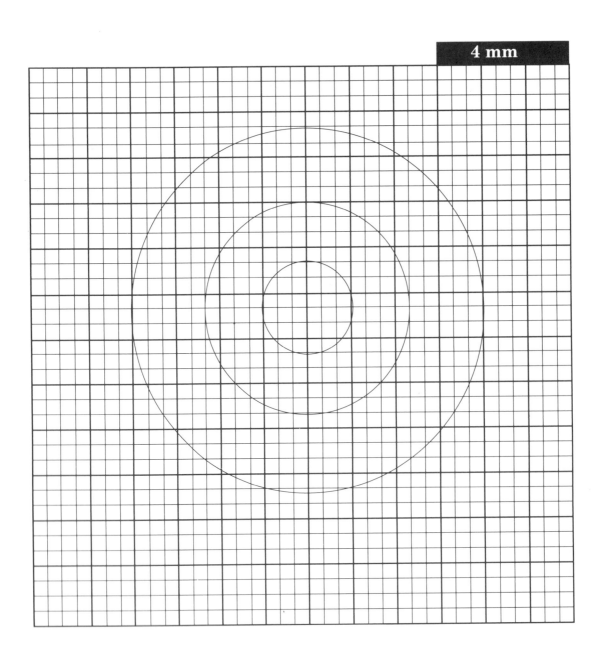

4 mm

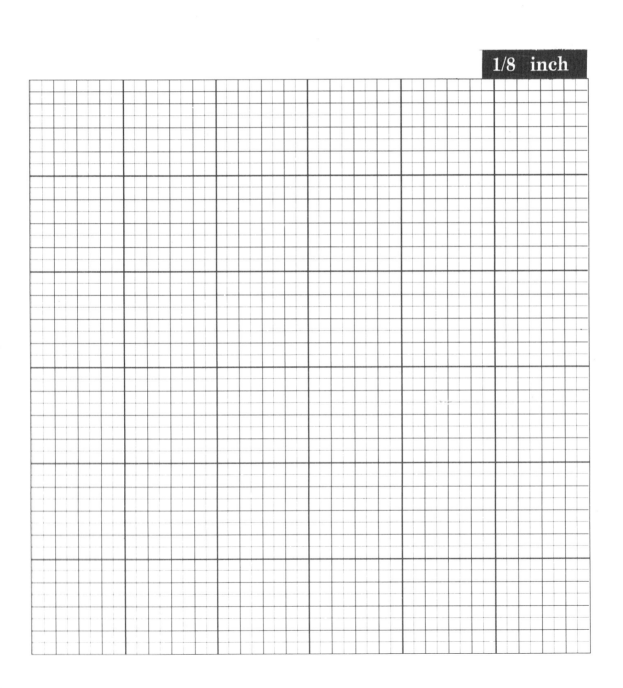

1/8 inch

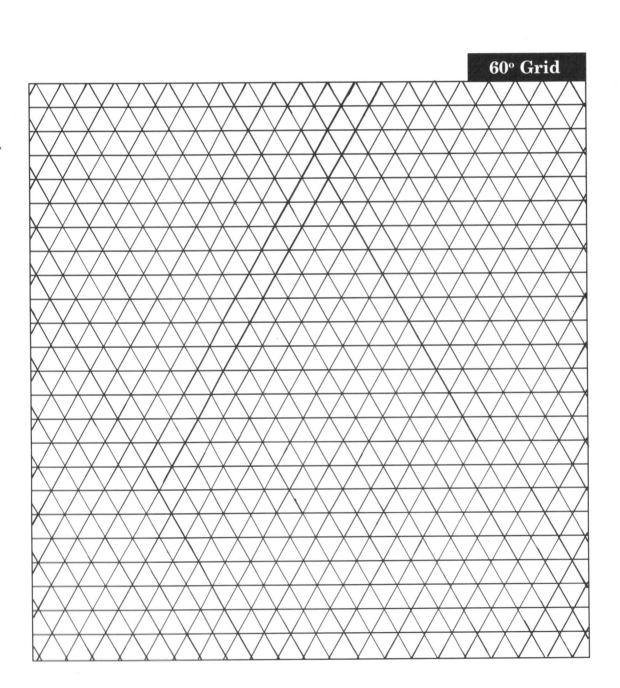

60° Grid

Index

Index